REALITY HACKER

How simple it can be to change the world around us.

Simon Gillmore

REALITY HACKER
The World is in Your Hands

Copyright © 2023 Simon Gillmore

ISBN
Paperback - 978-0-6458900-0-6
Ebook - 978-0-6458900-1-3

Simon Gillmore has asserted his right under the Copyright, Designs and Patents Act 1988 to be identified as the author of this work. The information in this book is based on the author's opinions and experiences. Permission to use this information has been sort by the author. Any breaches will be rectified in further additions of the book.

All rights reserved. No part of this publication may be reproduced, stored in or introduced into a retrieval system, or transmitted in any form, or by any means (electronic, mechanical, photocopying, recording or otherwise) without prior permission of the author. Any person who does any unauthorised act in relation to this publication may be liable to criminal prosecution and civil claims for damages.

DEDICATION

First and foremost I need to dedicate this book to my partner Andrea for her unending encouragement and support. You've read this work as many times as I have and never questioned the hours I've put into writing it. All of the things you do for me make me feel like a king. Also to Christine Gabriel for her meticulous work in editing the book – you must have been scratching your head sometimes to think that this bloke calls himself an author.

And lastly to my two Grandchildren – Huxley, and Kahalani. Never did I expect my eyes would be cast on something so beautiful. It wasn't until I met you both that I ever considered what I was leaving behind. You both make me feel so whole as a person.

CONTENTS

Dedication 3
Introduction 7
Chapter 1: Getting in the picture 21
Chapter 2: Our Big, Dumb Mind.. 66
Chapter 3: The Happening 96
Chapter 4: 'Reactionality' 136
Chapter 5: Memory Implants.. 151
Chapter 6: Light and Dark Emotions 169
Chapter 7: The Portal 183
Chapter 8: The Accelerator 206
Chapter 9: Intentionality 220
Chapter 10: The Hardest Work 237
Chapter 11: Our North Star 245
Chapter 12: We Matter.. 252
Chapter 13: Tying it All Together 294
Epilogue 307

INTRODUCTION

We live in a very different world to what we used to...

But of all of those changes, there are none more important and valuable to us than our advancements in the awareness of our own minds. For what has to be considered the next frontier of humanity – for in our current state of turmoil we have to begin to understand that part of us that creates the world as we know it. There is literally nowhere else left for us to go but within. If we all want to be able to enjoy a better quality of life in the foreseeable future, we have to gain a better understanding of what lies within us and the pathways to peace. And we have to be able do that regardless of our theological, or religious beliefs. We have to know ourselves better, and collaborate more effectively because the values and predispositions that have got us thus far, do not appear to be sufficient to guide us into the future. Our direction is not sustainable, and our hearts are slowly but surely breaking.

We have come so far, and know so much about the mind and the world that we live in, but our mental health is in the toilet. Where it is estimated that a staggering 30% of the population in the western world has been diagnosed with depression. And for depression to become the leading cause of health-related issues within the next few years. Medical research estimates as much as 90% of illness and disease to be stress related. Mental health is the leading cause of disability worldwide. With as many as 2/5 of kids under the age of 18 suffering from some form of mental health disorder. And these are the people who actually sort help. If we go beyond just depression and include the likes of bipolar disorder, attention deficiency, phobias, anxiety, and alcohol and drug dependency, we start to get a real picture of how little our improved sense of awareness done to benefit the overall health of our species. We may well know it all, but we appear to be in worse shape than ever. We don't know how to use our minds properly, and such a comparatively small number of people could be considered to have found some sense of peace or be where they want to be in their life. We are prisoners within our minds, with no foreseeable way out.

Of all the advantages we live with in this modern era – all the improvements we have been blessed with, it is the nature of our own subconscious minds and how it operates that would seem the most useful and important. The thing that creates the world according to us, and runs the program that dictates the conditions of our life. The 'God' mind if you will that creates the world as we know it. But this information isn't filtering down to the masses. It is well known but not broadly known. How the subconscious mind works isn't taught in schools, so it is not just that we are disinterested in the nature of this *world building tool*, we're systematically being distracted away from knowing about it. As Daniel Goleman suggests in "Focus" – *"Researchers have linked the high use of technological gadgets to obesity. The user's attention gets captured by many other factors, leading to low mental control and, ultimately, impulsive living".*

It is not just that we are ignorant of the information that could so simply improve our lives and the way we see our problems, our attention is bombarded by meaningless distractions. There would appear to be an enormous chasm in our understanding the differing roles and functions of the conscious and subconscious minds. Very few people understand the nature of the subconscious mind, or how this autonomous aspect of our minds works. How it proceeds to regurgitate an identical experience as a means of keeping us in a familiar seeming environment. We have to know how it works and be able to work with it, or we'll be forever beating our heads against a wall to feel better. We can't feel better by moving the furniture of our life around, because our state of mind is repetitively reproduced at a higher level of mind than the one we think with. We have this 'God' mind – that constructs the world as we know it on repeat. But for the most part people live with the assumption that there is nothing there – that what 'we' are is the mind we think with and there is no more to us than that.

It seems as if people don't care or know about the subconscious mind even though it should be considered like our 'primary caregiver'. It's the thing taking care of us, and controls perception, emotions and where our attention goes. This 'subconscious' thing is primarily responsible for all of human life on earth. It lays at the heart of our deciphering of the world, and holds the keys to our mental health. But for the most part, the majority of people are happy ignoring that there is anything there at all. They never consider that there's something there, replaying our thoughts and how we feel like a broken record that we can access to change what's happening in our lives. To have no awareness of the subconscious mind and its function is to doom ourselves living unconsciously. To letting go of the steering wheel of everything that is happening in our lives, and unknowingly handing it over to something that would resemble a robot that doesn't think at all. We don't even know we've let go of the wheel – it is little wonder we are emotionally unwell.

Or is this the workings of something far more sinister and systemic. Maybe it is not that the information isn't getting through, or that we're largely disinterested in our own minds, but that we've been duped out of the fact of our own intelligence. Sort of a sleight of hand magic trick - 'look over this way' so that we never see the truth of who we are. It certainly could be very costly for those in power if 'we the people' start getting along and begin agreeing on some of the major issues. If rather than being divided by issues that maybe aren't as meaningful as we're led to believe that we stand united by the core things that we all want and agree upon.

It is unfortunate but for the most part people seem to obsessed with the battle over their own minds to be overly concerned with bigger picture solutions. In this modern world our minds are hardly something we would very often consider to be a friend or wanted companion. So how did we arrive here? How did we get to a place in our evolution, where we ought to be on the cusp of a breakthrough in our understanding, but our lives and social system seem deeply embedded in a cycle of decay. For so many thousands of years we've been driven towards simplifying our lives, and improving our living standards, yet we've arrived in a hot pot of social and emotional turmoil. We're largely emotionally disabled, overweight, and miserable. We have the best dietary advice and scientific strategies at our disposal, but we're in the worse shape of our history. None of it seems to help.

And to me the whole problem exists because of the divide between the conscious and subconscious minds. Or the general lack of awareness of the subconscious' existence, nature, and the role that it plays in creating the world according to us. The problem exists because for the most part we thinking the thinking and choosing mind is free-reigning – is the extent of us. We're doing all of the thinking and making all of the decisions. We haven't concerned ourselves with the other aspect of mind that can and does control elements we may have thought beyond our control. That there is something we can tap into that controls our luck and what we thought of as 'fate'. But no – we prefer to believe that we're in charge and the world is just dodgy.

By far the majority of people live with the assumption that 'we', in the conscious mind is the extent of who we are. That there is no more to us than that annoying voice in our heads. We are the ones doing all of the thinking, feeling – making all of the decisions and choosing all of our behaviours. Where the reality is that nothing could be further from the truth. An estimated 97% of our thoughts are subconscious – that is, repetitive and the same as we had yesterday – and in many cases the same ones that have been bobbing around in our heads for years. We are not in charge of anything. Most of our thinking occurs without us even thinking about it. It is not us doing, it runs purely and simply like a machine replaying the same old jargon, regurgitating the same old feelings. We have what amounts to a robot upstairs, churning out the same old ideas and experiences without opposition or question.

So we have the same old outcomes and events replaying like clockwork without us even knowing that we played any part in it. Our lives are run by an underlying autonomously reproduced state that underpins how we think, what we do and believe, and every choice that we make.

Where our attention goes and the type of evidence we see in the world is not by accident or choice. Something is doing it and we better start getting to know it – getting familiar with it, and understanding how to use and communicate with it, or it will more and more seem like we are trying to chop down a tree with a butter knife.

97% of our thoughts come from 'the machine' and so too does how we feel. And that automatically produced feeling state corresponds to everything that is happening in the world according to us. If we don't know the nature of this machine that is running our lives, then we've let go of the wheel of where we are going, and we don't even know it. If we're not aware of it, there's nothing we can do about it. Are you still wondering why we are unwell as a society? Lucky for us the solution is very simple and so much closer to home than we may have thought. In fact it is child's play if we can just break free from our egos for a second. If we are not aware of the operation of the autonomous mind we will be left with almost zero control to change how we feel.

Because it is in learning to speak the language that this aspect of our minds understands that we stand any chance of living satisfying lives. Any chance of living contributing lives, which is of course the most crucial element towards our lives having a sense of meaning and fulfilment. Learning that this mind is there in the background, listening to every word we mutter, and understanding how we develop a rapport with it is the key to curing this mental health pandemic we are in the midst of. This book will grant you the simple tools that will turn those hard to break habits, and milestone goals into chunk size pieces that we will not only look forward to, but find simple to do. It starts with one baby step, and it will become something super easy to do. indeed it is by this very same process that we blindly stumbled into the lives, reactive patterns, and repetitive dramas that we find ourselves in today.

When we know the reason we want to do something, and it means enough to us, there is no longer any effort required. When we care about our results it doesn't take courage or motivation to perform a new behaviour. We don't even have to think about it or use anything we may have considered will power. It just starts to seem funny to is as to why we didn't change sooner. How the old way of thinking persisted for so long once we get a clear picture of what is at stake and how much it means to us. When we realise who else is affected and who else we are doing it for, old values, ideas, and behaviours just leave without even putting up a fight.

And while I am not a psychologist and haven't received any formal training, I believe the present era has made it absolutely possible for normal people to get their hands on and understand enough the subconscious mind to grant us a dramatic shift in controlling how we feel and the subsequent circumstances of our life. To understand enough about the part of our minds that is creating the conditions of our life that we can have a considerable impact on the level of peace we enjoy, and contribution we make.

The content shared within these pages is both simple and common to everything I have ever encountered regarding the subconscious mind, Law of Attraction, and mindfulness. Through my own ongoing battles with depression and feeling powerless over the circumstances of my life, the subject has been something of an obsession for the past 30 years. Hopefully I have simplified and distilled down the solutions I've come to sufficiently that you can also make as dramatic shift that has occurred in my life. It certainly won't take an obsession, or thirty years to understand what I share here. Most of my life I didn't feel the way I wanted to, but I am absolutely convinced that nobody in this era need live in emotional states they wouldn't have by choice. The information shared here is common and widespread, and I am confident that even people who haven't encountered this type of material will soon grasp the ideas. If not from this book or the many others on the subject, it will occur to them quickly and in the way it needs to. This is the golden era of awareness, and a glorious time for our species – I couldn't understate the majesty of the era to which we have arrived. A time of golden opportunity, where the window has opened for us to live what was once only considered the reserved privilege of the spiritual masters. If we have evolved beyond the age of reason – then surely we have arrived at the age of opportunity. I would not consider myself 'religious' by any standard definition, but I do consider the subconscious mind to be at the core of all things spiritual. The realm by which all things and ideas enter this world. While not religious I certainly have an appreciation for them all, and the similarities they share with personal development content.

It was said that the Buddha had entered a place where he was surrounded by beauty – where everything was full of life and divine meaning. Indeed that place abounds – it is right next to us, and quite obviously does not exist in the environment but what our own minds are able to turn it into. While I'd never dare consider to have realised enlightenment myself – surely every step we take towards an appreciation of what surrounds us becomes its own reward. While I'm not so naive that I think we will all be floating on a cloud soon and all conflict will vanish, I do believe the opportunity has never been more defined and real for us to understand how much power we have to create the world around us from the inside. While peace will always be a process, it is in knowing that there is a pathway that all people can appreciate that there is something sacred about us.

And call me romantic but it would seem the signs are clear that a better time for all of us is not only possible, but so close it might scare us. Isn't that the true and promised goal that has always been considered the outcome of the evolutionary process – a more spiritual form of existence? If we are to consider what that might look like in our own lives then we stand a chance to of seeing it. I think we owe it to more than just ourselves to entertain the idea that peace is possible for us, because surely peace on earth begins at home - in us?

But with mental health being the leading health concern of our time, (The only health concern of our time if we believe in the body/mind connection) you would think that by now we would be better at it. Why is awareness of the nature of the subconscious mind not mainstream news and filtering down to the masses? Is there some kind of conspiracy? Are we just not interested? Or is it taboo to talk about the subconscious mind – are people just not comfortable speaking of something that for the uninitiated might seem complex and beyond their depth of knowing? I don't know why but I ask the question because I'm as puzzled by it as you might be. It seems we have the instruction manual to take us into the next era, but we aren't even going to bother looking at it until we approach the runway. This information is the cure to our mental health pandemic, but *let's not talk about it*. It is not polite table talk. Something so fundamental to our shared health and survival yet it still appears to be locked in the vault of our minds.

The New Control Panel.

With the knowledge being so common it would seem as though we have got our hands on the buttons to control this apparent 'supercomputer' perched above our shoulders – but we're not using this 'apparently' amazing machine to our favour. It's our only doorway into the life we want, but we can't get it working for us. If we aren't living what we would loosely suggest is a satisfied life, then we aren't feeding the subconscious mind the right instructions – we aren't thinking right? Or is it that we simply don't understand the thing we are sending instructions to? That we aren't thinking in terms of something is up there listening, and turning our thoughts into the world as we know it, or into our reality? We aren't thinking subconsciously – with reference to our reality maker.

Can we address the elephant in the room here? We cannot say that we don't know enough about the nature of this part of the mind, to share relevant information en masse. How this part of our mind works is not as mysterious as we seem to be comfortable treating it. Why aren't the very basics that we can, and do understand of how it works taught in schools? Why aren't more people talking about it or interested in it? If this 'thing' is, as it is claimed, responsible for 97% of what is going on for human life on earth, why hasn't anyone been able to even pique the interest of huge numbers of people? If much of the crime, dissatisfaction, heartache, injustice, and apparently even physical illness, can be credited to an improper use of, or ignorance of its function, why isn't the whole world talking about it? Why isn't the whole world flooded with information that can help us better use and understand, our subconscious minds?

Sorry, but that really puzzles me – why isn't this the topic on the tip of everyone's tongues? Why isn't it being splashed all over the news, or talked about like it is of a higher value than any BS tabloid story, or conspiracy theory? I tend to think of this frank ignorance of the subconscious mind as being something very much like a conspiracy of sorts. "Let's all just pretend like this thing just isn't there – that there is nothing going on there – like there is no more to us than we are conscious of." What a great idea, to keep the awareness of the main functioning part of the human mind all 'hush hush.'

It is this awareness that can supposedly cure the human condition itself, but we treat it like it is taboo – it is like we have some sort of shared agreement to - 'let's just not talk about it.' WHAT THE? Porn is taboo, but I'm damn sure most adults have had far more exposure to it than they have to material that might help them live more soundly. It seems matters pertaining to the subconscious mind are the most undersold content on earth, if we are to consider it in the context of how mentally ill our planet is. Do we not know enough about it? Or do we think we have to be some sort of expert? Maybe a lot of people hold the position that 'I can't even figure my conscious mind out, so what hope have I got of understanding that thing?'

But I can assure you anything that I'm going to share in these pages is simple to understand – easy to use – and of every piece of related material I've encountered, all agree on the basic principles I'll share in these pages. I think the main thing we need to understand is that **this part of our mind doesn't 'think'** like we do in the conscious– it is not a logical deductive mind, like the conscious mind that we are more familiar with is. But this is our good news – this is why we really have the upper hand here. We can feed it anything and it has no means to dispute us – it can't question what we speak in the conscious as truth. It can't judge or dispute our words – it can't even distinguish what we do want in our life from what we don't. It can't even tell if the suggestions we are sending are making us happy or not. It's a machine – a robot – an autonomous experience replicating machine. To all of our proclamations about what is real and true, it only one answer – one response, "As you wish". It just keeps showing us what we think is true as reliably as the sun rise.

It is the dirt in which we plant our ideas, and it doesn't care what we plant, it just grows whatever we grant the prize of our attention. What we look at gets bigger – what we ignore gets smaller. This thing we call our life amounts to no more than what we grant attention and what we ignore. Amounts to little more than an unconscious pattern of reactions that we are the passengers to. Our experience is not as random, or chosen as we might have imagined. We have less choice in where our attention goes than we may have thought. What gets our attention depends on how we feel, which is the domain of the autonomous or subconscious mind. Or as Dave Allen has suggested - *"If you don't pay appropriate attention to what has your attention, it will take more of your attention than it deserves."*

Little Wonder We are Stressed.

It seems our species has arrived at a state of exponentially growing desperation. We have to change our minds and how we use them. Life on earth has changed so rapidly. We didn't even see the first camera phones until 25 years ago, but now every single move we make gets plastered all over social media. And most people's faces are now permanently glued to their attention sucking devices like it is the only place they can find anything worth knowing about. Our phones have become our window to the world, so much that we can't even see what's going on around us. It is as if our phones have taken the place of our eyes in a sense. We are now living in a fishbowl where everyone can see everything we do, and nearly all of the time. We are quite literally on 'The Truman Show' 24/7, but just not 'unaware' like he was. And is it good for our psychology? As much as we might love the spotlight sometimes, just when we think the camera is off, we are back on display.

As a consequence, we feel more judged, critiqued, and exposed than humans have ever been. There is more pressure to perform, succeed and we all imagine to ourselves that we could just be that next 'lucky one' who starts getting money for nothing – from doing something stupid enough to go viral in our normal boring life. As a result, we exist in the fight or flight mode nearly all of the time. We've reached adrenal burnout but we're not athletes or CEO's – we're just normal people who have become run down and highly strung as a consequence of the fishbowl. The psychological illness that we have always suffered from – believing people care what we do, has become considerably exasperated by the age of social media. We have evolved yes, but we tend to think everyone is watching us – waiting for us to fall, but they are not. People don't care anymore than they used to about what we do. It was bad enough before we were in the fishbowl, but with the advent of social media, and us seeing these stories of ordinary Joe's getting rich from nothing, we think there is something wrong with us if it hasn't happened to us yet.

We're exhausted, anxious and burnt out like we are in high pressure roles, but we're just normal people. We weren't built for this confusing type of lifestyle. We were designed and have evolved through many thousands of generations of tribal living, where we could trust our neighbours. Where our community had our backs, and we didn't have to prove or validate ourselves to anyone. We did our best, we got along, and it was enough. Things were quiet and we were free. This modern life has left our nerves frayed, and our adrenal systems spent.

No one could really want to be 'seen' that much – could they? Do we really want to be loved by more than just our friends and family. Sure we'd love to be living the life that we imagine the rich and famous are living — getting paid millions of dollars for just prancing around looking fabulous. We'd love to be 'special' enough to have money thrown at us for doing less than we are. But we don't ever feel special because of how much we've become accustomed by this social media age, to look outside for validation. How far we have drifted from the value that we placed on our own opinion of us. Is this a consequence of the era? Has this happened by the same gradual slip from reality that our unwanted habits slowly crept in? Have we fallen for the bait that other people are the ones who are best qualified to tell us what we're worth and what we are capable. I mean we fell for it as kids because we had no choice – we hadn't developed the rational mind enough to tell if they knew what they were talking about. But this shift has severed our connection with something truly sacred within us. What we've have lost is worth far more to us than any number of likes on social media. Our attention has been slowly lured away from our centres. What we have inside us is eternal and sacred – but we have lost all presence of it even being there. It is our only true source of value and confidence.

It is as if we have sold our souls for what is on sale at Target this weekend. We have sold what is eternal and sacred about us for the thin veneer of how we think we look to others. What a shame. Have we really trashed what is golden about us, for the hollow and fleeting image of us that we know flickers like a candle in the wind. The picture we have of ourselves that moves on the whim of our mood, or the slightest of occurrences, has overridden a much greater presence within us.

Do you think the internet has connected us? Or has it just brought the world into our living rooms, and given us more 'partial' friends. Given us more part-time friends who don't really have to offer us anything more than a thumbs up or, 'God bless them', a 'comment.' Do we sense there is a real difference between 'Facebook friends' and the ones we actually pick up the phone to – the ones we 'see' in person. I think the internet has made us more like dancing monkeys, desperately trying to reach out for that lifeline - some thread of connection with someone who 'gets' and knows us. Has social media improved our sense of connection and relationships? Put us more in touch with people? Maybe in some ways but in other ways, our relationships have become plastic, meaningless, and cheap.

We are on display – like it or not – and we are starting to get the picture that every single thing we do can be seen by the entire connected world.

But my plea to you, is to see those people who are really in front of you, because as twisted and complex as our reality might seem right now, they are the real ones. Is it possible for us to stop looking into the abyss of our devices expecting that we can find something that is more real than what is right in front of us? What we thirst for is real connection, but we aren't getting this most fundamental of our emotional needs, because we've lost track of where it really comes from.

And this is where I think that desperation to change our minds comes from. Our being starved of a connection because we somehow think we can channel it from our phones. We need to allow for that larger, and at peace part of our minds to enter into our conscious lives. Because, dare I use the word, God knows when it enters us there is no feeling like it. A feeling of belonging and being home in ourselves that cannot be compared to in the outside world. That sense of our lives being guided – and feeling comforted without anything in our environment needing to be different. We never even realised the price we paid - what we lost when we became obsessed with what's going on outside of us. What we lost was the sense of the subconscious mind – that something sacred and supernatural is there, listening, guiding, and delivering us to what is best for us. That can move things and alter our perception of who we are – and do it in the blink of an eye. It doesn't come from other people, but breaking the habit of who we were.

So that is the only real question – can we become more conscious of mind? How do we allow this thing to enter us, and sense its presence in our lives? And the stupid answer is – stop trying and just be quiet with yourself for a minute. Everyone has a connection to it, and it regulates what is happening in our lives just like a thermostat. When we sense that it is there our lives go beyond what we knew of as circumstances.

And that is what we crave – not a connection to others, but a connection to ourselves – to the sacred. Us sensing that thing that is there, watching, protecting, and soothing our berated souls. What we want is the state of mind that can only be felt in the remembrance of what we are eternally. And as we will see that is what mindfulness is – what it connects us to. Is our state of mind worth protecting more than anything else in the world? Can we elicit states of mind without reason – conjure up some fond memory or desire no matter what's happening around us. Or can we be calm in the midst of a crisis? These will become the simple choices that move the world as we know it.

When we understand what is at stake in our state of mind. When we 'allow' our conditioned reactions to run off with our mood it can have much more dire and longer lasting consequences than we may have realised. At the completion of this book you will never again let someone steal our mood over something trivial. State of mind is the window through which we view the world. That sacred 'Holy Grail' that transforms the world around us. Our vibrating heart that turns the world into what it is to us. The thing that makes certain elements of our environment 'stand out' more than others. You want to see love reflected back to you from the world? Real love? – allow what's inside you to come forward into your conscious life.

Yes, we are in a fishbowl – and we definitely get the sense that we are seen more than we used to be (maybe more than we'd like to be.). But that hasn't made us more conscious of what's inside us – it has made us less so.

"Forgive yourself now for what you haven't done yet."

CHAPTER 1
Getting in the Picture

"Clarity is the only path to personal freedom – to be clear on what matters to us, and move towards it with intention. Living intentionally is the only way to minimise how much of our life 'happens' unconsciously."

I have written this first chapter as something of an overview of the entire book. I wanted to put people on the same page – particularly if they hadn't encountered Personal Development, or Law of Attraction material before. I've outlined all of the main ideas so that they take less time later and connect with each other better as we move forward. Hopefully this will save time when these ideas are further expanded on as we progress through the book. It is in understanding how these ideas connect to each other that maximises their effect. I wanted readers to have all of these concepts clear in their minds, to help in realising just how they connect and relate to each other, before we embark on any deeper explanations of each of the topics. I'm certain that by introducing these main ideas first, the further explanations and how these ideas mesh will make more sense.

The 'ideas' I'm referring to here relate to what has been dubbed the Law of Attraction, however, I wanted to put this phenomenon of our perception into proper context so people can understand that it is not just some wishful waste of their time or 'dreamy' idea. Attraction is something that is constantly prevalent in our daily lives – and when we understand what it is and how it actually works, we'll be able to use it more consciously, and to our advantage. Attraction is the gravity of how the state of mind we come from, shapes what we see in the world. The world is an inner projection designed to reflect how we feel, or our unconscious expectation. When we are in a bad mood the universe will conspire to support this, and shine back to us reasons that keep that feeling alive in us. But this has been going on for a very long time and beneath our awareness – the whole world won't move with you the moment you decide to smile. (Even though it certainly helps.) Attraction is a Law just as sure as gravity. A force of nature I think is better described as the 'Law of projected energy.' As will become obvious through the course of reading, the world, and all of the people in it, respond to our energetic output. We can indeed change the nature of our environment, or at least how it appears to us, (what else is there?) when we change our energy – aka our state of mind, vibration, how we feel – whichever resonates best with your understanding.

> *"The mind seeks familiar conditions so that we can have knowable outcomes."*
>
> **Joe Dispenza**

State of mind is the lens through which we view the world, but it is not a conscious choice we make. It is a self-sustaining product that is governed at a higher place of consciousness. So for the best, from our understanding it is replicated and reproduced automatically by a machine-like process. It is the dominant mood that defines our character or 'way of being'. It is an unconscious function of the higher mind that regenerates itself from our memories and experiences. This 'automatic' mind can only ever present a mirror image of our past. How we feel is therefore very rarely a conscious choice that we make. It is essentially a conditioned energetic pattern that replays the same familiar experience – quite often for many years. The scenes we walk into are produced by the subconscious mind, and what stands out for us (what comes forth from the trillions of moving particles.) is not just relative to our conscious interests (agenda), but created beyond our conscious awareness by the unconscious programs that have been running in our minds for many years. The state of mind we call ours is just the consequence. It keeps itself alive by mirroring how we feel on the screen of our environment.

It may come as a surprise to us that how we feel on a daily basis, or the mood that characterises who we are, is not as much of a choice for us as we think. The 'world' pushes our buttons and tells us how we should feel, or rather circumstances do. Little do we know how internally generated those circumstances actually – how projected our perceived version of reality really is. Our state of mind is created by an unconscious function that plays like clockwork, but we certainly can make conscious decisions to improve how we feel. We just don't do it very often and, even if we have an awareness of how automated this replication of our state is, we are up against an aspect of mind that is deeply embedded in our psyche, operates on a level that is much faster than the conscious mind, and so is very difficult to change quickly.

Nevertheless we can always make those smart feeling choices when we can, and when this becomes our habit, or default, the process will begin occurring with almost zero input from us. It would seem even more reasonable to expect that unwanted situations would even come our way – even if they do we're going to equip ourselves with the tools to negate their affect almost as immediately as they arrived. But it is ordinarily the outside world that makes us feel the way we do. It happens unconsciously, so we aren't able to make the conscious choice to feel how we would want to. Circumstances are the driver of emotion because, up until now we weren't aware of the direct connection between how we feel, and what's going on in the world around us.

Yep, that time when everything just seemed to be going against you – or when you were late and seemed to catch every red light. It was all relative to what was going on inside you. Its why people tend to seem particularly irritating if we haven't had enough sleep, or we become easily bothered when we have something troubling, or important to us on our minds. But just like our breathing, (that other unconscious function of the body) we can make a conscious choice to boost our mood. Just as easily as we can take a deep breath, we can transport ourselves to a better feeling place. In the hindsight of this knowing this, it's a choice we are far more likely to now make. And when making that choice begins to characterise us – when it becomes a habit - we will almost certainly begin to see a very different world reflected back to us. Quite possibly a reality characterised by friendlier people, more opportunities to help, and more moments when we can deeply appreciate what is 'happening' around us. Depending of course on the type of things you value, are looking for and appreciate. So we have more control over what's happening in our experience than we might have ever imagined.

This book is designed to help us minimise how much of our life 'happens' unconsciously – without us thinking we played any part in our circumstances. If we aren't aware of our part in the creation we will be cursed to relive the same experiences over and over without ever having a choice in the matter. We can't change what we didn't do. We can only change what we understand our responsibility for. When we are able to see the events of our life as part of a long running pattern, we are freed from having this be our 'life sentence'. As stated in the quote at the beginning of the chapter – clarity is the key. The clearer we are on what is important to us, the more intentional, directed, and meaningful our energetic output becomes. To minimise how much of our life is happening unconsciously – with us as the passenger – is to live our lives intentionally. What we do because we meant to, can't happen out of habit. And the unintended consequences of remaining unconscious to what's happening in our life, can lead to far more dire results than we realise.

I will be so opinionated to state that I believe the core reason most of the mental health issues that persist in this day are relative to the degree to which we remain unconscious to our patterns, and live unintentional, reasonless lives. Where we make no claim to what we want, and what matters and has meaning for us. What we remain unconscious to, we can do nothing to change. Much of the mental illness that exists in this day, stems from people either not knowing what they want, and therefore not moving towards it, or not believing what they want is possible for them, and so fail to take any step towards it. They don't care about anything, don't know what they want, or imagine the thing they want is so far out of their grasp they have stopped moving towards it. We will never lift a finger towards something that we don't believe is possible. There will never be any effort where there is no perceived reward. Some people find it impossible to believe they can become the person they need to be. "I just can't see myself doing that". From their vantage point they imagine they've exhausted all options. Or as Abraham Hicks suggests **"You just can't get there from where you are."** Because we can never get to a better feeling place from a place of feeling bad. This is the acknowledgement of just how feeling dependant, or relative to how we feel the reality we experience really is.

What we want is what we turn the world into.

What we desire is what we turn the world into – what we program our mind to notice more of in our environment. The only things that are visible to us is what we are looking for and expecting to find. I accept that this idea may seem oversimplified if we try to consider its authenticity before being introduced to all of the tools that will be presented through the course of this book. Before we consider every tool at our disposal, and how quickly and easily these can be brought to the table of solving long-term problems. Understanding the language the subconscious mind understands, so we can communicate with it fluently – knowing what mindfulness really is and can do for us – and how the projection/reflection feedback loop we are poised in works, so we can start taking advantage of how simple our powerful mind really is. Or even more importantly, why it might be so hard for us to use this 'Law of Attraction' thing with the false idea we have of it in our minds. It can't work if we don't understand what it is. But when we know, we are able to sidestep that energy feedback loop and make every feeling choice at our disposal. In the light of awareness, these choices become as simple and straight forward as dropping a rock that is burning our hand.

There is something within us that wants the same things we do, but we have to trust that it sometimes also has a funny way of getting us there.

> *"First our minds must be opened – and then they can be cleansed."*

The choice we are faced with.

We have come to a period in our history where we stand on the precipice of great impending change. A fork in the road if you will, but the two choices that I think we are faced with will be framed throughout the course of this book. It is a question of us realising that we all play a part in and contribute in our small lives to the entire human fate.

This content is designed to help us be more in control of how we feel personally, but I have to think that it becomes a much easier choice for us to make when seen in the context of an even greater meaning. When we understand just how much what we do and how we feel matters and contributes. We've all heard the cliches' of 'be yourself' – but this will be as if more than just your life depends on it. Not in some overzealous and righteous sense – but in the sense that we have the absolute right, and duty to make ourselves the living expressions of our version of freedom. The freedom to be who and what we are lies at the core of living a conscious, intentional, and meaningful life. There are many doing it already with little idea of how important this is to the whole.

I'm certainly not trying to make anyone feel like they now have the entire world on their shoulders, but when we understand how much our seemingly small choices impact far more than just our families and communities, it will surely lighten the weight of many decisions we were finding difficult. Rather than us being in turmoil and two minds over things, the decision becomes plainer and more obvious when we see it in the light of this wider world view. This content is about helping us personally get to better feeling states, but when it's brought into the context of our communities and the even broader global implications those choices effect, they should become even easier for us to make and stand by. A question will be raised at the end of the book to help put us in the picture of just how much our feeling choices matter in steering a bigger ship. How much we are actually able to steer the fate of humanity by our once seemingly insignificant personal choices.

Once again, this is not to get all heavy - I just think we should be aware how much those apparently small, but life changing choices we make effect broader and longer outcomes than we imagined. When we understand this they'll be clearer and even easier choices to make, if that is, they were at all difficult to begin with. But in the context of the so called 'butterfly effect' that we all have over the whole, our actions are magnified by time and effect people in ways that could never be fully known to us. What we do becomes amplified by time and bumps into so many other energies that we have to know there far more at stake than our own personal reality. I think we have been coerced out of our voices, our meaning, and our greater intelligence. Convinced of our smallness, us 'little insignificant people' have been duped into believing that it is our scientists and politicians (The big players and smart people.) that have our back when it comes to the fate of humanity. That wise people who care about us and have all of the relevant information at their disposal are steering the ship.

They want us to believe that they have our best interests at heart, and wouldn't dream of taking from us, or putting one over us. They want us to agree to the 'fact' that it is not up to us, and that we should forgo our instincts – our greater intelligence. We have no intelligence on these matters, and play no part in the fate our kind. That what it takes to live in a decent world is completely beyond our scope and comprehension, so they'll freely take all of those choices out of our hands. Even though by far the majority of us all want very similar things in the way of freedom of choice, peace, and to raise compassionate, and contributing children, we seem very divided over some relatively trivial issues. I want to pose a question in the end of the book in light of what I hope we have become more aware of. A new sense of responsibility for how we feel, means so much more when it begins to spread in the lives and minds of the majority.

I have mentioned this in the hope that you will keep this in mind as you read. That information is not just so that we can manifest our new boat, or so we can get a greater sense of pride in our contribution. But also because I think it is vital to the human story that we start to get a sense that we can change the nature of our environment by the energy we project. The fate of nations is truly in our hands when we understand our choice to feel – our ability to create feelings without reason. And how much this actually affects the physical plane.

Attraction in Action.

It might be far simpler than we might have imagined to alter not just what's happening for us, but for whoever steps in our circle. When we get a grasp of how much the choices available to us in each moment to feel differently effect the environment around us, do we become the guardians of human fate? I know this might sound like more Law of Attraction BS, but my promise to you is this will be presented to you in a way that it not only makes enough sense to you that you can use it, but you will be witnessing it in motion, and in each moment sense its true impact. It will be undeniable to you, and we have all had experiences of this at work in our lives, probably without being aware of it. When we are in a bad mood it often seems like the world is conspiring to make matters worse. This is because our mood, or energy is being projected onto the world. Whether we feel good or bad, the world will always reflect evidence that supports that state of mind. But it is in awareness of this phenomenon that we understand just how easily we can turn our day around. And the truth be known, how far beyond just this day becoming more sensitive to our energetic output actually progresses.

You will see and experience the 'feedback loop' and understand why it makes changing how we feel seem so difficult. Why it puts the reality of us being able to change how we feel seem, by our design, beyond our reach, or choice.

Our environment must always replicate and reflect back to us, evidence that supports mood and expectation, but we'll get back to that in a minute. But if we are approaching this precipice in human understanding the doubters would seem completely warranted in the scepticism. We are approaching some kind of spiritual evolution and yet we witness more dissatisfaction in human lives than we have arguably ever seen in history. If we are waking up to this 'higher awareness', (becoming more conscious) you would expect there to be more peace in the world? We are supposed to be the most advanced, informed, and conscious our species has ever been – better equipped to answer all of the mysteries of the mind, perception and how to heal ourselves than ever.

But, in great contrast to these facts, we are at epidemic rates of depression and mental illness. Could the reason be so simple that it is staring us in the face? Could we really trust someone who proclaimed to know? Of course, I'm throwing in my 'uneducated' two cents worth, and you can be my judge and executioner.

The fact is we have **far more control over our outcomes and the reality we experience than we exercise our will over,** because we don't operate from the awareness of the relationship between how we feel and what's happening. Between our state of mind, and the reality or circumstances we experience. Or in simpler terms, we don't realise how the world seems to us, to be a product of our state of mind. My aim is simple – **To make that choice we have in every moment, to protect and improve how we feel, into a very simple choice to make.** To show us the moments when we aren't making those choices that we would if we were aware the tricks the higher mind was playing on us. If we understood the full gravity of what was at stake – how long these patterns might run for should we fail to act. And what we are also affecting by the energies we bounce off. I want to make it glaringly obvious to you how our conditioning operates beneath the surface of our awareness, so that we can take charge of what's happening in our lives. The enemy we don't see, or realise when or how it is talking us out of having a go at things that we could really be good at. It is the job of the unconscious mind to convince us 'nothing has changed' so there is no requirement for us to change anything or move from where we are. That any move out of the ordinary could be very costly and have dire consequences.

It is the job of the higher mind to create a familiar experience out of a world that is a constant state of flux. The world outside of us is trillions of moving particles that are constantly shifting and rearranging – and it is the minds job to make it look like it is standing still. 'Nothing to see here – just go about your business of reacting to the same old

BS'. It creates a familiar seeming world, out of the trillions of moving parts spinning all around us. To ensure us (in the conscious mind) that there is nothing to concerning and our ship is on an even keel. To convince us that we ought to be reacting the way we do, and what's going on in our life is fixed, rather than fluid. The conscious mind is much slower in operation than the subconscious. The signals from the subconscious are instant and automatic. We are not able to question what is going on, or see multiple perspectives of a single situation in the moment it's occurring. Reflecting on what happened and being able to see the event from different perspectives must come after the fact. But it is possible to make this process much faster when we live in the awareness that what's happening being an illusion of mind. We become less reactive and careful with our reactions when we are aware of what's going on at a higher level of mind.

> *"Until you make the unconscious conscious it will direct your life and you will call it fate."*
>
> Carl Jung

These are some simple choices for us to make now – but what makes them even easier again is the awareness of what is actually at stake. When we are aware not just of how much our state of mind alters the world around us, but the farther-reaching implications over time, and to the world at large. It is in an awareness of the broader effect of what we do that expands our sense of responsibility, and makes our reactions and behaviours less of a battle between two minds. How we feel turns our point of our attention – **unconsciously forces us to notice the elements in our environment that support that feeling state, we can only see what confirms belief. Beliefs are the reason we feel the way we do.** We aren't predisposed to be constantly questioning what we believe – we are just shown over and over by the mind what we already believe to be true. Our beliefs are automatically projected in the way we see the world, or what is referred to as the confirmation bias. If we weren't certain of many of our – if they weren't automatic - our experience would be chaotic. We wouldn't know what anything meant, or represented to us. We rely on our beliefs being automatic to navigate a carefree and safe life. We hand that stuff over to the 'driver' or the program running in the background. But when our small choices to feel better are offered to us in a new light of awareness of what is actually happening, they of primary importance. We are shifting reality itself when we wake to the games of mind.

When we get a grasp of the full scope of what we are actually bringing into our control, those seemingly small and ineffectual choices to feel differently become game changers. Just like how our tastebuds begin to change when our mindset does, we don't allow small things to keep unconsciously steering and effecting our lives. You wouldn't have such a sweet tooth if you had a sense of small behaviours becoming embedded as habits. If the wrong foods were seen for how they were going to affect us in the longer term, what tastes good to us changes in our minds. Those donuts won't taste so good when we understand that it is not just that moment we are eating them in – any action represents an unbroken chain of many actions.

Would you consider it a relief, or an uphill battle to alter the beliefs that have us locked in an ever-repeating Groundhog Day? Where every effort to improve your conditions seemed futile? **Would it be a relief to change the beliefs that have been making our life harder? Those choices will seem so obvious and easy to make, when we recognise the overarching effect they have.** When we can make choices that affect the very nature of reality, and what's 'happening' in our lives. When we can change circumstances that we've grown particularly bored of by the simple act of taking stock of how we feel in each moment, I don't think it's something anyone will consider a struggle to do. In fact I think you will be astounded by just how simple it can really be to make the simple choices that change what's happening in our life. It's easy when we get the sense how our everyday, and **easy to make choices really can have life changing implications.**

But at present we don't do enough to protect, monitor, or elevate our state of mind in the way that we might if we were aware just how much of our reality it rules over. Because our vibration is immersed in matter, our experience and how we feel happens almost entirely from memory. Our vibration is stored in the muscles and organs of the body – in the flesh, and matter is the lowest form of vibrating energy. Just like if you were to ding a tuning fork and then stick it into a bowl of jelly; the vibration all but stops. The vibration in us doesn't stop, but it takes a lot of energy to change. To alter our feeling states reliably we have to elevate our thoughts above matter, and into the ethereal realm. Think in terms of what we really know ourselves to be.

Just as in Newtons first law: **"An object at rest remains at rest, or if in motion, remains in motion at a constant velocity unless acted upon by a net external force."**

Our energy doesn't change unless acted upon. That is, unless we have a reason, or someone or something pushes us. But when we act with regard to changing our energy, rather than trying to change our perception of circumstances from within the conscious mind, it is as if we have hoodwinked the subconscious mind. We are now the ones tricking it, because of an awareness of its nature. We don't have to consider all of the ways how we might see the event in a better light – we just have to feel better, and the process happens of its own accord. When we elevate our feeling state the shift in perspective is automatic. The subconscious mind lacks the ability to reason – it doesn't know or care why we've made the decision to feel better. Energy is far easier to change than circumstances. I will go so far as to say that I will prove to you that working on our energy first, is the greatest return on effort you will ever come across.

Without awareness we don't recognise the tiny choices that we could possibly be making in each moment, for the profound opportunities they represent.

We don't realise how overarching the effect of state of mind has over what we see, how we think, and what we give our attention to. How it shapes what shows up and becomes visible in our environment. We forgo that, would be easy choice to make, and opportunity to improve our conditions, because we don't prioritise vibration, or guard our reactions. **We don't recognise those choices as an opportunity to alter meaning, not just in this moment, but from this moment on.** A choice that becomes so much more apparent and easier to make when we know just how much we are affecting, and get clearer on what's important to us. When we take into consideration how many other people benefit from us creating the best feeling states we can and following through on our intentions.

I'm not trying to make this sound super easy to do. Becoming more certain of what we want and what matters to us is an ongoing and lifelong process. But I have to think that knowing how much simpler, and guided our life becomes when we are clear on what's important to us, then being clear on what we want kind of jumps the que in our priorities. Discipline needn't be the grinding torture it may have seemed, when we are clearer on our reasons. When we form a proper sense of the true consequences of chasing short-lived sensations all of the time. Such reliance on those overly stimulating tiny Dopamine hits, actually takes us further away from experiencing joy. Life is never easy, but it is always so much easier when we have a clear awareness of the reasons we do anything, and understand the longer-term consequences of our choices. I promise you that it will be easier than you ever thought when we understand the power in our hands to change the nature of what 'appears' for us, by small and easy to make choices.

> *"Do not waste one moment in regret. For to think feelingly of the mistakes of the past is to reinfect yourself."*
>
> **Neville Goddard**

I love how many people, and how many different ways the truth of attraction has been communicated. There is always another way that we can put it - one that just clicks for people. An analogy, a story, a perspective that makes the idea click – where we now see and understand the gist of it. We've been spoilt for choice really, the same principal put in so many different ways - broadcast across so many years, languages, and cultures. Needless to say though that while we still have any level of mental illness – while there remains anyone who doesn't understand the choice to feel, there can never be enough people trying to spread this news in anyway it can be understood. We need to get smarter in our delivery, so that this truth can be more broadly understood, known, and practiced by all. The mind is telling us a lie about our apparent conditions, and a lie about who we are. It is hiding and denying our connection to something sacred, but trying to wake us up in anyway it can.

I am super confident this book may just be the way it clicks for you. The five key pillars I use to illustrate the power in a conscious choice, will put your ducks in a row. That you will rarely if ever have to suffer at the hands of circumstances again, and will realise quickly how close your place of solace is. We can quickly withdraw into the protection of our shell if we ever lose the sense of how truly sacred our perceptions are. If we forget just how mind created and mind changeable, the outside world really is.

I will show you...

1. Such a unique take on **state of mind projection** (Law of Attraction) that you will actually be able to use it.
2. What **mindfulness and meditation** actually does for us and permits us access to.
3. How getting **clear on what we want** actually alters what 'shows up' in the world around us; channels our efforts, and allows the unimportant parts of our lives to just drop away without pain or any sense of loss.
4. What **our conditioning** actually represents; in the lie we believed about ourselves for so many years, and how it infiltrates our defences.
5. the chasm of difference between what are **internally, and what are externally created emotions**. When we get the sense of just how different they are, we will tend far more to the light than we've probably ever known in our lives.

I just know that this will make sense to you; enable you to change your mind and way of thinking enough that you can feel the way you'd choose to more of the time. But it is really about the awareness of the eternal nature. Of what we are connected to just by the virtue of having a mind – and sensing that thing that is there guiding us and creating the world around us as an active presence in our conscious minds.

I certainly don't want to make it sound like this truth should have occurred to us already, but I would like to assure you this will seem like a 'no brainer' choices when we recognise the opportunities available to us for what they truly are. The opportunities that will aid us in defying the logical mind, and move with ease towards a better feeling state.

If the word 'vibration' sounds a little 'new age' for your liking, by all means substitute it with state of mind, state of being, frame of mind, or just simply how we feel. Our 'mood' or emotion is of course far more variable and temporary than the momentum of our dominant state, but everything we feel adds to the mix and has the potential to become a permanent part of our experience. Everything we feel becomes a part of our karma, or the energy we project. As does any dramatic event carry the potential, or dare I say has the tendency to replay in our experience perpetually. That is of course, until we 'get the lesson', or work out the purpose this emotional pattern serves. Sometimes this is as simple as asking ourselves the question of what purpose does this serve? Reality is the most convincing of all illusions. One giant ploy designed exclusively to sustain the *state of mind coding* that underpins our survival.

Why would we not want to know about this 'world creating' operating system below our awareness.

It is not just that we don't understand the effect how we feel has on reality, or how our mental experience is happening on the inside of us. But also our ignorance, or general lack of interest in the very thing creating the 'setup' or is it that the majority are still oblivious to the illusion. The general lack of interest in how the subconscious mind operates must be the largest contributor to why our mental health has become the issue it is today. As I've mentioned, I'm not a psychologist, but that is my point. I don't believe we need to be 'experts' in the field to have a 'clear enough' understanding of the subconscious' operation that we can implement lasting changes. The very beauty of the age to which we have arrived is just how common, knowable, and usable awareness of the subconscious mind is. Awareness of the nature of the subconscious mind has become so simplified and digestible that it is ready to eat. Changing the culture towards our general lack of interest, equates to us being able to cure the human condition itself.

Why must we continue to live ignorance? Because we imagine the conscious mind is the extent of us, and all we are working with. That we think we can change our lives with positive thinking and effort is killing us. We have to get to the core of our perception mechanism. Not some mysterious place at the end of some wild pilgrimage; a place in the quiet of our minds. We have to get to know us, and intimately. Hear that voice of providence in our heads like it is an audible friend. Because battling on without engaging our inner essence can't make us feel better, no matter how hard we try. It is precisely because we cling to our ideas that there is no such reality creating part of mind – because of our ignorance that human predicament persists.

For me, it is like WTAF is going on here on our planet; that an interest in this phenomenal tool, (our subconscious minds) lies right in front of us, but so few consider it a topic worthy of interest.

The Ferrari of dreams.

Imagine if there existed a Ferrari that was serviced, full of fuel, and all we had to do was step on the pedal and it would speed us to that place where all your dreams had already come true. **Wouldn't we at least want to know about it?** Wouldn't even the greatest sceptics be asking, 'yeh right, where is this magic Ferrari then'? This is truly what the subconscious mind represents – us being able to rewire our minds and thinking. So imagine the surprise if we were to find out that this 'Ferrari' was already parked in our garage. That it already existed within our own minds. And I think not in the power of the mind, or positive thinking; or any of the cliché's we have probably grown a little tired of. **But in how we use, relate to, and create our emotions.**

Wherever it is we imagine we want to be; that place, or position is only representative of an emotional state. Where we want to be is a place characterised by a feeling state – the state of 'having'. It is why in the earlier quote of Abraham Hicks "You can't get there from where you are." We can't get to a place of feeling the way we'd like to if it's not the way we feel already – if we not sure how it is that we want to feel. What's stopping you feeling the way you want to, and doing the things that you want to do now?

This Ferrari is real – it is living in the light of a created emotional state, rather than forced into how we feel by conditioning or 'circumstances.'

Everything we want is because of how we imagine it will make us feel. If it didn't make us feel awesome, we'd never want it. And it is in the creation, or imagination of that feeling that the reality or pathway opens up to us. We have to know the feeling first, and the clearer we replicate the feeling the sooner wit surrounds us. The sooner we live with the reality that the desire is actually there. How this Ferrari becomes real for us, is in our recognising the enormous difference between **emotions that are internally created**, and the ones that seem **forced on us by conditions or circumstances**. We are so convinced by the higher aspects of mind that our circumstances are not only real but unchangeable. We rarely even allow ourselves to challenge the idea of what is real, or entertain the thought that our view on the matter can be changed. If we want to change our minds and start to think like we are someone else, then everything must become fluid, and up for questioning. Particularly if it doesn't hold us in high regard.

What is commonly known and freely available for anyone who wants to understand our ability to shift the world around us, is both very simple and universally agreed upon.

That said, I don't think there is a literate person on this planet that doesn't know we have a subconscious mind. And even if they've never heard anything how it works, they have some awareness that it creates the world as we know it. I mean, we all know we do many of the things in our life 'subconsciously' – that is, without thinking about them – purely out of instinct or habit. We understand that large parts of our lives are lived out of habit, rather than deliberately; most of what we do, believe, and consequently feel, happens without us even thinking about it. We all know what it means to do things 'subconsciously', and we all know we do it, but **would I be correct in assuming that we think we have to be highly educated to know anything about this aspect of our minds?** That we would need a high degree of education in order to use it to implement desired changes. Or do we just not want to know this stuff until we become so hung up that we walk into see a therapist, who must know all of this stuff and can explain it?

Is it some kind of conspiracy to supress the interest in the subconscious mind? Or do people not want to know for a reason?

It puzzles me that, so few people have an interest in this thing if it is clearly what dominates our life experience/s but I guess that's my problem to deal with. And forgive me for repeating but you would really have to wonder how, with the huge impact the subconscious mind has over life on earth, that no one managed to sell this idea mainstream. Why isn't it being sold as the next big thing. It is the corrector of all of our problems and the maker of dreams, but people are interested in, well, just about everything else. The cure to the human condition itself, but let's just leave it on the sidewalk. It will forever be a thorn in my side – my puzzle to solve and mission to make this awareness interesting and worth learning about. To make this 'Law of Attraction' stuff usable, and I've got some big surprises in store that I think just might give us the upper hand on something that has kind of being screwing us over most of our lives.

The Position We Are In.

In light of the current circumstances in which we live, where we have become privy to an encyclopedia of personal development knowledge, and have tapped into the best of every creed and culture who has ever attempted to rectify this human conundrum, you might assume that we'd be better at it. That we'd nearly be there. Or is it that we exist right beside this knowledge, but at the same time are only really interested in polishing up the 'veneer' of what we look like to others? Are we ever more concerned, or should I say unconsciously compelled, to act out of fear of how we look to others (our group in particular)? Even though we proclaim to not give one f$#k what people think of us, we are unconsciously lured by our need to form bonds with others, belong and adhere to group norms.

Our survival is far more reliant on our relationships and connections than we are probably able to admit to ourselves, and we are prodded by forces beyond rationale to find, connect and stick with our tribe. Once upon a time to be exiled would mean almost certain death. We couldn't survive on our own, and we are still privy to those same instincts that have persisted through thousands of years of our evolution. We have an unconscious need to belong to a group of some kind and to be doing what everybody else does.

Compassion is the only measure of a soul's development.

It is a long-standing belief in 'spiritual' circles that the measure of any soul's evolution can only be known by its level of compassion. So it begs the question, does that happen because **as we become more spiritually awake**, we understand how intimate the connection between us and the world around us? We realise that our skin is not the limit of us? Or that as awareness grows we understand ourselves to be a part of everything, and connected to a far vaster source of energy.

That acting purely out of self-interest could never satisfy the higher and wiser aspect of us?

Not getting all 'judgy' here, just stating the commonly understood 'rationale' that we are intrinsically a part of what appears to be the outside world. And **to embrace this awareness would also mean that tapping into a much vaster source of energy than is available to us from the perspective of separation.** When our purpose is to lift others, don't we get a little bit of the energy from those we pose to help? It is not just us that we are doing it for, so we do it with gusto. **To see other people benefit from what we've done is the real treasure that cannot be measured in currency** – all the better if they never knew it came from us. It would seem that when we have an earnest interest in serving the greater good, we inherit the energy of the greater good to help us.

> *"To do something that helps someone else – that genuinely helps them. I defy you to find another experience that is as satisfying."*
> Jordan Peterson

Our Greater Body

The outside world is what I will refer to in this book as our 'greater body'. And the subconscious mind is what I will refer to sometimes as the 'big' or collective mind. I know this may not fit with many of the experts who may insist that the subconscious mind is something far different from 'universal consciousness' but this is how it makes sense to me. That said, I think it is only **by knowing ourselves in the context of something larger that we can feel our lives have meaning. That our work and contribution can feel like something of a calling.** That said – I'm also fairly certain that our lives shouldn't become a 'look at me' contest where we think we have to be seen to be helping huge numbers of people to consider our work meaningful. Getting attention doesn't necessarily mean we, or the work we do is better than someone else's. our work shouldn't have to attract huge numbers, or our effect to be miraculous to consider our work purposeful.

I really think this is a big part of the problem – we either don't do the work, or we don't put our souls into what has meaning for us because no one else see's us as some kind of miracle worker. Whatever ever the role be that we find ourselves, I believe the aspect of it that is **'spiritual'** always comes from the deepest part of us. No matter what work it is that we love doing it comes from the same place. But if it doesn't feel right to us, then maybe it is not what we were supposed to be doing. What makes the work spiritual is where in our hearts the intent comes from – not how many people think it is good. That we always come from a place of genuine interest in others and bring to our workplace a 'light' that is uniquely ours. We could be a nurse, or a garbo - a high court judge, or a truckie - but our work is equally as 'spiritual' because of what we bring that lifts the spirits of others. In whatever situation we find ourselves, **we are a part of something larger, and to feel that is what spirituality is really about for me.**

> *"You see, it is the love with which you do things that radiates - it is not the things you do."*
> The Ra Material – the law of one

State of Mind is the Regulator of all Experience.

State of mind is not just the filter of our experience; it is **the trophy** of our lives. The 'holy grail' to be held above all else. If our lives cannot be full and realised - conscious and joyous, without us having a great state of mind. Surely it must be placed above all else. If it colours and permeates into every single thing we do, why does it not come first in our priorities, and why do we so easily give it up over dumb things? Why is it so easily sacrificed? When we accept it as what underlies everything we do and every experience we have, shouldn't always be the first priority we consider. Everything that happens falls under its spell – flies under its banner. And when we come to realise just how changeable it is – how often we let it slide for dumb reasons, we might actually get a picture of why our life seems out of our control and dissatisfying. When we are able to see what's happening when our buttons are getting pushed from an observer level of consciousness, then surely we are at least dawning on a life of meaning and satisfaction.

Surely when we see state of mind for everything else that it influences, we start doing everything we can to manage, protect, and elevate it – and what's happening in our life responds in kind. When we begin to create great states of mind beyond what we even have reason to, just because we know the effect, and no one can stop us. This is indeed the true essence of Attraction – our ability to create the feeling without reason. That is the meaning of faith – we just know it is coming – we just know that it is possible.

The subconscious never knows or cares where our visualisations are born. If those pictures we have in our minds are generated from imagination or real-time memories. Whatever be the source the effect is the same, and so the effect on our reality is the same. Can you feel great from a memory, or imagining that you have just received something long waited for? Now you're starting to get it – now you're starting to force the world to your will. And wasn't it all so easy? Wasn't it effortless?

Getting in the picture.

When we really get in the picture that the sole function of the subconscious is to sustain vibration. (Keep us down?) That its aim is to reassure us that nothing in our world has changed, even though we are doing everything in our known power to try and change it. Then we might start to see those unwanted, yet familiar patterns of jealousy, impatience, and frustration for what they are. What this awareness is aimed at granting us is to take a step back and see what is happening from a more detached perspective. What we thought was happening in our lives is far from the truth, and never deserved the emotional devotion we had been granting it. It's not as real, or final as we thought it was – and no matter what happened we can make it right. We don't have to repeat history, but that's exactly what we do if we fall into a whole over over it. If we fail to forgive ourselves, we almost guarantee we will fall victim to the self-loathing pattern that feels so familiar to us now that we would wonder who we were without it. Just to question the fact of what really happened is to pull ourselves out of the whirlpool we were getting sucked into.

From the observer perspective of our lives – from that state of detachment, we peek behind the curtain of where reality itself is being constructed. We become the emotion free director of the show rather than the drama infused actor. We are freer to decide how we might respond, rather than being kicked in the gut with no choice. When this becomes our pattern, we have formed a life altering pattern the grants us a director's chair in the movie that is our lives. We are not numb to our feelings - we are just freer to act and choose in spite of them. **Without effort or thought, we begin to live more tolerant, patient, resilient and peaceful lives.** Kind of like, as a consequence of being gifted a backstage pass in the production of our own lives, we 'automatically' become less reactive, and more centred and calm. And it has nothing to do with trying.

We are surrounded by all possibility.

From the millions of possible outcomes – the 'infinite possibility' that surrounds us – we make visible what is front and centre of our experience. From the blank canvas, of the 'everything' and the 'nothing' emerges **'our something'**. Much like those 3D pictures reveal their imagery when we blur our eyes, we are the ones who bring forth from 'the everything' from all possible outcomes that swirl before us. Whether it is a beautiful world of opportunity, or a horrid and unjust hell, the difference is not in the environment but in us - in the filter. And filters can be changed. When a salesperson, a mother, and a teenager enter a shopping centre, they are all see different things, relative to their interests. From the vast display of sensory info, certain elements stand out and become more prominent to them because of their interests and agenda. Because of how instinctive their minds are as to what is of importance to them. We see what we look for, so what is it you would like to see more of? Because these proclamations are precisely how we program the part of mind that we have limited access to. The part that creates the world as we know it. We can change the parts of our minds that we aren't conscious of, and **it is no more difficult than 'what do you want?'**

It is our deeply emotional nature that makes some decisions more difficult than we think they should be. It is never just an easy choice to break a habit that still serves a very important, unconscious need we have. To break the habit we have to go inside to know the need that it fulfills for us, if we are any chance to fill that need with a better behaviour. We have to see for ourselves how ironic or flawed our means of meeting the need by way of the current behaviour. Is there a better and more suitable way to meet that need? We can only consider this once we know the need we are trying to meet.

The need will always remain, and so too will the habit if we don't first understand all of the reasons we do it. Much of the angst that we suffer from is because our values evolve and change as we get older, but our habits remain. We try to meet evolving values by way of static behaviours. We are slow to realise that we want different things that can no longer be met by behaviours that have become engrained in our lifestyles. What always worked for us now feels like we are smashing our head against a wall. 'I know I need to be more relaxed, but no matter how much I've increased my beer intake I just don't seem to get the same amount of calm I used to.' Go figure. With every evolving value, comes a whole new menu of needs to be met.

In this moment, there are choices you can make — simple choices — to look forward to something different happening. Choices you can make to feel better, improve your mood and expectation. Choices you can make to 'control' the type of things you see in the world. To take charge of your feelings is to take control of your reality. The ability to elicit states of mind without reason goes beyond the effects we are conscious of.

It's 'happening' unconsciously.

As the word 'unconscious' would suggest, we have little to no idea the parts of 'what happened' that come from us and so can do nothing about changing it. We don't sense what's going on as a by-product of our energetic output or our unconsciously created expectation. There is no choice in or control over what we aren't aware came from us. But when we change the energy we project, we change the world according to us with it. We make what was once unseen into something visible. **This book is about presenting those very simple and easy-to-make choices we have that change the world around us. We will begin to recognise these choices as opportunities to change far more than just our mood.** But without insight, we are locked in one of the most powerful, perfect, and convincing feedback loops that exists on our planet. A feedback loop that has us convinced that there is very little we can do to improve our plight. Nothing we can do to improve how we feel, what we deserve or how other people seem to treat us.

But, in reality, there is lots we can do, and these are certainly not difficult choices to make when we more fully understand the underlying emotion and the role our reactions play. There is no requirement for us to do anything as noble or brave as 'facing our fears', or grinding from dawn until the early hours. When we grow in awareness of just how make believe the story we've been telling ourselves is and why, that apparent 'lion' we were afraid of turns into a mouse. Meaning we can indeed still go after and even live the life we've been fighting for - it just seems so much easier for us to imagine now. We can imagine it into being. That huge mountain we assumed we had to climb, shrinks once we see new pathways to the top. We realise that there is always an easier way and if it has seemed impossible for many years, maybe that wasn't even what we were supposed to be doing. It was just that our ego's got the better of us. We realise that there is no shame in who we are and what we've done. And everything we've done has brought us to this great place – where something far more divine than we can realise wanted us to be. And we have the audacity to find shame in who we've become?

Often a door will appear in a wall – just when you thought you were beat. But if the opportunity isn't presenting itself you can be certain an even better one is on its way – something far more suited to your skillset, and far more rewarding.

> "Intellectuals solve problems, geniuses prevent them."
>
> **Albert Einstein**

That hard slog of work you might have assumed you had ahead of you can often be turned into something we can achieve in just a couple of days. The obstacle is often just a failure in our perspective – a problem exacerbated by our way of looking at it, and not what we think it is. Lifelong phobias have sometimes been overcome in minutes. There is a reason our fears are existed that sometimes doesn't make as much sense as we think we do – and when we get to the feeling or energy of being in the solution the answer is often revealed to us in the simplest of terms. A completely unconsidered way to solve the issue just appears to us like magic. A switch gets flicked, causing you to accept the reason you were afraid to make absolutely no sense at all. You have done things very similar to this – even harder and more challenging than this with absolutely no problem.

The reasons we were worried don't make anywhere as much sense as we thought they should. Filters and our conditioned way of seeing the world can be fixed, and changing our beliefs can be fun. If we just keep our desired outcome in mind and see beyond what we think are the immediate issues. What is our life like when we get past this? What does it allow us to do once we get past this next stage.

We turn the world into what we are looking for in it.

The key of course is in understanding that feelings are never things we should wait for the evidence for. They are tangible and real pieces to our puzzle that we can create without the evidence. **We don't have to wait to feel like we have those things we always wanted – and that feeling is the most direct route to seeing the physical evidence that reflects the feeling start showing up in our reality.** If we feel the way we want to already, the desire loses its power over us. We no longer need the 'thing' because we can create the feeling even in its absence. We want for nothing. We've literally cheated the system, and shortened our way to the result. We have managed to create the feeling without the having – the more realistic the feeling and the more often we practice it, the sooner the reality you desire has no option but to appear before us as real. If we have the feeling, we don't need the thing. Here's the thing - we don't get the things we want - we get what we already believe to be true. We attract the reality of the person we believe ourselves to be in this moment.

The only thing we really need is to be **clear on the details of what we want and recreate a realistic imagination of how that would feel.** If you have not encountered this type of 'work' before that may sound a little bit like BS, but it will become much clearer to you how and why this is how our mind works to make an abstract feeling materialise into something real. I know that people can have a much greater **return from their efforts** than they are currently going about getting what they want. This isn't 'hard work' as you used to know it, but it is the greatest return on effort you will ever encounter.

> *"You are already that which you want to be, and your refusal to believe it is the only reason that you do not see it."*
>
> **Neville Goddard**

The 'work' that changes everything doesn't come in overalls, but it certainly will require you to be ever more focused, clear, and sensitive to the energy you are projecting than you probably have been. It will require you to have an open mind and a willing heart. This stuff might seem all too 'witchy' and hard to believe at the moment, but I promise you that it will all seem clear as we work through the principals in the book. I'll make it so clear that you can use and see Law of Attraction in action instantly in how your view of the world and you problems, begin changing once you're able to shift from the conditioned state of mind. Changing how we feel was only hard before we knew what was on offer right in front of us. The 'hard stuff' starts to 'lay down' right in front of you, so you can walk over it with ease. New doorways will appear, and chance meetings will arouse your suspicion that there just may be far more order to this chaos than you suspected.

Becoming more conscious will become your new favourite thing to do.

What do you want? This seems such a difficult question for so many people to answer, but why. I'm all for keeping our most personal desires to ourselves, while we work on them. **But knowing what we want is the very thing that makes our life easy** – that channels our efforts into one meaningful direction – that alters our perception of events and, most importantly, changes what we look for in the world. Being clear on what we want is the very thing that enables us to 'bend' the meaning of an event to suit us as a learning or a boost up. Everything that happens is part of our path and helps us get where we want to go faster. Everything that happens is brought into the context of meaning by is it bringing me closer or in my way? What is the lesson can only be known and learnt in relation to the goal. Everything that happens shortcuts our results. We can only understand the meaning in relation to how clear we are on where we want to go. We see the world and everything that happens in it for how it helps or hinders us towards meeting our goals. The world means nothing until it relates to our agenda. If it's not important to the goal, it becomes less visible to us.

Our goals are how we decipher what is meaningful to us, and what is not. And the clearer we are, the less bothered we get over the trivial and unimportant stuff. The clearer we are on agenda, the more we are able to bend the meaning of an event to our will, and to suit our needs. What things 'mean' becomes a decision rather than an unconscious and forced reaction that we have no choice in.

Knowing what we want is not just what makes our life easier and more directed, meaningful and time rich - what we are looking for is what we turn the world into. Out of all possibilities, what we see has everything to do with us – our energy and what we have told the subconscious mind we'd like to see more of. 'Seeing' is an intuitive and emotional faculty – a projection of the mind. **We change what is in the world, by what we look for in it**, what we give our attention to. What we make into a more prominent part of our experience. It is how we gain control over what would otherwise be happening unconsciously. By what we are grateful and looking for more of, we take back from that 'automatic' part of our minds what is happening without us. We do this by getting clear on what looks better to us and declaring what we would rather see. Nothing is out of our control when we become 100% responsible for how we feel.

> "Death is not the worst thing that can happen to us – but to not know why we lived."

Disclaimer

Is the universe friendly?

The one small choice that has the most significant effect on our experience.

I'm not so naïve to believe there is no darkness in the world and that it will just disappear if we don't look at it. That there is darkness in the world is the reason I wanted to write this because you just may be the last hope someone has to remind them of the goodness that still exists. Being able to show them that there is still some good in the world - a glimpse of the light - might be all it takes to lift their heads and start seeing it all differently. To shift the trajectory **of what happens for them from that moment on.** You may be all they need to push on for one more day that gives things a chance to turn around or for something unexpectedly positive to occur to them.

There is darkness in this world – there is even darkness in our homes, and in our own hearts. We ourselves live with destructive, repetitive habits and are our worst executioners - we are our worst enemies and the only saboteurs of our growth. There are those on all levels of government and even in our own workplace that don't want the best for us. This may seem odd when denying us some benefit comes at no cost to them. But that's just how some people are.

Can we fix every wrong in the world? Can we ensure that nothing 'bad' will ever happen to us by just 'projecting' good energy? Is it your fault everything you consider bad ever happened in your life – that it's your fault – you asked for it, and you should just 'get over' or deal with it? Of course not. Just as sure as doing all of this work will not ensure nothing undesirable ever comes your way. But you certainly have better tools to deal with it, and are willing to understand it as being a part of your way forward – as somehow woven into your destiny. Elevating your vibration will not cease all human suffering. Nor will buffer us from ever experiencing any pain. What this does represent is us understanding that we can change the nature of the material world, by changing how we feel: **change our energy and we change the world according to us.** By the energy we add, the whole shared vibrational mix becomes a little bit different.

Nature gave chameleons this wonderful gift of being able to blend in with their environment – a dynamic camouflage. But nature imbued us with an even greater gift: that we change the 'colour' and nature of our environment by how we are, and by the energy we project. The world moves in relation to our energy, in response to us. We can't fix everything that is wrong in the world, but because the world expands outwards from our own hearts, we should concern ourselves with what we are adding to the mix? Because, like it or not, it makes a difference.

Bad things do happen to good people.

Many bad things have happened to some very good people, and they don't always have a silver lining. Mums and Dads have lost children to cancer, car accidents, abusers, and killers. Lots of people have experienced horrific things in their lives. I'm not suggesting if we turn a blind eye this will all disappear like magic. Very few people ever make the choice to be strong – most are forced to become that way by circumstances beyond their control. I'm not asking people to pretend bad things don't happen when we are wishful. Or that we can just slide down a rainbow onto our unicorn, and ride off to our awesome job, where everyone is lovely. I know as well as you do that's not the real world.

> *"There are only two ways to live your life. One is as though nothing is a miracle. The other is as though everything is."*
>
> Albert Einstein

What can you do about all of the darkness in the world? Shine your light and be what the circumstance calls for. And I'm not throwing a blanket over all of the evil in the world, and imagining it can all easily be solved by way of a simple solution. There are those in the world who would definitely love us to give up hope. That want us to stop caring and shining and lose our compassion, so they can say "see, I told you so – the world is an evil place." There are those who would love nothing more than to see us at each other's throats, as proof that we are not capable of governing ourselves and see that as the justification for further reducing our freedoms. They may even try and convince us to give up our choices and control for the 'greater good' – that it would be irresponsible and antisocial to think that we can have some say, input and choice in how the human drama unfolds. It is also true that darkness can reach maturity much faster and easier than the light, but it also perishes at a much greater rate. Love builds slowly but remains. Evil grows quickly but has weak foundations. Just as the truth always prevails, but lies are very hard to hold.

We evolved because we give a shit about each other – because we learned to work together and collaborate our efforts. And whether or not you consider our population growth to be our ultimate downfall, the truth is that **we have thrived**. We thrived because the light is greater than the darkness. **We are collectively and unconsciously centred on curing the conundrum of human suffering – making life better and easier for everyone.** We wouldn't have come this far if we weren't predisposed to value compassion or that we are, at our core, caring souls. We've come too far and achieved too much to allow the conspirators of evil to extinguish the hope in us. All I'm asking for is to realise what hope offers and what it costs us. It offers everything and cost nothing. Make those simple choices to feel better and as well as you can, and for a far better reason than you may have ever imagined. This is for far more than just you.

There were many who came before you, who paid the ultimate sacrifice in the name of keeping hope alive. Who risked their life for what they believed was right. Are we, in our wisdom, prepared to say that there is nothing worth fighting for or nothing worth saving? That because bad things have happened to us and in the world, we should tend towards imagining darkness will win, and there is little to no point to what little difference we can make? If the naysayers or unfortunate circumstances have managed to lead you to believe that, then they have beaten you by some very underhanded tactics.

I don't mean to get all heavy here before we even get into all the light stuff that I intended this book to be about, but I understand that there will be critics and doubters who want to insinuate that I said, "You asked for what happened to you by your energy and destiny, so you should just deal with it and be happy." I am far from suggesting that and I certainly don't have all the answers as to how people might integrate all of the crap times they've been through and make 'lemonade' out of it.

> *"The single most important decision any of us will ever make is whether or not to believe that the universe is friendly."*
>
> **Albert Einstein**

It is because that choice will colour everything you see and want to do. We never lack the courage to do the things we want to: we lack hope. We will never lift a finger in effort towards something that we don't believe will ever come true. It is never courage that we lack to take on bold pursuits – **it is that we don't care enough about the result.** We haven't considered the other people in our life and who else might benefit. If we lack faith in the fundamental goodness of our fellow humans, then we will be reluctant to think that we ourselves could improve anything, or that our life could be of meaning. It's not that we lack the courage to do things - people, or the circumstances of our life, have just managed to suck all of the 'care' out of us.

Is what happened, or may happen, your fault or the fault of your energy or destiny? Probably not, but what you do about it is. And I'm not saying 'get over it' – or try to see the good side of every shit story. I'm just saying if we're to give up hope, then meaning goes with it. And isn't that what we really want just as much as to think that our life has purpose. That we are in the pursuit of something meaningful – we're doing something we care about. If what happened broke your spirit is all the more reason to fight for all the broken spirits out there. Who else have they got? To live in a world that is either supportive, or out to get us, is a far more powerful choice for us than we might have imagined. I wouldn't see any point in trying to add something of value to a world I imagined was 'out to get me' either.

Empathy is strength - empathy is how we connect and become trusted, and needed in a relationship. How many people have ever been listened to and understood? Empathy is how we be what the what the circumstance needs. It is far from a sign of being soft or overly sensitive. It is a quality that only the strong can tolerate, and only changemakers are willing to embody. We have to have a sense of social conscience to do meaningful work. If the world is to be slightly better for us being here, we have to be able to sense what it needs. But if taking on too much of what others feel – if empathy becomes our curse then who can we help? Who can we help if we are buckled and afraid?

I've been buckled and afraid before and it is never an easy thing to trust someone who's trying to convince us that "everything is going to be alright." But that they were there meant everything to me at the time. When we are drowning, sometimes all we need is that small reminder that we can float. And to be that person for someone when they need it is a privilege. Finding the way we can do that discreetly without them losing face is the highest skill of all.

> **"Not - this is misfortune, but to bear this worthily is good fortune."**
> Marcus Aurelius

Some people may never recover from the torment they have been burdened with. The guilt, the trauma, and the frank injustice, particularly when children are involved. It's hard to imagine that there is a point to that level of suffering – to be born only to carry the burden of losing a child in any way. I can't imagine how that would feel, nor do I think anyone who has felt it would ever wish it on another. I honestly don't understand why it happens, or if there is any meaning behind the atrocities and injustice that seems so commonplace in our world. What is the point of our souls spending what seems like an eternity in hell? So, we can do tours through that horrid place? And I certainly mean no disrespect to anyone who is living through something horrid right now, but it is only the people who have been through the fire that can help the people that are. That can comprehend, relate to and guide people with faith that there is hope on the other side of what's happening to them now. It is only the fire-proof that can walk us through the fire and be trusted that there is life on the other side. Maybe not joy and happiness, but a life lived with purpose just the same. If we know the 'why' or the reason, we can bear any 'how'.

> *"I am not what happened to me, but what I chose to become."*
>
> **Carl Jung**

The manipulation of meaning

> *"I have always believed and still believe that whatever good or bad fortune may come our way, we can always give it meaning and transform it into something of value."*
>
> **Herman Hesse**

Bad things can and will happen – so is what I'm trying to communicate just coping strategies? Not in my opinion. Because I've seen this stuff work firsthand. I have a very fortunate life, and great connection with the people who want to be in my circle. I've come to trust in the effect of monitoring and raising our vibration. That our state of mind can be chosen much more of the time than we ordinarily practice before we are conscious of how much it actually effects. I know that how we feel has a defined effect on the events, people and circumstances that are drawn to us, and what becomes visible to us. This is one giant leap beyond positive thinking, but does it guarantee that we'll never again experience hardship? Probably quite the contrary – "God gives His hardest battles to His strongest soldiers," as it is said. And I can only speak from my faith and experience that a positive expectation not only changes the world we see, but far outweighs the alternative.

More to the point, it enables us to manipulate the meaning of events by the effect being a conscious decision rather than an automatic and unconscious compulsion that we have no choice in. being clear on our agenda is the thing that helps us consider everything as somehow woven into the path of our destiny. If something seems unwanted and pointless – like a tragedy that couldn't possibly hold any lesson or benefit then we really have to go a level deeper inside to find the lesson. Without the compass heading of our agenda we would never even bother looking. And instead just remain angered or upset, or often crippled by an event that was sent to change us. Everything is sent to prepare us for what we said we wanted more than anything. But the unwanted stuff must be held up to where we think we are going for the meaning to ever be received.

It is by the clarity we hold of where we want to go that we can very well bend the meaning of any event to meet our needs. It is all meant for us, even if we can't see the immediate gain. This is the true power of a clear agenda – with it we can bend the world to our will. This is what is meant when they say 'bending reality'. When we change how we feel about, look at and interpret an event, we are moulding the events meaning to our reality. The event becomes part of our clay that we are working on. Rather than it be something we had no choice in, we have transformed the event by integrating it into our story. Any change in how we make in how we feel about something and what it means, alters both the event and future events like it from that point on. We've changed what will happen in the future by how we changed the event.

A Fork in the Road.

Our goal is always the same – take back the power from what is happening in our life unconsciously.

Spoiler alert – the message of the book comes down to this. The difference between handing the wheel over to the unconscious and conditioned patterns of our life – where everything seems unwanted and there's nothing we can do about it. And living an intentional life because we want to do things we care about. One pathway follows our desires and the other is to let go of the wheel without even knowing it. One is to pursue what has meaning for us and know why we do things, and the other is void of meaning. To follow the intentional path of meaning and do what matters to us, is to consider that our life is guided by a force beyond our knowing, and can do some hard things without effort. We've let something else drive too – but something beyond our scope of knowing and we trust in all of the outcomes it produces to get us there.

What will it mean for us when we get this thing, or this thing has come true? This is all that we must keep in mind to keep us on the path. How will our lives be better and different when we live in the manifestation? This is all we need to know in order to persist and be guided past any obstacles. If our reasons are not clear we'll be letting the conditioned patterns do the driving, and it may be a long time before we realise how out of our control our life has become.

One is the pathway towards getting what we want that proves conditioning wrong, and is meaningful and satisfying. The other is to allow how we have been conditioned to drive. The false ideas that were deeply embedded in us before it was up to us. It is a life void of meaning where circumstances remain beyond our choice or control. There are very few opportunities because we are trapped in our movements by our reactions. If we want to reach for the wheel that will change how everything goes from this point on – what do you want? Why does this matter to you? And how will it change your life and the lives of others when it is true. If we know then it has already happened. All we need do is stay calm and the universe will show us the way.

The Sad Truth.

How much of our life happens instinctively – out of habit or goes on automatically without us thinking we played any part in or had any choice in the matter? The real curse of our lives is that we live inside a conscious mind that has been generationally trained to ignore the presence, influence, and role the subconscious mind plays in our lives. We know it's there, and some of the basics of how it's working in our lives, but we seem to have this unspoken agreement that it doesn't exist or affect us. We pretend, or act like there is no subconscious dominance acting over our life, and we are the ones doing the 'driving' and making all of the decisions. It is little wonder we are not well as a species. I would even go so far as to say the degree to which we have managed to 'hoodwink' ourselves that we are completely in charge of, and running our lives in the conscious mind, and disregard any influence of the unconscious, is to the same degree the dissatisfaction we might experience.

We have to accept that the emotional and instinctive mind has the reigns, and we are really just along for the ride. We have to work with the thing that is in charge and treat it like our ever-willing companion. Or we can live without concern of how it operates and takes instructions – we can imagine we are all alone in this world with nothing and no one helping us. The subconscious mind creates the scenes of our lives with lightning speed, but then steps back saying "It wasn't me." Such is the nature of the illusion. We live under the pretence that we live almost the entirety of our lives **deliberately**, paying no mind to the subconscious aspect that lies at the heart of our every circumstance, habit, pattern, and decision in our lives.

To me what is happening in our lives on autopilot is the definition of living in hell. We have no choice in or control over the things that happen automatically and unintentionally. And that hell is not created by the mild and familiar feeling we experience, but by that growing sense that 'I didn't do this' and there's nothing I can do about it. What's happening will always tend to feel like there is no way I would have asked for this if I had a choice. The hell I'm referring to comes from the idea that we played no part in what's happened. We can't change the nature of the event and have no choice in our reaction. What's happening in our lives, without us having any awareness of the part we played in it may not always make us feel bad. But it is opposed to a life lived intentionally, and what we do intentionally is **always in our best interests**. Is always towards some defined and desired end. And there is a giant chasm of difference between what happens automatically and what we do consciously that will shock you to realise when we go into more detail on it later in the book.

Living automatically

How much of our lives do we 'do' without question? Because it's what we've always done, or because it is what everyone else is doing? This is not to say we are 'sheep' as there are very sound and complex forces at work in our lives to ensure we do the things our group does. But many of us can and do, live our lives, almost completely on autopilot. And little by little our lives become less than satisfying, until we find ourselves a long way from satisfaction, and wonder how we ever got there. We never sensed those small choices that were being made for us by that 'trusted' subconscious driver, and when we were moving unintentionally by the hand of fate. And I'm not trying to give anyone advise as to what they should or shouldn't be doing.

Most people have very sound reasons for doing what they do. But if we aren't conscious of those reasons, we will never perform our actions with the gusto, and enthusiasm we ought to. It brings to mind the story of an experiment conducted on two groups of housemaids in a hotel. The first group was subtly reminded of the physicality of the job they performed, and how a single day's work equated to 4 hrs of a solid gym workout. The second group – the control group — wasn't told anything. At the completion of the study, it was found that the first group that was given awareness of how much exercise they were actually getting at work, experienced a far higher level of satisfaction from their work, were markedly happier, and actually lost a considerable amount of weight through the course of the study.

It is amazing what a little bit of awareness and reminding ourselves why we do what we do adds to both the process, enjoyment, and the outcome of our work. What we do with intention lights us up - but what we do automatically or out of a sense of obligation (no choice) makes us tired very quickly, and never feels satisfying. I'm not suggesting that we can cease everything we are doing in our lives by reflex in an instant. But raising the awareness that when we become more conscious why we do the work we do, we take our lives back from the automatic - it gives us the sense that we are in control, and feel inspired by the work. It makes us feel better. This is simply bringing our attention home to the things we do already but without knowing the reason.

When we do the small things with intention, the big things we might have only ever dreamed of doing will become a more obvious and clear choice. A natural by-product of living more consciously if you will. Look after the pennies and the pounds will look after themselves, as it is said.

The word 'consciousness' parallels 'choice' – what we do consciously, we do with considered intention and for good reason. Instead of doing things out of a sense of obligation, or because we think we have to without ever really knowing why. If we don't have a mindset of playing a conscious part in our lives, then we become susceptible to the types of people who are determined to try and control us. These people are masters of deception and the hypnotic effect, who will try and convince us that we don't have a choice. We are offered two bad options and are made to feel like the choice is ours.

That there are many things happening that we don't really feel like we have a choice in, is a phenomenon that exists because of we have a long running history of us doing most of our lives automatically and out of habit. They have used insight of the subconscious influence and the nature of how blind we are to our choice making mechanism to trick us into believing we only have the options they present to us. They've effectively conned us out of our right to choose, and like the subconscious that drives our lives, many people aren't even aware that it happened. But there is a deep psychology behind being able to take advantage of how mindlessly we normally operate. We believe the choice isn't really ours. Many of the issues that divide us as a society have been purposely installed to trigger conflict between us.

We have been conditioned to believe that we have 'no choice' because of our tendency to leave so much of our lives up to our robot mind, or programming.

If we don't make every small choice that is in our best interests, we inadvertently lose the ability to know the big choices that are also optional. Take control of all of the small things, and we are far less likely to ever be 'conned' out of our rights and personal sovereignty. We have been systematically blindsided out of our personal choices, not just by governments and authorities in recent times, but also by the trickery of psychology trained advertisers. And of course, how unconscious our addiction has become to our mobile devices. It's considered normal behaviour now to stare at our phone screens for hours on end. The architects of these apps are highly skilled at subliminal manipulation, and tasked by their employers to make their products more and more addictive.

We're are unfortunately lambs to the slaughter, because of our drive towards always picking the low hanging fruit. We are wired to notice patterns in our environment that get us the easiest access to our sustenance. And a big part of what sustains us is not just the food we eat but the neurochemicals we find delightful. We have these little devices in our pockets that have us drip fed on dopamine – so much so that we don't look up from those devices often enough to grow and seek the bigger hits that we used to. We've been lured just like the pied piper did with the rats and all too easily. *'If you just keep them spell bound by social media they will never bother with wanting to know what their life's purpose is, or notice the sinister game we are playing right under their noses'.*

There is sadly a very limited awareness of how much AI is already impacting the lives of humanity, and how much these seemingly 'harmless' Apps are able to sway what we think, feel, and believe, by manipulating the content on our feed. The algorithm knows us subconsciously, and far better than we even know ourselves. What we click on and for how long – we are all being profiled and not just so they can target us with ads. If we don't want to be blindsided by this technological era, we need to be as intentional as we can be with everything we do.

"The greatest tragedy of our time is that we have no interest in the subconscious mind that controls every thought, emotion, and occurrence in our lives. But the tragedy is not that it is unknown to us, but that this information is right in front of our faces. It is not hiding, or hard to know and understand, yet we don't even see it."

Chapter summary.

- State of mind is the underlying cause of all experience – how we think, what is going on in our life, the outcomes, and events we experience, how people treat us, and the type of evidence that stands out in our environment are all a product of this automatically reproduced state.
- State of mind is not a choice for us but recreated by an autonomous and machine-like part of our minds. It reproduces by projecting itself onto the environment – the 'world' makes us feel the way we already do – keeps the feeling inside us alive.
- Has the primary job of the subconscious mind is to turn an ever changing world into a familiar seeming experience. Which is why we find it so difficult to improve how we feel. Without insight into this operation we can be forever stuck inside a subconscious feedback loop. It can drive us crazy if we are trying very hard to change.
- But when we understand just how much of our experience is a repetition of state of minds recreation process, we can do a lot more to consciously choose to feel and react better, and at the same time alter what is happening in our lives. We can elevate our state of mind even when we don't see reasons to in our environment.
- Every change in feeling has a reciprocated effect on the reality we perceive.
- This is really the essence of Law of Attraction principles – to create a feeling without real evidence, **because of a consciousness that the feeling is what makes the evidence show up.**
- That we have a limited interest in the subconscious mind despite it being largely responsible for our mental health, perceptions and human life on earth would seems puzzling. Particularly when we don't need to be a scholar to realise the very simple and basic things that will help us understand its operation well enough to get it working for us.

- Truth is we can change our life in enormous ways by way of small incremental improvements in consciousness. Without doing anything as drastic and brave as 'facing fears' we can change how we feel and consequently the world according to us – aka our reality.
- To live intentionally is to minimise how much of our lives is happening unconsciously – without us thinking we played any part in it, and so consequently can't do anything about it.

CHAPTER 2
Our Big, Dumb Mind

"The mind that thinks, doesn't know, and the mind that knows doesn't think.

Simon

Something is listening.

> *"You cannot entirely control your subconscious mind but you can hand over to it any plan, desire, or purpose which you wish transformed into concrete form."*
>
> Napoleon Hill

We all know we have a subconscious mind, and we all know we do things 'subconsciously'. It is the higher aspect of our consciousness that lies quietly in the background of our mind creating the world according to us. The aspect of our mind that possesses a seemingly God-like power to shift how we see the world, and our ability to overcome our issues. Isn't that really what defines something to be an issue – we aren't able to see it in a way that looks like a solution. We find things difficult to do, because of our way of seeing. Because of the way we are used to looking at things, and tackling the problems that we can deal with. It is our way of looking at the thing that is at the heart of any problem – the filter through which we see the world. It is only a problem because we can't change our way of seeing it.

I'm sure most people will be familiar with the analogy of the baby elephant who when it was young was able to be restrained by a small peg in the ground. But as the elephant grows to the size and strength that could easily rip that same pin from the ground has been conditioned to think the same small pin can hold it where it is. Or the fleas that when placed in a jar with a lid on it for a couple of days, would only jump as high is the lid even when it was removed. And we humans are the same. Have been boxed in by our thinking and way of seeing the world by events that happened so long ago that the causes of our pain or humiliation no longer apply. They apply but only secretly and in our imagination. We can't sense what is there as an ongoing reaction to a now unrelated event, but it still manages to corner us into thinking that if we try it, it will all go wrong. We are conditioned by our experiences to be subconsciously afraid of situations that we have much less cause to than we imagine.

We have grown into completely different and more competent people, but those same old fears illogically spoil what we'll take on without us even being aware of it. unfounded fears that would run like cockroaches if they were ever exposed to the 'light' of our questioning – or seen for what they were. If we were to ever ask ourselves with some sense of honestly, 'what's stopping me'? What we may have imagined beyond our capability could be flipped on its head far easier than we ever thought, but the platform from which we think just keeps churning out the same thinking patterns over and over like they are real. But they are not – they are no more real than the lid that was removed from the jar of fleas. It is not even there anymore. So anything that we really want to do can be broken into steps that gradually prove to us just how unfounded our fears are. If we have an end goal in mind that excites us, we owe it to ourselves to change how we can look at it. Any endeavour we imagine desirable can be broken into a series of doable steps if we take the time to reflect on it and come up with a plan. Most importantly, if we keep in mind that there is something lurking in the backgrounds of our own minds that would like nothing more than to show us the way.

We really need to understand this subconscious mind thing as a guide and a friend – it absolutely wants the best for us and the very same things we do. We would have never come up with the wish if we had not already experienced it on some level in our lives. We just need to learn the language it understands and begin speaking in a tone it can hear. And that is the language of emotion. **If we can imagine how it would feel** to be living in those circumstances today like they feel real, we are talking directly to the thing that can change our reality in an instant. We are speaking the language the subconscious mind understands as clearly as English.

We don't live in a physical world – we live in a psychologically created experience. We live in what our minds have made it into. And we can turn it into something vastly different, and not by what you know of as hard work, but by getting closer to part of us that is making it seem the way it is. If what's happening in our life is less than we'd like, we only need to become more sensitive to the messages, or 'instructions' we are sending with our feelings. You are seeing a reflection of how you feel in what you know of as the world. How our thinking makes us feel becomes the world as we know it. If we can change how we feel, the thoughts will change themselves, because emotion is the underlying platform from which we think. How we feel provides the scaffolding if you will for our thoughts to exist in. If we are bold enough to imagine our grandest plans coming true, the thoughts will change themselves.

As Robert Kiyosaki stated in his ground-breaking book "Rich Dad Poor Dad", the mindset of his two father figures was vastly different. Where one would say 'I can't afford it', the other would say 'How can I afford it'. And while the difference in these statements may already seem obvious to you – being that the first one stops the mind thinking, and the latter starts the mind. We can quite literally turn the mind to 'go' by way of a simple choice of words. But we so often miss these profound opportunities because we don't hear ourselves thinking, or consider them to be the instructions we are sending the subconscious mind.

We really need to understand the fundamental differences in how this part of the mind operates to get it working for us. The things by which we would measure someone's intelligence in the conscious sense (recall, logic, ingenuity) don't apply at all to the subconscious mind. It is an altogether other breed of intelligence. It accounts for all of what we know of as our lives, and has a warehouse full of storage space. It doesn't decide what things mean – meaning is instant and automatic – meaning is known, not deduced. The subconscious arranges the particles surrounding us to take a familiar form. It doesn't think in terms of what we understand as thinking – it just 'is'. It operates thousands of times faster than the mind we use, and builds our world in a split second, but for all of what we may consider 'intelligence' it is sadly lacking. For what we understand as 'intelligence' the subconscious mind has none of those attributes. This world creating part of us is basically very dumb.

It believes everything we tell it like a gullible child and is powerless to challenge even the most fundamentally flawed reasoning we can hold. Earl Nightingale compared the subconscious mind to dirt when he suggested 'that it doesn't care what you plant'. It will produce weeds just as readily as it produces crops. Whatever we give our attention to gets bigger and becomes a more prominent part of our experience. To get this world changer working for us we have to understand how different it really is from the mind we think with. It can make our lives immeasurably easier if we make friends with it and start talking to ourselves like some big magical 'Genie' is listening. We have to realise that it can't argue or dispute us, whatever we feel is true becomes our reality. If something isn't going right for us, it is only because we've become too distracted to hear the messages that we're sending. It is not the subconscious mind that is at fault, but what it is hearing. It grows whatever we give our attention to and focus on, with no idea if it is good for us or going to make us happy.

It only has one reply – 'as you wish'.

If we really want something and persist in that very same desire over long periods of time, the subconscious will organise our experience to come across the right information or people who bring that desire into being. It may take less time than we thought, or it may take more – the point is that if the desire is persisted in, it must happen. **There is an awe-inspiring force listening in the background of our minds that ensures what we feel in the moment is reflected in our reality. What we think becomes real in our world.** It works in ways that are far beyond what we can understand to reconstruct the scenes in our life, and make the right things cross our path at precisely the right time.

The conscious mind can't know of the magic and mysteries of how this all comes into play – nor should we ever concern ourselves with the magic at this level of mind. We need never concern ourselves with 'how' this could possibly all come true, but just persist in the feeling that it has. The subconscious has us on a collision course – the shortest route possible to have the experience we've been asking for. What we see before us always reflects of our present vibration. And it is our ability to imagine desired states as if they were real that overrides anything that can be done by us to bring about this shift in what we see before us – we don't change the presented evidence the subconscious mind does.

But the mind has our back. Any time we don't feel the way we want to, or find ourselves short in any way from the desired state, we will always be presented with how or what needs to change in our way of thinking. Or we'll be introduced to what we need to learn in order for us to make it seem real. Whatever we ask for, or claim to be real will become real. 'I create as I speak', is the true meaning of the Aramaic word *Abracadabra*. Whatever we state to be true – so shall it be.

The life we have has been brought into reality by what we believed to be true. If this isn't what we want we only need to redefine what we want to be different.

The conscious mind doesn't know how this 'reality' thing gets created. We don't have an 'all access pass' to the great creative mystery to know it works. We don't have access to the subconscious or the mind that 'knows'. And I say 'knows' because of the unquestionable nature of reality. What Einstein referred to as *the most convincing of all illusions*. The subconscious is the mind that knows, but it cannot think, and leaves the conscious mind exasperated, thinking 'how the hell did I get here' – or 'surely I wouldn't have asked for this if I had a choice'? All the conscious mind can do is decide what looks desirable and move towards those things in the best way we know how to. Or to do the work we imagine needs to be done. For us in the conscious mind we do the work – we start digging a trench or we take up a course of study in order to get our results. In contrast, the subconscious isn't a logical, decision-making, or 'rational' mind. It doesn't care if what we want is good or bad, or rather it can't tell the difference. It has no way of knowing if the pictures in our minds are real-time memories or come from our imagination. It is so 'dumb' that it can't tell fact from fantasy.

It has no means to decipher if the image we have in our mind has come from a real time event, a memory of our past or a desire for the future. The subconscious has no **critical faculty** – it doesn't think like the mind we operate with and for the most part, know of as who we are. It doesn't think, it just creates reality in the image of what we subtly suggest to it to be true, by how we are feeling. By how our thinking makes us feel, and what we know to be 'the way things are'.

As daunting as it may seem – that we have a screaming infant at the wheel that makes up the world as we know it, this is also what provides us with the greatest mind hacking opportunity of our time. We can lie to our 'reality maker' as to what is happening and who we are, and it has no option than to take us at our word. It doesn't just believe us but turns that information into our complete and convincing reality. Turns it into something we ourselves can't tell isn't true. The subconscious has no means to tell truth from fiction, and we'd be crazy if we didn't use this to our advantage. If we persist in any line of thinking it becomes an undeniable reality for us. It can't argue with us – doesn't care – just presents onto the stage of our life whatever it is we state to be true. The subconscious just personifies the words we speak. This is what I have to think is **the most exciting news of our time** – the underlying 'good news' that this process of consciousness represents. **A reclamation of our own minds,** because we can now understand this vital difference, and connection between us (conscious mind) and the thing in charge of what's going on in our life. (The subconscious mind.)

> *"The subconscious does not originate ideas but it accepts as true those which the conscious mind feels to be true. And in a way known only to itself objectifies the accepted ideas."*
> **Neville Goddard**

The most important insight of our time is to understand the distinction between these two aspects of mind, and how we can get that big, 'dumb', reality creating, mind working for us. Make a friend of it rather than the foe that I imagine the majority of people feel it is.

Certainly anyone who doesn't like how their life seems, or the frame of mind they're in. It would seem that for far too many people our minds have become an unbeatable enemy. As does my own at times – but I am waking to it – I am building my defences. I am rallying what I now know to be at my disposal to catch this monster when it is unintentionally running off with my mood. I am now aware of the trickster, and I know that it is only in awareness that I have any chance of winning the fight. If we don't understand the nature of our reality creating mind - how automatically our feelings are recreated – how our feelings are projected onto our environment - and the choice we have to consciously produce emotions without reason – then it's like we entered a boxing match but have no arms.

When I say something is listening, I refer to the awe-inspiring power that is the subconscious mind. That force living in the quiet of our minds that always says 'yes'. If we say to ourselves that, "I hate this job" – we'll be given even more reasons to. If we say, "I never seem to be able to get ahead and save some money," it will be reflected in the reality we experience - it will always come as **"yes, this is true" or "as you wish."** The subconscious has been compared to a wish granting genie, and when we become conscious enough of our own thoughts, then we start to sense what it is we've been asking for. We place our order not just by how we feel, but how well we describe the life we want. What does our dream consist of? Write it down even, because the 'magic' as they say, is in the details. How clear are we in the instructions we're sending?

Are we just repeating some expressionless and 'blind' affirmation, in trying to create a more desirable future? With no real intention, belief, or expectation of seeing any real change? **Or is it heart felt and 'expected'?** Is what we are asking for something we truly anticipate and have a keen eye out for the evidence appearing? Because we don't get what we want - we get what we feel in our heart is already true. We don't attract what we want, we attract who we are. Do we feel like we already have this thing in real time? Is it spoken about in present tense as if it were already here? Or what is sometimes referred to as future written goals - to speak from a place that assumes the thing we wanted was already here. Like we have already got past the end goal and this is what we are now experiencing. "I'm so glad that I have now arrived at this place where I don't concern myself with how I am seen, because it allows me too..." - fill in all of the blanks for yourself. Remember, the mind can't argue with us.

This is the essence of future written goals. To speak to ourselves from the perspective that our desire is no longer wanted – it is here. As in 'Now that I have... I'm so glad that I can'. We are so grateful for what this next stage has allowed us to do. We are so thrilled for what this achievement has enabled us to do. The opportunities we now enjoy, the people we are able to help, the health and free time that is already commonplace in our lives. Don't ask or question how it all works and will come to fruition. Our job is only in the creation, and the belief that it has already happened. We are in a very real sense high jacking or tricking the subconscious mind, and it has no means to dispute us – it doesn't want to, it just makes it so. It is never a thought of 'if this were true' – but 'now that it is true'.

Can you imagine what having this thing in our life now allows you to do? This type of trickery is the most direct route to seeing whatever we want showing up in real time. This work is not aimed at making us crazy trying to tune into every tiny thought that we mutter in the silences. But the more conscious we become of thought, or the more we understand the emotional effect of our thoughts, the easier we can weed out the habitual and sabotaging stuff that doesn't align with who we truly are, and what we truly want.

This is a book about consciousness – about being more conscious of thought. Even more, it helps us understand the feelings created by our way of thinking. And what we may be unintentionally asking for in our habitual and lazy modes of thinking. It is us realising that there is something 'listening in' that can perform the seemingly miraculous and turn all of this around for us in an instant. It hears everything we think and is building the world as we know it as a consequence of what it hears.

How do I know this? Because I talk to it often and it's never let me down. It has provided me with so much to be grateful for, from the asking that I have persisted in. But it has also taught me patience, humility, and a deep respect for the people in my life. Taught me things that are far more valuable than getting what I want all the time. I have sometimes been that kicking and screaming child, and my mind has helped understand what I gain from growing up and being responsible for how I feel. I couldn't be more grateful for anything in my life than my humility. Sometimes we get even more than we bargained for – more value than we have even asked for.

Enabling mind. Is the subconscious real?

The subconscious couldn't possibly even do anything for us if we don't think there is anything there. If we don't believe that it even exists or can open doors for us where there weren't any, we disempower the greatest force know to humankind. How miraculous this thing can be, depends on us starting to open our minds to hope and possibility. If there is nothing there, then nothing can help us. But ask it to show itself and it opens the door. Ask it to show you one thing to prove it is real and build your faith, and it just might. But go on doubting, and you will kill any ability you yourself might have had to open a door that goes far beyond the possible. Imagine what you want just might be possible, and you may be very surprised how much light creeps in when you just prise that door open a bit. By opening our minds and hearts it becomes real. We evoke the spirit of possibility when we allow it to show us a taste of what it can do.

And by all means ask it to prove itself to you. Demand of it to 'Show me the money'. But we must also practice patience and remain alert to all of the small signs. To the weird ways that it tries to guide and reassure us. We must keep the faith and follow when we are guided. We must give thanks for anything it shows us in order for it to keep showing up. If we ignore the signs, or boo-hoo the results, what do think is going to happen? If we don't even see the sign we asked for, we probably aren't going to see the next one either. So, get to asking

– start with the small stuff and increase your faith in the wonder of what is possible. Don't let the reality of what has happened be the killer of what can happen. Ask every day to be shown something of its immense and mind opening power. It cannot do anything for us until we allow its wonder into our imagination, via faith.

This is what was really insinuated in the Disney movie 'Pinocchio' when Jiminy Cricket suggested we should 'wish upon a star' because when you do, you open the mind to the realm of infinite possibility. You think far enough outside what you thought was possible that you 'permit' the miraculous to happen. We allow them by belief, faith, and our willingness to dream. If you don't believe anything is there that can put doorways in walls, or move the whole system of meaningful chance, **then your belief becomes a self-fulfilling prophecy**. Allow it into your life – let it show you what it can do. Do the asking and stay open to the signs. Be expectant of being shown something of the way it can do things that both defy logic and go beyond the scope of what we can achieve through hard work alone. Be open to the magic and watch as it unfolds. And the final part to this process is the acknowledgement. Make a big deal out of it when it happens if you want it to keep happening. It will show you more but not if you're like 'mehh – what else have you got?' We are trying here to prise a door open into something wonderous – to enter another kingdom – be at least a little bit surprised and happy that you are not as on your own as you may have thought. Allow it to keep coming into our life.

We all have access to this incredible part of our mind.

In our present era, we don't have to be Doctor's of Psychology to know enough of the basics of the nature of our subconscious, reality creating, habit driven, and illogical mind to have a huge influence over changing the results we are getting.

Why wouldn't you be interested in learning how to think in terms of what's listening and creating our world as a consequence? Something that can move mountainous problems with a tiny lever. Why wouldn't we want to learn to speak in the language the subconscious understands as fluently as English? The language of emotion. To be able to literally just walk into our own minds and place an 'order of experience' as if we are guaranteed to be able to sit back and watch it come true? Why wouldn't you want to be expectant of all the best this life has to offer.

Our big, dumb mind

> *"Honestly sometimes I get really fed up with my subconscious. It's like it's got a mind of its own."*
> Alexei Sayle

I'm certain by now that you understand that I mean the subconscious no disrespect when I refer to it as 'dumb' – only that it operates quite differently to the conscious mind that we think with. If we were to meet someone with a subconscious mind in the place of their conscious mind, we would consider them to be, well, short of the full quid. They would not be able to think for themselves; they'd be mind-numbingly gullible and couldn't tell good from bad, where they were, what is real, or have any concept of time.

Maybe I am jumping to conclusions here, but I imagine that the overwhelming lack of interest in the subconscious mind probably stems from the fact that we seem flabbergasted to even work out our conscious minds. And as a consequence we imagine this 'subconscious' one is completely beyond the ability for 'normal' people to grasp. If we are at odds to even work out our own mind, or make decisions, what hope have we got of ever understanding the parts of our mind we aren't conscious of? And I think this mindset is precisely why our mental health is in the crapper right now. **This is where the confusion lies.**

We live almost exclusively in the conscious mind, and have an almost complete disregard for the subconscious and the role it performs. As a consequence it seems that we are forced to be the puppets, rather than the puppeteers of our reality. This confusion and general lack of interest is precisely why we are incapable of feeling the way we want to most of the time. This rank division between the two minds that are supposed to operate in unison lies at the heart of all mental health issues, and the widespread dissatisfaction that typifies human life on earth right now. The chasm between the two aspects of mind and or our blind ignorance of the subconscious isn't just why we don't get what we'd like to, but lies at the heart of every physical disease in the body as well. We've known of the bodies intimate connection to the mind for a very long time. The body is the mind, and the stresses and problems we have in our psychological lives always develop into physical illnesses. Our planet is inconceivably unwell, but we aren't addressing the issue at its core. The ignorance of the operation and nature of our reality creator.

The ignorance of the subconscious mind lies at the heart of every form of mental illness, and is the reason for physical disease manifesting in the body as well, yet we still don't give it a thought? Everything that goes wrong in the software of the mind becomes a physical aliment in the bodies hardware. But it seems as smart as we are that we are only interested in patching the hardware when wounds start to open up in the body. The subconscious mind will always get us to do what it wants us to do, be that by aliment disease or sorrow – but if we only listened to our bodies and hearts more intently maybe we could avoid the extremes of ill health? it opens up a wound. I'm not trying to make out that I have all of the answers, but this refusal to acknowledge the presence and role of the subconscious is what is making us sick and feel disconnected. Have we completely lost our minds, and our connection to something sacred with it? We'll leave that to the end shall we.

We think we, in the conscious minds are 100% in control and responsible for what is happening, in our lives. And only hard work and therapy can get us back to health, while at the same time we ignore the one thing that can save us. We think we are the ones doing the driving in our life, and wonder why it is so short of fulfilling. We have no idea what we are driving or how to steer it. What we are in charge of.

And for all intents and purpose the subconscious (that can't think for itself.) assumes we know what we are driving. It is like giving toddlers the instructions of how to set up the nuclear power plant. What hope do we humble and uneducated people have in understanding a bigger, faster, and more complicated subconscious mind? Which is so far from the truth that it seems an injustice.

As I mentioned in the introduction to this book, we've arrived at this very fortunate time in our history. An alive and evolving process of consciousness that we witness daily. We are privy to all of what we need to know of the nature of the subconscious, but we are far more interested in new phones and what the Kardashians are up to. Information pertaining to the nature of the subconscious has become ever more common. It is as if we have all been invited to what goes on inside a therapy room and the summation of how the mind works, but we've somehow managed to look the other way. We are no better off for the awareness that has dawned.

I have mentioned all of these already, but just so we can see it all in one place, I'll sum up here what I think the main important aspects are that have become commonplace about the nature of the subconscious so we can begin working with it, or rather exploiting its apparent 'gullibility'. Shoot for the Achilles heel so to speak. This is what we know and is common to every piece of psychology or personal development content that I've encountered. We know:

- *It has no **critical faculty** – it can't think, decide, or rationalise like we do in the conscious mind.*
- *It has **no sense of either time or reality** – doesn't know if the pictures in our mind have happened yet, or are what we'd like to happen. It cannot tell if the images we have in our mind have come from our past, present, or future/ if they are 'real' or imagined.*
- *It **learns by repetition**, not by a textbook or being shown once. The more times we do something the more engrained and habitual the behaviour becomes.*

- ***It speaks in pictures and emotion*** – *doesn't really understand words. We have thought in images since long before we ever used words.*
- **Cannot tell if what has happened is wanted or unwanted.** *If it holds our attention, it will be used to recreate the familiar. The mind will keep showing us everything we believe to be true as a way of stabilising and normalising our experience. So we don't feel like we don't know where we are.*
- **Once we learn a skill, or come to a firm conclusion that becomes our subconscious experience.** *What things mean isn't a decision – life and what things mean happens instantly, because it is made at a higher level of our minds. Our experience of life happens almost entirely by habit.*

Compared to the mind we use and know of as ourselves, its powers of deduction are non-existent. It has no sense of logic and can't do anything towards creating a more desirable experience without better instructions coming from us. By us providing a more defined details of how we would like to feel, and what we are expecting to see/ looking for. The subconscious mind is powerful beyond imagination, but it only serves one simple purpose: the recreation of a familiar experience. The **most convincing illusion of all.** It does all of this in the name of maintaining our dominant vibration, or our normal way of being. The outside world is used by the mind as a mirror to reflect back to us, how we already feel. How we feel shapes our perception and gives form to the **reactive pattern** we refer to as our life. It is a feedback loop we cannot escape without insight.

Is it working against us?

"The moment we work out what is happening in the world as an infant, we only notice and look for those very same patterns. From all possible realities, we turn the infinite amount of sensory data into that same old pattern we were first so excited to have worked out. We bring forth from the forest of all potential what become the 'trees' of our experience. From the everything and the nothing, we turn it into the something, which is our lives. **Of course we 'know' what's 'going on'** *– we are the ones who made it so."*

The subconscious mind serves one pivotal role – to sustain vibration.

Because our vibration state is our survival gene. Our vibration is encoded with and run from all of the core beliefs that keep us safe. Why is this so important that this higher mind dominates our perceptions? It houses the instincts that help us sense danger. Our instincts stop us from walking down dark alleys, be they metaphoric or literal. It's why some people give us the shivers, and why we will back out of business deals if they don't feel right to us. Of course our instincts are not always on point – we sometimes do dumb business deals and choose abusive partners, but we can change these subconscious patterns whenever we're ready to. But this part of our mind is making millions of tiny calculations every second using the benefit of our experiences to, as best we can, keep us out of harm's way.

We wouldn't be able to intuitively surmise friend from foe, pleasure from pain, or what would be seen as appropriate behaviour if it weren't for entrusting enormous amounts of what's happening in our life to this automated part of our minds. If we couldn't trust our intuitions to stop us from doing dumb and unacceptable things that might land us hot water. We are designed to leave the driving to this faster and experienced part of our minds, or we might risk our social standing - or put ourselves in even more embarrassing situations than we already do. Or more importantly, we may lose the sense of our deepest core values – this kind of stuff just can't be up for grabs, or debated and uncertain – it must be known, defined and automatic or instinct. Our values must be held deep within our reserves of mind, where they come to us naturally and without question. So it is kind of hard to fight those feelings held in the subconscious even if we have become to better equipped by our learnings to deal with the risks that our fears are trying to warn us of.

We may risk being cast out of our tribe, if it weren't for those antennae that remind us of the ways in which we need to remain sensitive to social norms. Even though it has been a long time since we lived in tribal societies, we still live with a very deep sense of wanting to be a part of a warm circle of friends. They offer us emotional nourishment that is just as vital to our survival as food is. We are encoded with what we need to do in order that we can maintain that sense of belonging because isolation is something we equate to death. Our vibration carries a very powerful momentum – if you think of a mind that operates thousands of times faster than the conscious one, effectively pulls off reality as an unquestionable illusion, we start to get a picture of how difficult it can really be to create any change in our state of mind. How difficult it can really be for a depressed person or addict to consider feeling differently to be a simple choice. That is unless we are operating with some insight of what is going on behind the scenes and why. When we have awareness we have a much broader perception of things. If we know the trickery going on within our minds, and that it is just trying to warn us of things that may not be as dramatic and life threatening as they seem, we have a broader range of emotional responses available to us.

The subconscious mind, or the inherent instincts and beliefs that it is designed to protect, tell us instinctively what is needed in every situation without even thinking about it. Our instincts come from the fast brain, and our ponderings, desires and direction come from the slow, or conscious mind.

That vibration is so critical to our survival that all of the programming and instinctive stuff – that our core beliefs are kept off limits to us. We are not aware of them as beliefs – they are just how the world is or what is true as far as we're concerned. If it were easy to rewire this circuitry I think many people would find themselves in more danger than they could handle. We don't always understand the hidden dangers of taking giant leaps forward in our status – the other things that we might sacrifice at the same time. Like friendships and all of the things in our life that we don't realise how much we value. How raising our status makes us more vulnerable to criticisms that we're not quite ready for. That we don't understand come with package we're asking for. We can't just expect to move into these glorious lives without knowing all of the things that it will cost us – so the mind shows them to us as we take those baby steps forward.

We don't always realise the price we might pay for getting everything that we want in a very short space of time. So our beliefs are there to test our resolve. We say we want 'x' but are we really willing to sacrifice all that will go with it in the process. So it makes sense that those deeply held beliefs live where they are protected from us being able to change them on a whim. So that we might avoid finding ourselves way out of our depth, or doing dumb things without giving them much thought. So our beliefs (particularly our deepest and highest values.) are buried so deep and entangled into our way of thinking that we rarely ever even suspect it to be our beliefs that are causing us issues, and the undesirable outcomes we're having. The mind has them wrapped so perfectly into our stories that we hide any idea that any part of us had anything to do with what happened. If this stuff were at our fingertips and we saw our own beliefs as what was causing the drama, we'd be changing our minds so frequently that our lives would turn into a chaotic mess.

That's the job of the subconscious mind – present reality as it seems. And then convince us we had nothing to do with it. 'It wasn't me'. Not just to sustain our vibration, but ensure that in the conscious mind we still feel like we're the ones that are doing the driving and in control. The subconscious is the very clever thief in the night that is highly skilled at disguising the fact of it's existence. So maybe it is little wonder of the widespread limited interest about it. It might well be the master of disguise, but I'm pretty sure we are catching on?

These instincts remain in the untouchable realm of our mind and could never be suspected as the cause of our grief unless we do the consciousness work to bring it to the surface. Until we are willing to ask ourselves those tough questions that we may not like the answers to. What's the root cause of these results that I no longer want to experience? We cannot get those answers, or begin to delve into our own circuitry **without being clear on what we want,** and be willing to explore what we think might be stopping us. Until we are willing to clearly define the goal and what the obstacle may be. And even though it might be starting to sound like we are doomed by these beliefs because they are so deep and untouchable that they can never be changed, there are certainly many ways we can bring these to the surface – that we can get to the core of what's not working for us.

And by the end of this book you will see that it isn't as difficult as it may seem right now. Our beliefs are off bounds, but it is far easier to talk ourselves off the ledge when we realise that these instincts are usually overzealous, and these instincts are far better suited to warn us of dangers that are no longer present in the way we live now. These instincts have a far exaggerated sense of the real dangers we are up against. We have a bigger safety net than those instincts realise, particularly in light of being able to choose and create emotions without reason.

There are a multitude of ways in which we can meet, befriend, and even trick this part of our minds. And I'm going to show you the simplest and least painful that I've learned and have worked for me. But we must first understand what we are up against – how ordinarily off limits the 'reality show' really is, and how the mind keeps it that way. How crucial it is to our survival that we live with some sense of stability, even if that stability has been for a long time distasteful to us.

The mind is just trying to be sure that the thing we want is right for us. It's looking out for us like a protective parent, and wants us to be aware of everything that comes with the desire so there's no surprises. That we anticipated all of the parts of what we wanted that we may not have been seeing. If we want something that might seem way beyond our scope right now, it will give us all of the skills and lessons we need to get us across the line. We need to be patient sometimes and pick up every skill and every lesson along the way. We're getting the picture aren't we. We need to be able to predict all of the outcomes that we might face – some of which are made up by our wild imaginations but making any kind of a drastic change is never easy and for good reason.

Breaking long running habits is never easy, but if we know the reason why and what we gain in the process we take that to mind. That's what we tell the mind when those emotions are pushing the button of cravings – desperately trying to keep us in old patterns.

Which certainly brings to mind some even better reasons to make changes. That we often don't consider all of the benefits, and wider range of choices available to us when we are able to exercise a greater self-control. With it comes confidence, and the trust we gain in ourselves. There are many more benefits to breaking habits and delaying gratification we may haven't even have thought of. Who we become as people is far more than the bit of weight we lose by having better eating habits. Keeping promises to ourselves lies at the heart of confidence and any plans we can make going forward. There is a lot that is off bounds to us if we can't trust ourselves.

But the mind will use whatever **'reality chips'** it can find in the environment to restore the status quo. It will shift what comes to our mind, or focus our attention on anything that reminds us things are as I expected so we never feel out of our depth. And sometimes that means finding anything in the environment we expect as the familiar - looking for signs of rudeness, intolerance, injustice. We walk around, going, 'have a look at this dickhead' which translates in the subconscious mind to 'the world is full of dickheads. So, of course, the answer comes back: "As you wish."

If it's on our radar, it will be used as a means of preserving the momentum of our vibrational state.

Entering the Matrix.

The subconscious mind turns an infinite experience of unlimited possibilities and things we could notice, and narrows our point of attention down to notice only things that keep our story of how things are in place. From all possibility, we draw forth a world that seems familiar and creates a reaction in us that maintains the status quo of our vibrational momentum. To put in maybe more understandable terms – our energy projects out into the world and reflects back to us in familiar wave patterns that **make us feel the same way we already do.** The most precise and perfectly disguised feedback loop we could ever imagine. It is 'perfect' in every sense except that it has us trapped in a cycle where we find it very difficult to improve how we feel. And sometimes no matter how hard we work, and wish or pray for things to be different that same old world keeps getting reflected back to us. It's enough to make you cry, when you're trying with every ounce of effort you can muster, but see no recognisable sign of things getting better for us.

> *"We are caught in these familiar feedback loops and don't even know it."*
>
> **The Matrix**

How we currently feel is projected outwards and reflects back to us in the circumstances, events, and conditions of our life. The situation you imagine you are in has almost nothing to do with your environment. So, how does it help us to know this if it is not to our liking? The outside world and the circumstances you are in will subtlety change every time you make the choice to feel better. Without reason or evidence we change how the world responds to us. When you go inside to create an emotion you would like to have and cease being party to the reflected illusion. It gives us the knowing, and the ability to 'call reality out'. Our subconscious mind uses the world as a mirror on which it projects our vibrational state, causing an unconscious and conditioned reaction in us. But now we are awake to its little game, reality becomes ours.

We ordinarily have a very limited awareness of how much the cause of the reaction had to do with us. This is the most essential aspect of the illusion. That the conscious mind doesn't catch on to the ploy of mind – this is what ensures vibration continues in a perpetual cycle. To disguise the minds part in 'what happened'. If we knew, the feedback loop would become flawed and invalid, the system would become unstable. But to the point that interests us, when we wise up to this little plot of the mind, we become less affected by our 'drama' and have more ability to feel as we would choose – more ability to manipulate the meaning of events, and reality itself. If the subconscious loses its ability to push our buttons with unconscious and automatic/instinctive reactions, we inherit the power from within the conscious mind to be more in control of **not just our feelings but our destinies.**

We turn the 'everything' into the familiar – all possibility gets turned into patterns we have seen before, so that we know what's 'going on.' Of course we know what's going on – we are the ones who made it into what it is.

When we get a sense for the trick being played on us by the subconscious, it starts to seem like we are watching it happen to someone else. Like we are the less affected observer of our lives, rather than the ones flying off the handle without a choice in the matter.

The real question is, how often do we find the life we are living to be what we'd consider chosen and desirable? Breaking this often-torturous feedback loop, through awareness, is possibly the highest form of 'work' and endeavour we could ever partake in. In the name of living more satisfied, peaceful lives, and feeling the way we can honestly say we'd choose to as much of the time as possible. Once the 'jig' is up and the conditioned, automatic cycle running beneath our awareness becomes exposed, we've taken back our power. Maybe even unintentionally, but just the same we're back in the driver's seat. In every small way – meaning by even the most subtle of reactions, we understand that we are grabbing the steering wheel of our life. We are less blown about by what may have seemed to be happening on the outside. We are the ones who can stand firm in how we would choose to feel, even in the midst of a storm. We are less exposed to what is happening in our lives that is seemingly against our will.

Of course this is a process and never something we can ever reach perfection in, but we certainly can grow exponentially into beings having a more chosen experience. Or as it is often put, into living our lives by design – by our choice. That we can't be perfect is no reason not to move towards improvement and maybe even mastery.

Nothing changes – we still 'carry water, and chop the wood.'

I think that the most important element of this awareness is that nothing in our life/environment or what we do needs to change for us to reclaim our right to feel as we would prefer. That no matter what we do for a living or who we are the highest possible internal feeling isn't determined by our status or other peoples view of us. It is a choice to feel differently without reason – a remembrance of our sacred beginnings and what we are as beings. This doesn't require special knowledge, or anything we do or anything in our surroundings to change. It is a knowing and the result is instant – the moment we understand what we are connected to how we feel becomes far less conditional than we thought it was. How we feel becomes more chosen than automatic, and that choice changes everything on the outside.

We're not instantly going to be famous, rich, and doing a job we like better – becoming one with the mind that perceives everything as it is goes much deeper than the veneer or image of our life. A surrendered acceptance of circumstances being the way they are merges us with the part of mind that made it as so – a part of mind that is always chill. We still are who we are, and do what we do, we just feel better about it. And that feeling alters what's going on for us. We can feel enormous regardless of the job we do, or don't do – or the size of the goals we have for our life.

What I wanted to share in writing this was how under considered Imagined states of mind are in how we go about our lives, and how we approach the treatment of mental health problems. Attraction isn't airy-fairy stuff, it is a science and a real-life law that should be applied to all levels of how we go about our lives. But the crux of it is simple – we can feel the way we want to without reason. No matter what the world is doing – no matter who thinks what of us, we can become present enough in our own minds to sense that thing that is listening, and when we do we see the actual futility of all the externals – of everything that seems to be going on.

We allow it to be the way it is, and we are still at peace. So many people I speak to say they just want to be happy. Well, there are no conditions to that. There is not one thing stopping us. We say we want peace of mind above all things, but then get stirred by the most trivial of things and put this huge list of demands of the things that must precede peace. On the conditions we must be in before we allow ourselves a second of peace of mind. And as plain as that might seem from the outside, we don't see all of the ways we block it from the inside. We do have to live intentionally to feel like we are going somewhere that is chosen – that we have control over that. But every step along the way is ours to enjoy – ours to connect with the part of the mind that has made it what it is. We'll go more into this in the chapter concerning mindfulness and what it actually grants us, but all we ever lack if we are in pain, or haste, or don't like what's going on for us is presence of mind. A separation from the subconscious mind.

> *"People are strange: they are constantly angered by trivial things, but on a major matter like totally wasting their lives, they hardly seem to notice."*
> **Charles Bukowski**

What I'm getting at here is that you will never again trust reality as a constant, particularly if it feels like it is trying to destroy you. It is not reality bringing you to your knees, it is old outdated conditioned responses that for a very long time haven't suited the things you have grown to now value. This is as much a part of the problem as the gap between the conscious and subconscious minds. We are driven, no sorry, we are 'forced' by habits that we even know in ourselves are never going to take us to the places we now want to go. To the places that by our process of maturing we've now come to value. Our values have grown and changed, but the old forces of habit we are conditioned by seem to push directly against our will, and sabotage our best efforts.

It is like we are bystanders sometimes as we watch ourselves smash a hammer straight into our head. The horror of it all is that we can never get to new ways of being, via old ways of doing. What we used to do no longer works, but our habits dig us into ever deepening holes.

What I am offering in these principles is the very real capacity we have to combat any enemy that we may not have even realise existed. Not just the forces of habit, but our conditioning itself. Our conditioning – hmmm – let's just think about it for a second. The core beliefs we carry about ourselves and what we are capable of that we never had a choice in. That became buried deep in our psyche by the suggestions of others, long before we ever developed that part of mind that could rationalise those suggestions as rubbish. Conditioning was never a choice we made. But something someone who hardly knew themselves convinced us was true about ourselves. And the tune has been playing our in our lives ever since – most often to our detriment. Most often ruined all of the moments of our lives to feel like we couldn't have something, or perform in the way we wanted to. It is those very suggestions that became our torturer – that are our judge, jury, and executioner. What is on offer in these principles is that you will not only start to distrust the reality that has had you beating on yourself, but you'll have the tools to disarm the invisible thing that's been hurting you.

Without a fight, any effort, or facing enormous fears, you'll recognise darkness in the tiny simple choices we can make in each moment to shift the nature of the world around you. You'll realise just how unsubstantiated this 'reality' thing really is. And how pure and magnificent any choice to feel that is born in our desire truly is. The **truth of who we are, and our reality are worlds apart,** and you'll have the tools that can recognise them for exactly what they are.

You will never again trust 'reality' for what it is and come to a place of absolute faith in how much of what we see can be altered by a simple and easy to make choice to feel differently.

The tables have turned – it's all moving in our favour.

The mind has been inadvertently putting one over us for all of these years and the tables have just turned. We only need to understand this one small fact about its nature to step into ownership of what's 'going on' in our lives. As previously stated, the subconscious is not a logical mind – it doesn't think, in the sense of what we understand as thinking. It cannot tell the difference between past and present, real, or imagined; it has no ability to sense the difference between what seems desirable and what doesn't. it is unable to judge if something is good or bad – if it is something that would make us happy or not. It just grows whatever is on our mind. If it comes to our attention and we wallow there, it will become a semi-permanent part of our experience until we get fed up with it enough to change it. Until we 'get the lesson'? I hear it put this way sometimes and I think to myself of how hard I have had to learn some of the lessons in my life before I would no longer tolerate them. I've repeated some really dumb stuff for years. The simple rule of thumb so to speak – if it gets your attention it will be used in the preservation of your vibration. It will be repeated.

But this all-powerful, reality creating mind can't argue with us. It truly resembles a gullible young child and takes everything we say about the world, and ourselves, at face value. We have to understand this if we are going to get one up on it. If we are going to make it our common practice to use this fact about its nature to our advantage. So go right ahead and tell yourself you're a legend and that you are worthy of the best life has to offer. The mind might be some super powerful magic making genie, and the maker of everything that is real in our life, but it has no defence against what we repeatedly state as true. In my mind we really can put one over 'reality' much easier than we might have thought.

If this subconscious mind thing is responsible for the quality of every person's life experience, and it is far from what you could consider complicated to understand, then we would be crazy not to use this to our advantage. Understanding these simple things I've shared here could have a huge impact on us living more meaningful and contributing lives. And if we know emotions as a choice that changes much more than we were aware of and we recognise why that choice might be more difficult that it seems, surely that could go a long way in our treatment of mental illness. When we use our mind, or rather work with it rather than against it. If we understand that in each moment we are gifted a choice that can change everything – that can disarm the very monster whose been mucking with us – **aren't those easy choices to make.**

How many people have just been telling themselves the wrong things out of habit, and for so long that it became what they thought was their life? It seems like we got high jacked by what's happening in our life 'automatically', but don't really have a sense for how it happened. But we can ask the question – if this subconscious mind thing is responsible for 97% of life on earth, could this awareness possibly be utilised in reducing criminal behaviour and the folly of what might have seemed to be an 'easy way out?' If this awareness can lead to us having peace in our hearts - with us being ok with who we are, surely it could lead to a shared peace for all people. A more peaceful, tolerant, and sustainable future for everybody.

Why has awareness of the subconscious mind not been able to be brought into the context of a broader mainstream interest? For me this is the definition of a tragedy. We can't say we don't know this stuff – the information is everywhere. The key aspects about the nature of the subconscious mind are so commonly known and it would seem like awareness of it is an easy fix. It is this 'universal cure' that somehow manages to hide behind the thinnest of veils. Can this not be communicated, or shared in any meaningful or useful way?

Why has no one been able to sell this as a game changer. My mind boggles – we've struggled to even drum up any interest in the thing really. If you talk about the mind being in charge of or responsible for our perceptions – what more is there to our lives than how we perceive them? Or to life on earth really? We all know there is more to our minds than we are conscious of, but most prefer to believe that **'there's something out there'**. Not something within us. I thought we should have grown out of the infancy phase of our awareness by now. I mean, we have been gift wrapped all of the knowledge. Many would even regard the personal development movement itself as a form of religion. And the principles of mind are not dissimilar to anything that can be found within spiritual ideologies.

And I'm not talking about using the mind and Law of Attraction so we can all become rich and famous. But we should, at this very late stage in our evolution, have some peace in our lives and understand the value of living intentional lives. Instead, it seems we are just beckoning the world to consume us, as if we think there soon won't be a human future. It is like we just want to be sucked in, spat out and forgotten. I sometimes wonder, if this is the extent that our human culture has developed into, is it worth preserving? With all that we have achieved here on earth, we should care more and be prouder of what we as humans have done and represent. We would not have come this far if we didn't value compassion, collaboration, and our connection to each other as highly as we do. But we seem so divided and disinterested in the big picture.

> *"Who then is invincible? The one who cannot be upset by anything outside of his reasoned choice."*
> — Epictetus

Chapter summary

- We don't need to be Drs of psychology to understand enough about the nature of the subconscious mind to start working with it, instead of it putting one over us.
- We should think in terms of there being something that is listening to our thoughts and creating the world as we know it from our declarations. How we think is the instructions we send to our world maker.
- The subconscious doesn't think in the context of what we know of as thinking – it doesn't make decisions or come to rational conclusions like we do in the conscious mind. So it can't dispute or argue with anything we tell it is true. So go ahead and tell yourself you're a legend.
- It has no concept of time and cannot tell (doesn't care.) if the pictures in our mind have come from real-time events (memories) or from our imagination (desires). They all have an identical effect on how they make us feel – on the reality that we attract.
- It is much faster in operation than the conscious mind, but it has no critical faculty. Like a gullible child it cannot tell if what is on our mind is something that we want or don't want. If it is wanted or unwanted. If it gets our attention it will become a more permanent part of our experience.
- The subconscious is like the dirt we plant our ideas in – it will grow weeds just as readily as it will crops. What gets our attention gets bigger in our life.
- We can enter and know this part of our mind anytime we get quiet and slow our thoughts down. When the conscious is quiet the subconscious comes to life, and becomes more open to our suggestions.
- Far from being our enemy it is our greatest friend, constant companion, and the only real resource we have in creating a desirable life. What more is there to life on earth than

how we see things – and the subconscious makes how we perceive the world.
- It can change our perceptions and what we may have thought impossible or troubled us overnight. While we sleep the subconscious can change our world.

CHAPTER 3
The Happening

What's 'happening' depends on how you feel about it – if it doesn't bother you, it never happened. We change the event itself when we change how we feel about it. What's happening is something far more changeable and up to us than we may have thought.

What is Happening?

We've all had bad days, right? The ones we would have absolutely avoided if we had any choice in the matter, or we knew how to, right? The theme of this book is that we have far more control over the outcomes we experience than we exercise our will over. Because we don't operate from the awareness of how much our state of mind, or mood and expectation, affects the scenes and situations we find ourselves in. We don't realise how much our energy actually builds the whole experience. We ordinarily don't operate from **the knowing or make the connection between how we feel and what's going on**. If we knew, we'd be far more careful with our energetic output. And as we'll see later in the light and dark chapter, we'd pay far less mind to our knee-jerk reactions or 'reality.' I guarantee even by the end of this chapter you'll be far less at the mercy of outside forces than you might have been.

Allow me to paint this picture of some poor bloke having a bad day. We'll call him Michael - and he's just had one of his worst days on record. One he would certainly like to forget and definitely wouldn't ever wish to be repeated if he had any choice in the matter - If he thought it was within his power to change. It all begins with Michael sleeping through his alarm. "Oh shit, shit, shit." It's Michael's turn to carpool, and for the third time in a row when his turn has come around, 'something' has conspired to make him late. He's developed something of a reputation that he'd rather not have. A reputation that is almost certainly a long way from the person he knows himself to be. He sees himself as someone who is reliable, prompt, and sharp – the kind of fella who won't let you down. So, when his self-image gets dismantled, seemingly against his will for the third time in a month, he is really starting to question himself. How he's feeling is a long way from what he'd consider a choice.

He races out the door, with unkempt hair, mistakenly picks up yesterday's shirt, and doesn't have time to prepare the salad diet he's been priding himself on sticking to. He races to his first colleague's house, and enroute realises he hasn't picked up the USB stick with today's presentation on it. "Dang – I'm freaking late already,". But it's the day of the presentation, so he makes an illegal U-turn, and you know who's waiting at the next set of traffic lights: That normally invisible constable on a motorbike. "Goddammit – I haven't had a traffic ticket in years." By the time Michael has picked up his three work mates, none of whom has been afforded the time to stop and pick up their customary morning 'pick me up' coffee, he's feeling a little frazzled, hated on by his mates, and not exactly oozing with the confidence he might have liked for the day of the presentation. The sales pitch he was heading up that his whole team had been putting together for the past month. Michael is positively rattled. He'd let his team down, his mates were in his ear, he was hungry – not to mention slightly bothered by getting that traffic offence that he really couldn't afford at the moment. He's not really what you'd call in the 'flow.'

So, he gets to work, surprisingly only marginally late considering the setbacks, and has to sneak sheepishly into the morning meeting. He does his very best not to be noticed but with his recent track record for being late, this is hardly going to go unnoticed. The meeting concludes and Michael is summoned to have a little chat with the boss. "Michael," the boss says. "I really hoped we wouldn't be having this little chat, but this is the third time in a month you've failed to be punctual. This is certainly not what I would have expected from someone that I thought might be thinking about his chances for the upcoming promotion. You know as well as I do, we'll be looking for a new head of department when Syd retires, and I was thinking that might have been you."

"I know sir," says Michael, "believe me this is so out of character. I can only reiterate as I did last time that this definitely won't happen again."

"We will have to see. In the meantime, you can see what you can do to patch up the Collins Account." This particular account just so happens to be the most difficult to deal with client the firm has. Michael just knows this isn't his job, but it's been dropped on him as a form of penance for the untimely tardiness. He needs to get on top of this today if he's ever going to redeem himself as the boss' first choice for a new office, pay rise, and all the perks he'd looked forward to for the past 2 years of hard work and good service. That is now at risk of being thrown out the bloody window by a cruel twist of fate.

To cut a long story short, Michael's presentation was not everything he'd hoped it would be. He could smell himself in yesterday's shirt, he copped a ribbing in the lunchroom for being late, being reprimanded about it, and for skipping out on the salad lunch he'd laid bets on sticking to when no one thought that he would. The Collin's account phone call didn't exactly lift his spirits either. Maybe it was his mood at the time, but that phone call nearly cost him his entire career. Not exactly the build-up he would have liked going into such a pivotal presentation. But thankfully his colleagues picked up the slack with making the presentation something of a success. Then he arrives home to find that his teenage son hadn't mowed the lawn as he was asked, and a fight ensued with his better half over it. One more night on the couch with a sandwich for dinner.

Does this ring any bells for anyone? How easily things could have gone differently, and how often we seem to sabotage our choices seemingly against our will. How differently might Michael's day have gone if he hadn't made that first 'rookie' error with his alarm clock? Not just in a "Sliding Doors" sort of way – but if things didn't continue to stack on each other to conspire against him? What if, even though he had failed to meet his own mark on a few occasions, he'd managed to brush it off, and regained his composure? Would he take less offence about the remarks about his salad lunch failings, if the Collin's account phone call had not gone so 'pear shaped?' Would he have ended up sleeping on the couch if, even after every other mishap, he still managed to master the presentation, and restore some self-confidence?

Of course, these are all impossible things to know, but it brings to mind the question – do you think our reactions have the ability, or the tendency to 'trend' and compound on the one before? Is a bad start to the day doomed to just keep getting worse? When we are in a bloody big hurry, it just seems like there's some kind of evil plot against us ensuring we catch every red light on the way? Let me put it another way – when you have reached your boiling point, and you're on a hair trigger, how likely is it you'll notice that smiling baby in the pram that might lift your spirits a bit? Or spot that bottle of your wife's favourite wine being on special on the way home? Because that is what this Law of Attraction stuff is about in a nutshell. We tend to see evidence and find ourselves in situations that reflect our mood. **We can only notice evidence in our environment that supports our state of mind.**

When we're angry, we're confronted with other angry people. When we are depressed, we tend to see even the smallest of things as seeming like an insurmountable mountain to climb. We pick up on all of the stuff that bolsters and supports our feeling state. We can only see things that keep the feeling alive inside us going. That's how this attraction thing really works. It is not some dreamy idea that we just imagine living in a castle and the next day it becomes real. It is an underpinning law of the universe that has been communicated to us for centuries, in spiritual texts and a myriad of cryptic ways. We look for and can only see a world that rationalises and preserves the feeling alive inside us. We seemingly 'attract' more reasons to keep the feeling alive in us going. How we feel runs in perpetual motion.

In his best-selling book *Emotional Intelligence,* Dan Goleman claims that even our 'memories are very state specific – we have what amounts to a box of good mood memories.' And many people experience mind blanks when put under the pressure of exam conditions. 'It's as if stress makes us stupid.' The principles that define this apparent 'Law of Attraction' are not dissimilar – we see a world that supports our state of mind. We can only see the things that support and confirm how we feel at the time. How we feel dictates the memory bank we have access to, the type of evidence we see in the world, the situations we imagine ourselves to be in – also known as 'what's happening'. These are all a consequence of our state of mind.

And, of course, these principles are echoed in the idea of the confirmation bias which further re-enforces the idea that we tend to only see evidence, or notice results, of the things we believe to be true. If we believe that pretty girls are mean, or teenagers are lazy, we tend to find confirmation of these beliefs, rather than evidence that opposes what we've found to be true in our experience. And we all know that people are by their nature almost incapable of accepting ideas that challenge their experience and opinions. Most are certainly very unwilling to. We could stack undisputable 'proof' in front of them, but if it subconsciously challenges their beliefs and long-held views, we may as well be talking to a wall. What we might be open to as credible sources of proof, won't even be recognised as anything more than some type of conspiracy non-sense. We live in a world now that is 'seemingly' filled to the brim with these 'conspiracy' nuts, because the majority opinion has become so widely influenced by the narrative of mainstream media. And it's no surprise that we are left scratching our heads as to what the 'greater good' actually refers to anymore.

Keeping in mind of course that we are never up against the truth but what the majority have become convinced of as truth. If we are trying to convince anyone of our apparent 'conspiracy' we need to keep this in mind. It is not a question of how true something is anymore, but how many people buy in to the idea. We aren't able to research every single issue and government conspiracy, and by some strange freak of nature we seem to only be drawn to, and encounter forms of evidence that support what we currently feel. If we think we can convince someone of something they weren't aware of, we need to keep in mind that you're not only up against what they have heard, but a natural proclivity towards what they majority have been convinced of. You are not armed with the 'truth', and you are not up against the truth but something far more primal and stronger than we are conscious. Very often we must be content with planting the seed, and letting people know where we stand.

What we have encountered and learnt isn't true in anyone else's experience. What we call the truth depends of course on what we have seen with our eyes, known to be true in our experience, and of course what we regard as sound evidence. We can't dispute what we see with our own eyes, so we should keep that in mind when we are sharing perspectives. (Or arguing our point.) People may very well have better reasons than we think why they believe what they do – a lifetime of proof, and learning can never trump what we consider 'facts'. That is not to say that we can never change minds – even our own. I found it very interesting to discover that one of the ways in which psychology measures intelligence is open mindedness. Indeed how could we consider our opinion sound or well thought out if we weren't open to how new ideas can improve the ones we already have.

My point is that beliefs needn't be our enemies if we remain open to them being wrong. If we remain pliable and allow the jury to be out on many of the most important moral questions we have. Even phobias are irrational beliefs that successfully shrink the world we live in and things we are able to do. But when those beliefs become challenged and brought into the light of questioning, the beliefs crumble from the foundations up. We start to wonder why we ever had the belief, and such is the case with all of the beliefs that unconsciously cause us to feel in any way like we wouldn't chose to. People with a phobia of spiders have entered programs where little by little their fears become exposed for the false conclusions they really are. And in the space of a few hours can find themselves allowing tarantulas to crawl over their bare hands without any discomfort at all. What if we could remain open to how irrational the things that scare us, and understand that they can be broken down by a series of easy steps. Would it change the plan we're making of what we want to do.

I'm not suggesting we are absolutely broken, just point out our subconscious tendency allow beliefs that are harming us to exist in us without question. We are not looking to prove the conclusions we unconsciously live with to be wrong, or we'd find ourselves in a very confusing world. Deciphering what was dangerous would become so difficult for us that our minds would never be at peace. But what if because of what we understand about this subconscious trait, we shifted to being a little more open to being wrong about the things we don't like or scare us. Seems we'd live in a slightly broader landscape and could have more fruitful and engaging conversations.

If we have an image of ourselves as being weak-willed and lacking in discipline, it will be near on impossible for us to behave in any other way. We are forced to act in line with how we subconsciously identify ourselves. And it is not like this is some strange Law that doesn't make any sense to us. As mentioned earlier - A salesman, a mother or a teenager will all walk into the same shopping centre and see an altogether different place. Because we don't just look at what interests us, but what subconsciously draws our attention. The things that resonate with our vibration. The same shopping centre, but they all see a different world because different things stand out to us and draw our attention in beyond our conscious control. Our attention is subconsciously drawn to things that might matter to our agenda. We see the world relative to our beliefs, goals, interests, and how we feel.

And of course this idea is not dissimilar to what is known as the observer effect. The idea that we actually alter the results of an experiment because of the hypothesis we are trying to prove, or the bias of our expectation. **We change what we look at because of what we expect to find.** Common to the old saying that *we don't see the world as it is – we see it as we are*. We change what is on the outside of us by what we are looking for in it. We influence the results of our lives by what we look for and expect to happen. This is a subconscious process so we aren't even aware of it happening in real-time, but when we understand how much we can actually impact those subconscious functions, seeing different things in the world, and becoming an altogether different person isn't as much of a stretch as it might have seemed.

I don't believe there are any weak people. We don't lack self-control so much as we fail to see the true price we pay in the moment we lose restraint. We aren't weak, we just don't see the reward that is invisibly on offer, or the true price we pay for losing respect for and trust in ourselves. There are no weak people – only ones who can't see the reward as being worthwhile. **Where there is no perceived reward there will never be a single breath of effort.**

It may have been the long way round to making the point, but what is 'going on' in our lives has everything to do with our energy and how we feel at the time. We will recall different types of things happening at the same wedding event we attended, depending on how we feel now. We quite literally tell a different story, and remember different things relative to the mood we are in. We don't just recall different parts of the event; we'll twist the story and its meaning to suit our current mood. The event itself changes, not just over time, but from the emotional place we're in when we tell the story. Our memory is very state specific, and we will have a different recollection based on how we feel. The 'details' depend on our mood, as does the story we tell ourselves about what's going on in our life. If something doesn't bother us – doesn't form a blip on our radar – it is as if it never happened. And similarly, if someone was to launch at us with an off-handed comment, it only happens to the degree to which it bothers us. We could hear the exact same comment come from someone else and we are ready to rip their heads off. Our emotional reaction defines the meaning of the situation. What's happening depends on how we feel about it.

The 'happening' is born in how we feel, and the type of situation we find ourselves in, depends on how well we think we can deal with, and defend ourselves. We can quite literally change an event itself – change what it means to us, not just by how we see it but by how we choose to respond. And I understand we all know this and how simple it really is, but how often do we use this reality altering skill – the superpower that perspective really is, to manipulate what seems to be happening in our lives. Like the stroke of a paint brush we can tell ourselves a better story of what apparently happened, and this powerful mind thing just has to take us on our word. Every time we make that small choice to feel even slightly better in any moment that we can, we move the world and what's happening in our favour. We spin that perceptive machine on our shoulders to notice a completely different world. This is not to drive us crazy and be on edge all the time, about our reactions, but to realise the powers we never knew we had to change the world according to us. We can literally change the nature of the physical world around us, by changing what is apparent in it. Even plants move away from pain and towards the sun.

> *"Never does nature say one thing and wisdom another."*
>
> Juvenal

Changing more than just ourselves.

It is not just what's happening that we affect when we have a change of heart. When we change our point of attention, and or perspective – when we make that choice to feel differently we also change how other people seem to treat us, the memories we have access to, how we feel about ourselves, and what we think we can accomplish, etc. We change the nature of the world around us and our place in it, all by changing what may have seemed a completely insignificant and automatic reaction. I wonder what might have happened to Michael, who we met in the opening story, if he'd done a ten-minute meditation instead of taking his pie into the lunchroom. You see, in every single moment of our lives, we are offered opportunities to change so much more than we may have expected. The less we are swayed by or forced to feel by the reality of the 'situation', the more we control reality itself.

Holding our state of mind on a higher level of importance than the petty 'goings on' that normally frequent our minds is what personal freedom is all about. It is what reality hacking is all about and as we'll see by the end of the book, we actually gain some degree of control over those apparent synchronicities or chance encounters that we have always suspected to be completely beyond our ability to influence. But I'm sure we're getting the picture of just how much those tiny little micro reactions are spinning off into our environment.

We see how much power we actually possess by some simple-to-make choices and how, over time, we can position ourselves into a completely different future and emotional space. The dimension of emotions is the underlying blueprint for the entire connected universe, and we can now pay it the heed we should. All those subtle little reactions we are making add to the field of all potential outcomes. I only wanted to share this with people so that this choice we have to be less reactive, shift our perspective, or turn our attention really becomes an easy choice. We can change everything that has been going on for us, we can turn our attention from anything we don't like or want to become a pattern in our lives.

From this moment on.

Our life is a replica of our expectation – the pattern that we first 'worked out' as small children, has been replayed ever since. We don't look into the world to spot differences; we look into the world to see familiar patterns that first revealed themselves to us when we made sense of the chaos around us. In the name of bringing the vast amount of sensory information around us into order, we slowed it down to our level, and a pattern emerged. We 'discovered' what was happening and from the millions of bits of sensory data that still surrounds us, we turn it into our lives. From the millions of possible circumstances we could find ourselves, we've turned it into this one, based on that pattern we 'worked out' all those years ago.

We know what is going on in our world, not because we are clever but because we are the ones presenting it at another level of mind. We know what's going on because we are the ones who made it. But we are also the ones who can change it, and start to notice different and more pleasing patterns. We can change what we are looking for, and we can change the meaning of whatever seems to be going on. And in the process of doing so, we're not just 'bending' our reality, but increasing the likelihood of seeing more of what we'd like to. we have downloaded a new pattern recognition software. We don't just change the event in that moment but every event like it in the future. We are starting to understand how this **reality shape-shifting skill** can be adapted and applied to every other aspect of our lives.

When we change how we feel, **it is never just in that moment**. We change what we will now see, and what will happen or the likelihood of drawing to us **evidence that matches the new state** – our new emotional preference. Do we want to keep seeing this old pattern reoccur in our lives? Do we want to keep noticing this very same pattern that is more truly the result of some ill-meaning adult who imparted some disturbing vibe on us? Because when we understand the power we have in noticing new patterns – and that this also breaks the spell of the unconscious feedback loop, we've taken control of what we may have thought will forever be beyond our control. When we fully get the sense of how much control we have over what is an subconscious experience, the world starts to slow down. We get the sense of it all moving in relationship to how we are. We have stilled the world by stilling ourselves.

And I don't know about you, but I'd rather have absolute control over how I feel than all the tea in China. No job, boat, or holiday could compare with that. I mean, we see the pictures of the Maldives, or a pool overlooking the Greek coastline and imagine these places as an absolute paradise. So we go and do some overtime at the job we're not overly fond of, and sacrifice many of the luxuries we might have otherwise afforded, so we can sit on planes and in airport lines to get to 'paradise'. But we get there and yeh, it is truly breathtaking. I'm not saying these places aren't beautiful, but we still feel the same.

We still have those same old subconscious patterns running our lives that probably even get compounded by the traveling, and the withdrawals we get when we get back to work. We never consider it an option to get closer to ourselves, or go on that inner journey that can change our perception of what we have and where we are. We never think to enter the mind – that next frontier that could have turned our backyard into paradise, and our friends into nobles. Our normal life into something astonishingly special. It never occurs to us to go on a vacation to our inner worlds - one that can transform who we are and what we do – and at a substantial discount from the Greek Isles.

In visiting these inner worlds, and doing the reflective work on what matters to us, we are learning to control an unconscious part of ourselves. A world that we had resigned to being completely beyond our choice or control. But this is what 'more conscious' means and offers. That is the good news this process of becoming more conscious represents. A vacation to a part of our minds that knows peace as the norm, and an appreciation of every 'thing' and person in our life for the sacredness they truly symbolize.

What we are not conscious of, or what is unconscious to us does not mean beyond our control when we understand how a few of the moving parts work and mesh together. We are still going to have bad days, and we are still going to have moments when we forgo or forget our choice to feel – moments when it is much harder than others to try and just flick a switch and feel good. That is a given - but we are gaining the tools, the ascendency, the momentum to change what is happening for us from this day forward. Unconscious no longer means beyond our control, or that 'You can't touch this'. We realise that we can pause in that moment of fury, and in doing so shift both the momentum of our lives and at the same time the chance encounters, or synchronicities we're likely to experience. We are enacting our will on the matrix of hypothetical chance. Something we may have never considered could be contained in such a simple choice.

What will our world be like when this becomes our practice. Practice leads to permanent. Can I be so bold to predict that when we understand our choice to feel that reality itself will lose its power over us. As will those who have preyed on the weaknesses in the nature of our operating mode and have managed to influence us beyond our will. That have succeeded in forcing us to abide by laws and follow rules that are definitely not in our best interest, or the interest of the 'greater good' for that matter. Those who use fear tactics and advertising trickery to pull emotional strings that we didn't even know we had. They will be at a loss to manipulate us in the way they used to. I imagine the outside world at large will become something more resembling a playground that we have no necessity to own.

We will not have the same need to stand out, or be heard or right. No need to control or get others to see our way. Much less need for approval or validation - for the opinion of others to remind us of our worth. The world will indeed be our oyster when we are no longer at the whim of circumstances for our right to feel the way we want to. We will understand our birthright to feel exceptional, regardless of any perceived social standing or circumstance. We will have this little reminder present in our minds that we are home no matter what might seem to be going on. And I for one think that this is both close and believably possible – that it spells an exciting time that we live in. Maybe I am a little romantic, but for me the times we live in represent a revolution in consciousness. An evolution of people being able to feel the way we want to more and more of the time. It represents a time of true human freedom.

When we will no longer have to be dance to the beat of the outside world, or be the dancing monkeys of the fear mongers. When we realise our worlds to be internally created – that we live in a psychological space and not a physical one. When we know our power to feel without reason or evidence, then we have figured out what I think freedom actually means.

By our natures the best part of our lives will still be handed over to the subconscious processes, but this is our awakening. We are the living witnesses to how automatically we live our lives, and the illusion of the matrix coming apart at the seams. That's the process of becoming more conscious. Waking up to the long-formed habit of denying or being unaware of the presence, role, and effect the subconscious has over what's happening in our lives, finally arriving into the light in our conscious minds. Seeing exactly how we've been sabotaging ourselves, and cursed to dissatisfying lives. Humanity is breaking a powerful long-term habit of ignoring the part of our minds that can unlock us. And it is happening all around us.

We are becoming more conscious on so many levels of the parts of our lives that were happening subconsciously. How we can in the conscious mind affect the subconscious processes that regulate our fears, primal needs, and perceptions. What was once the business of the highest and finest intellectual minds is coming to our 'table' – to the choice and attention of everyone. When we can accept the idea that we created what's going on in our lives at some level, we can change the very nature of both what happened, and what we see in the world from that point on. In becoming aware, **we have already changed how we feel, and how we feel is that unconscious driver of our experience.** We can control what may have seemed, and what has been for a long time believed to be beyond our control.

Intelligence is self-control — control of the habits, reactions, and impulses that we might have suspected weren't in our best interests. We know many of our thoughts and reactions aren't in our best interest, but we seem powerless to behave differently. But when we become practiced and understand the reality shaping things that those small choices also affect, self-control takes on a whole new meaning - a 'next level' value. Self-control becomes that bit easier when seen in the light of how much we are able to change the world by our self-control and our feelings. ***How much we are able to bring forth the 'invisible' from the field of infinite potentiality.***

Our Conditioning – The enemy within.

> *"Our identity is fiction, written by parents, relatives, education, and society."*
> **Genesis P-Orridge**

What is our conditioning? The beliefs about ourselves and our place in the world that was forced on us before we had any choice in the matter. I say forced because these were the suggestions about who we are and what we can do that went deep into our psyche before we had developed the reasoning mind that could reject these ideas. Someone told us who we were, and we had no option but to accept this as true. These conclusions have put a wall around what we will attempt and what we think we deserve that has tarnished every single occurrence in our life ever since. We will never even attempt to be an athlete, or a performer or anything else that might make our heart sing because someone managed to convince us, at a very early age, that this will never be an option for us. The suggestions still lives in our hearts, and what we know of as the pain in our lives is the impenetrable and invisible walls these ill-formed opinions have formed.

That is the real agony of our conditioning. That we cannot see what it is that still has this hold on our life – we have no idea how these ideas still taunt us. How this force actually uses our voice from inside our head. Mimics the very same voice that first inspired us, to talk us out of our dreams and make quitting sound like not just a perfectly logical choice, but the smartest thing to do. There's little wonder we can't defend ourselves against this cruel foe. We beat the shit out of ourselves, and have our moments spoiled by nerves and fears – the unseen faces of the beliefs who hide in our minds, disguised as **the way we think.** The suggestions that hide where they can never be found, challenged, or brought to justice.

When we entered this world as infants we came in as a blank canvas, and most of what we first learned was absorbed vibrationally from our parents or other adults that we had contact with. Many of the stresses, fears, and conclusions that are locked into the deepest levels of our consciousness – that are stored in the flesh of our organs, occurred when our learning was purely subconscious and instinctive. We inherited the vibrational coding of our parents. And although those feelings that we cloned or moulded into our own ways of being were responsible for what patterns stood out for us, those patterns still didn't have a meaning attached to them. The meaning that we assign to those patterns comes when our mind develops the ability to rationalize and reason, so we can try and make some accurate predictions about the outcomes of our behaviours.

As our young minds develop we are still filled with innocence and are predisposed to living in our imaginations. To thinking the best of the world, the people in it, and don't really have the cognitive ability to form complex situations in our minds. We haven't developed enough of our identity to draw strong and defined conclusions about the circumstances we're in. The 'what's going on' conclusions we now live in are only born when we become more certain of our experience – when our minds begin to 'set' and there's less guess work and curiosity. When we start to form a defined picture of who we are – or who people tell us we are.

When we are born and still 'wet behind the ears', we've only just come from the 'other-side' – a place of pure joy and unfettered creation, where we could imagine anything and have it manifest right before our eyes in an ethereal form. Our imaginary friends were real. Even if they didn't have a body, they had more personality than a hologram. So it is a shock for us to grow and realise that out here in the physical world of matter - a much lower vibrational dimension, things take much more time and persistence to materialise. More time than most people have patience for.

While this may all sound to some like hocus pocus the only point I want to make is that something happened to that young, pure, and fragile mind that caused it to set, almost in an instant. And we formed a very strong underlying conclusion about how the world is, from that point on. Something (or someone) ripped us from that magical land we were living in and shattered our innocence forever.

Of course as soon as we left the womb there were all sorts of new sensations – the pain of hunger, piercing sounds, and sights that were completely confusing to us. But we still held that innocence that everything was going to be alright, and we could be whoever we wanted to be. That is of course, until we got hit with the terrifying realisation that we were almost defenceless in the world of big people. Some of whom didn't really seem to like us very much. And I am a believer of that large school of thought who think that this shift from innocence to defenceless, happened in one terrifying single event. We were dragged out of 'heaven' screaming when it first become astonishing clear to us maybe not everyone loves and wants the best for us.

And please don't get me wrong here, I'm not insinuating that we were all abused as children, nor am I downplaying those that have endured terrible things in their childhood. But I think every young human once crossed some threshold between what was a beautiful world, and what became a dark, lonely, and scary place. And maybe this event didn't even resemble something anyone would regard as sinister – it probably looks more like an unsuspecting parent, or some adult having a bad day who unintentionally lashed out. And left us wondering 'what the hell have I fallen into here', as our bottom lip quivered. And maybe this theory is wrong, and it was a whole series of smaller things that slowly destroyed our innocence, but the point is the same. Those early conclusions that were forced deep into our psyche have stained, shaped, and spoilt our every ambition and life event since. It framed what we expect to see, and what we would forever be on the lookout for. And as we have discovered, what we are on the lookout for is what we turn the infinite of all possible outcomes into.

Boo hoo you say – that's life, and indeed it is, but what I'm hoping we can understand is how much this first impression is still running and often ruining our lives. Understand the cryptic forms this emotional impression takes, what our conditioning looks like when it enacts on our life. How this 'lie' about who we are, is a deeply subconscious underlying story that can be managed much better when we are aware of it. This impression was not grounded in any form of truth about how the world actually is, and it represents our one and only true enemy – the conclusions that were forced on us before we had a choice in the matter. Conclusions that screw with everything we want to do, how we deserve to feel, and the evidence we are seeing in the world to this day. We have to know there is a very real and deceptive form of darkness within us that we can in fact do something about.

For most people we don't even remember it happening. We don't remember it as an event, because for most people it was so long ago, and we did all we could to immediately block it out of our minds. Probably in the hope that in forgetting that it won't affect us. But unfortunately that impression remains in us as a feeling and a belief. A sentiment that remains entrenched in the patterns we call our life. We need to understand this so we can take on this BS enemy and get to the heart of ripping this thing from our lives. It ruined us, but it needn't keep 'flavouring' our life. As traumatised little children, we transferred or translated that emotion into what we know of as our beliefs. Beliefs that the world's a scary place, we don't deserve anything good, and we'll never do anything of any notable value. What do you think that did to our lives, and every experience since then? Those beliefs became our prophecy. But I think that it is far worse that we never had any idea this needn't be true, or the parts of that event that were still alive in the life we were experiencing. We just tend to call it reality, when there is this devil inhabiting our heart forbidding us to even contemplate that we have value and deserve joy. That little person that we were is coming back with a vengeance.

So someone came and ripped us out of 'imagination land' and to this day, that impression continues to overshadow our experience 'unconsciously'. Meaning we are not privy to the ways in which this affects us - our conditioning has done a complete number on us. We don't sense that it comes from us, or how far from the truth these beliefs are. We don't realise when that event turns into that voice of ill-formed reasoning and prevents us from doing something we might like to. It comes through in our mind as some unfounded conclusion that, maybe we were wrong, and should feel as guilty, or sorry as someone is trying to force us to. We don't get when or how it is actually us subconsciously sabotaging our results, as a consequence of what we 'forgot' happened all those years ago.

I don't know about you but it kind of makes me a little mad of how many people suffer for the things they never did. And not for a day or two, but for a lifetime. Sentenced for a crime we never had anything to do with. The little kid that we were, not only got shat on when there was no one there to protect us, it's been negatively impacting our lives ever since, and we don't even know it. Kind of makes me want to say, **'Get out here and show yourself, so I can show you just how scared I am of shadows – of things that aren't really there, and aren't really my fault.'**

I'll shed some light on the form this 'beast' sometimes takes so we can at least do battle with something more real. So we can get clued up on the tactics it uses, arm ourselves when we need to, and let go when it makes more sense. I said before I don't know anyone who I would regard as weak, and in the same context I don't know anyone that I would call cowardly. We just fail to identify and be able to take on the enemy in the form that it takes. Most people I know would run at the beast without fear for life if I was able to identify for them the very thing that had been wrecking not just their life, but the lives of everyone in their life. When we can see this beast for what it is we can dig in and have a foothold in the battle. Might be better to take your anger out on something that can actually change things for you going forward. We do have to understand the nature of the enemy and the peculiar ways it is able to disguise itself. There is an art to war and picking your battles. As Sun Tzu suggested in 'The Art of War' that we never take on the might of an enemy – all great victories must be tactical.

> *"The supreme art of war, is to subdue the enemy without fighting."*
>
> Sun Tzu

Our Automated Hell.

"I have seen your enemy, your oppressors — they are not who you think they are, and I know how to beat them."

My name is Simon, and it is my aim to make things 'simple.' I want to make it simple what mindfulness allows us, what purpose offers us that we may not have considered. I want to show you how attraction really works, the enormous difference between internal and externally created emotions and the nature of **our only true enemy – our conditioning.** I want to simplify the beliefs that automatically run our lives behind the curtain that were inputted to such a deep level in us long before we ever developed a logical and discerning mind.

Long before we ever had a choice in the fact – the limitations that unconsciously handicap our lives formed a dark, heavy, and melancholy cloud over our experience. It is the purpose of our lives to become less affected by the undesirable effects of that conditioning process – or to become more conscious of their operation so we can either change the beliefs or rise above them. It is not a life to be locked in a self-supporting feedback loop that we weren't conscious of.

"The purpose of our lives is to become conscious of what is unconscious in us."

The Greatest Secret.

In Earl Nightingale's recording of 'The Greatest Secret', he tells the story of a young man, fresh out of school who is down the street one day when an old friend suggests to him, "Why don't you go down to the mill, I hear they are putting people on?" And so, the young man does this and in time, he has a wife and children. He comes home each night and watches television for 5 hours, until his wife suggests that he should go to bed because he has to work tomorrow. And so he does this every day for the next 40 years until he retires. It was never a job that he wanted that much, and he never once thought to question why he did it – he did it because that's what everyone else was doing. But it is the things we do without questioning why or simply out of habit that leads us down a far darker path than we may have ever realised.

When we never question or never do things deliberately with purpose and intention, we also forgo the sense of what else lurks in those subconscious processes. Acting and thinking with intention is thinking consciously – like we meant to. And what brings those irrational beliefs out into the light of day where they can be met and challenged so they don't go on blindly spoiling our lives. If we live each day without question and purely out of habit, or because it's what everybody else is doing, we are in effect allowing the beliefs at the heart of those unwanted events to hide in our psyche. We had nothing to do with any unwanted event that might happen in our eyes, nor are we able to turn anything about it to be in favour of our agenda. When we live on autopilot we don't have an agenda. We can't manipulate the meaning of an event. We didn't know we could or have any reason why we might? We don't give our lives too much thought at all. What 'happens' just seems unfortunate, but expected, because 'shit like that just always happens to me.'

What we do out of habit, unintentionally, and without giving any thought to why we did it, has far greater consequences than we may have realised. Takes from us a great deal that we maybe had never considered. Dare I say they place us in real danger of being manipulated beyond our will. We can't change our lives if we don't know what we are changing them into. And living our lives 'accidentally' can never take us towards something desirable. Can't take us towards a life of meaning, or anywhere we'd chose to go. My aim is to help people to minimise how much of their lives is happening automatically and beyond their choice. That's happening unconsciously – where we are awake but sleep walking. What is a life lived without question or reason.

Just like when we are on a long drive and draw a complete blank if we have driven through that small town we were coming up on. Our lives can happen in precisely the same manner if we aren't clear on what matters to us and moving towards it on purpose. What we don't do with intention we do automatically. That is, like we are not even there. And we have inadvertently handed the steering wheel of our lives over to that devil we were just speaking about who certainly doesn't care where we end up. The clarity with which we live is the only path to a personal sense of freedom, and taking back from our lives what is happening unconsciously. The best defence we have against the conditioning that automatically constricts the choices we can make.

Taking the power back.

Ever since our programming became solidified, and those deep automatic patterns began to do the driving of our lives, we've been locked in a battle to counter that conditioned feeling state. We've been trying to improve the quality of our life, our results, and feel as good as we can. And for a good part of it we've succeeded. We've learnt about the things that most interest us, and we've come to know what is of the highest importance to us – what has meaning for us. In this pilgrimage we call our life we've tried to make ourselves as competent and useful as we can be. It's in our nature to want to help, and be able to do everything that we can do for ourselves. And every time we take on that challenge to expand ourselves it is in the name of proving we can do something we weren't sure we could do. Something our conditioning was making feel hard to do. We a drawn by our natures to do what bothers us most. What is that part of us that we see as flawed and move to correct it. The obstacle is the way as they say. What is the hardest thing for us always points towards our greatest sense of freedom.

How good does it feel to overcome a challenge. To do something maybe a lot of people said that you'd never do. To prove them wrong. And sadly lots of people get drawn down pathways that aren't right for them just to prove that very point. We get so strong willed and determined to 'prove' them wrong that we lose sight of the fact that to do this thing is not really something we personally value anymore. We think it means more to us to prove a point that no one else actually cares if we do or not. We really do have to reel in how much we think other people care about what we do. Most are so self-interested they couldn't care less, and not because they are evil, but because they are focused on their own stuff. They've got enough going on to even notice what we do.

More to the point though this battle we are engaged in to feel better is never going to happen for us no matter how many things we accomplish, or hills we climb. If we don't get clearer on what matters to us and reflect frequently on our direction, we might find ourselves down that path – where no one cares about what we are doing but neither do we. If we want to feel better – if we want better things reflected back to us, then it is never by the 'grinding' that is often suggested we do, but remaining crystal clear that the direction we are aimed in holds value for us. And more to the point of what we are speaking about here, if we realise we are pitted in a battle against none other than our own conditioning, it must seem obvious to us now that we can take some shortcuts. If we keep an eye out for how this tricky beast of our conditioning tries to put one over us, we don't have to enter any battle arena, we just have to be more conscious of our reactions, how we feel, and be sure what we want to do is important to us. Then we can drop everything else without a thought.

Our conditioning will always be trying to convince us of things that aren't true about us, and sidetrack and distract us with second guessing and conscience. Make things seem overly dangerous and dramatic. That beast who presents as the things we were convinced about ourselves that weren't true is one hell of a trickster, so if getting our own back is making the best choices for ourselves and feeling relaxed about what others might think are bad choices, then we are staring straight down the barrels of this beasts shotgun and smiling. In knowing some of the tricks it pulls, we can play a few of our own.

If 97% of what happens in our life happens subconsciously – without us knowing that we are even doing it – then it is only in becoming more conscious or should I say more sensitive to how we feel that we truly take back the reigns. It is not a battle or courageous endeavour, we just calmly and politely chill down into the 'saddle' of how we feel. Because what 'happens' in our life automatically, subconsciously, robotically, forced purely by habit, is what truly defines 'hell.' And taking our leave is not a title fight or a fire we have to walk through – it is reflecting on our life, doing what's important to us and sensing the real stillness of what lies in the background of our minds. It is knowing that we are guided by something more well-meaning than our conditioning, and are never alone even when it feels dark.

But what we don't know we played any part in, we have no choice in and so it must continue to happen until it comes to our awareness that we played a part in it and had a choice. If our habits are not formed intentionally and monitored and reflected on as taking us to meaningful goals, then they are carrying us to somewhere we would rather not go. If we don't live our lives intentionally, we will be constantly reminded by our circumstances that 'I didn't ask for this; why would I want this if I had a choice?' Nothing that happens unintentionally will ever feel desirable or of our choosing.

Feelings and reactions that are forced upon us by people and events outside of us are always the result of conditioned reactive patterns. Any feeling that is **'forced'** upon us, is the opposite of **'power'** or what comes from the inside, or by our choice. I will speak more about the difference in these internal and externally created emotions later, but it is crucial as we go forward that we sense the difference between these two types of feelings. One that is a choice, and we like and the other that is not. The latter can only come from one place, conditioned and unintentional emotional responses. This is one of the masks our conditioning wears - the feelings we wouldn't have by choice.

When we have a reaction to anything that has happened on the outside of us – be that events, people, or situations it is born of the autonomous program running in the background of our lives. And sometimes these are instincts that are designed to save our life, and sometimes they are wake up calls to remind us that our behaviours have taken us from our intended path. But if these reactions can be seen as part of an identifiable cycle in our lives, then we can at least start to see them from a distance for what they are. And in being able to step back a little from what seems to keep happening, the solution might come much easier than we thought. How to end the patterns we're not overly fond of is sometimes as simple as spotting them. As soon as we see them we understand the flaw in our reasoning.

The lesson we've been so stubbornly avoiding, or is tangled into a huge knot of conflicting ways of seeing starts to become more glaring as soon as we change the place from which we look at it from. And in what may seem like a simple shift, what we are actually engaged in by questioning our reactions and becoming more aware of how we feel, is unravelling a pattern that might have otherwise carried us away, wasting our time and best efforts indefinitely. I'm not exaggeration here - some of the patterns running in people's lives can carry on unchallenged for decades. It becomes their version of normal, and is by what they use to keep their whole unpleasing story in place. But allowing it to continue is neither kind to them nor necessary. They are not learning or growing – locked in the most futile of all battles, like a rabbit running from its own shadow. It's a recurring pattern that many people never even realise they have a choice in.

Some people, dare I say a lot of people, can cope with mildly dissatisfying lives and they don't really even notice when that pain increases incrementally. They may not even notice until decades later when they wonder why they stayed where they were or how they ended up where they are. Most people are never willing to take that first step of change which kind of demands of you that you admit you don't like where you are. Some people never want to face that kind of discomfort. To be fed up with where you are now is the necessity of any real and lasting change.

> *"I've never seen any life transformation that didn't begin with the person finally getting tired of their own bullshit."*
> **Elizabeth Gilbert**

We start to get the picture though of how difficult our lives can be when we are at the whim of these unconscious reactions. If we have no choice in what seems to be going on. Without us even knowing it, we've entered a 'hellish' world without having any say in it. But in something as simple as frequently practicing the 'take a breath' and realise we could move towards a response that is more in line with our choosing, we begin to generate a more chosen and less conditioned experience. Something that comes from within us. As subtle and insignificant as this might seem, we are waking a giant **to defeat our only real enemy – that we have no choice in how the world is forcing us to feel.**

This force always comes from conditioning, and what happens in our life automatically defines hell, because we start to think that no matter what we do, we can't change it. If we get to the point of thinking that what we do doesn't change anything or matter, **then nothing we do matters.** And if it makes no difference what we do, then **all effort becomes pointless**, and for me that is the definition of hell. If we can't affect the world or change in our lives, what is the point of living?

"The trouble with our habits is that they make big things seem small. They are driven by big mind, and they only seem to affect one tiny moment, but they affect a lifetime."

Freud stated that the aim of living is to become more conscious of what is unconscious in us. Everything undesirable that is happening in our lives, is the result of the automatic and conditioned patterns running our life. Patterns that we feel like we have no choice in or control over. The beliefs that became deeply entrenched in us long before we had a choice. We can chant all of the affirmations under the sun, and still manage to sabotage our goals because of those beliefs. Our beliefs are not evident in what we say but what we do. As I've mentioned, we like to imagine we are the ones in charge of and running our lives, but we need to look closer at how we behave to get a look at our beliefs. Who is the one making your decisions? We like to think we are, but when was the last time someone got under your skin, or who decides whether or not to have that second helping of desert, or watch Netflix instead of doing the study you were supposed to. we have to pay homage to the dominance of the subconscious over our experience if we are ever going to bother with understanding how it works enough to get back some of the control.

The solution to all manner of bad habits, unsatisfied lives, and mental illness alike is universal. In any of the ways that it makes sense to us of how to become more conscious of the mind that is doing all of the creating. The methods are varied but the theme is always the same, and never as hard, or as far from where we are now as we may have thought. To be clear on our goals – because that's what we are programming the mind to look for. That is what we are turning the world into. That is how we are able to see what wasn't there before we targeted our mind to see it. To be less reactive or to take a breath when we are in the midst of something that feels uncontrollable.

To never to beat ourselves up for any way that we are or thing that we have done. To forgive ourselves is our only hope of avoiding the cycles of guilt and repeat. When we feel bead we act bad. We are never behind on the scoreboard – we are not playing catch up. We are precisely where we were supposed to start from. And these may very well seem like insignificant changes, but we are changing the trajectory of our lives. This is how we end up in completely different and places we might never have imagined we could. These are the very simple ways in which we are becoming more conscious of the mind that makes the world as it is. And we'll explore some even more profound and easy ways shortly. That help to remind us that all that stands between us and our life being closer to our dreams, is a thin veil of perception. Of us being able to see things differently that are already beside us, right now.

> *"When you change the way you look at things, the things you look at change."*
> **Wayne Dyer.**

We are designed to pick the low hanging fruit. To make our lives easier and simpler. But that is also the curse of our life, because we are by design supposed to always take the easiest option. What's the simplest way we know of to get the same result. We are wired to entrust the largest part of our lives to the automatic mind. To allow it to run all of the big stuff – to trust that the track we are running on will get us where we want to go, so we can just enjoy the ride. But it's also why we think we had nothing to do with anything that we don't like that's happened in our life. Because we give our lives over to the autopilot we need to be sure we periodically reflect that the pilot knows where we're going to the same place.

It may not look like the true face of 'evil' but what is happening in our life automatically, and forced by the outside world, is the very conditioned responses that are at the heart of every ill-feeling, and every event of our lives that didn't go as we would have wanted it to. Our enemy is well disguised, but what we don't like always comes from the same source. Any emotions we have that we would not have by choice comes from conditioning, but we are armed with a new sword in awareness – in being able to recognise the true face of our enemy. Recognise the enemy as any way in which we are forced to feel that is not of our choosing, and we are ¾ of the way towards defending ourselves with the full might of source energy.

Our Emotions are our Compass.

Another quick disclaimer here that I am not suggesting that we shouldn't be bothered by anything. Our emotions are our compass and the only means that the subconscious mind has at its disposal to warn us of danger, alert us when our values have been compromised, and guide us towards following our life's purpose. Our feelings are not the enemy, they are our guidance system. What I'm suggesting is that we don't dwell on them or let them be our ruler, or allow them to spoil our time and consequently our life. Allow poor and unchosen reactions to become a permanent part of our experience without us thinking we played any part in the countless number of annoying things 'out there'. Things are supposed to annoy and bother us. The things that bother us most are how our subconscious points us towards what we are supposed to do. What we came here to do. An unbothered person is an ineffective person. I'm not asking anyone to subdue their passions and fire. Only to spend less time bothered and more time doing something about what bothers us most.

What's happening in our life automatically is the beast we are trying to slay. And being clear on what we want and living with intention is our weapon. Defining the obstacle we think we are up against is how we bring the beast out of hiding. And in my experience when the light is shone on the beast – on what we thought it was we feared, it turns out to be a hell of lot smaller than we thought it was. Shadows cannot exist in the light, and quite often all we need to do is ask the questions of what is stopping us and the rationale for what we were worried about just crumbles. Those fears we couldn't see because they were tangled up in a myriad of cloudy ways of thinking, run like roaches when they are exposed to the light of our questioning.

The beast is very clever in how it hides – it is masterful in disguising every way in which the blockage could be in our way of thinking. It is our way of thinking itself that is the problem that can't be seen. How can we see our own way of thinking to be a problem that can be solved? Our problem is an anomaly wrapped in an enigma, but that can be avoided with consciousness. By elevating emotional states we don't solve the problem – we just wonder where it actually went. Or we often need to think like our own coach, or view the issue like we are a bystander to let the real obstacle to become clear enough that we can do something about it.

Sometimes the beast sounds like our own voice of reason, convincing us this goal isn't worth all the anguish it has cost us. And sometimes it takes the form of the people who say we can't, or laugh at our pursuits – the ones who have different values or wouldn't be able to do it themselves. Sometimes it's those moments that destroy our confidence and cause us to roll up our map and stop searching. It very rarely seems as though what is stopping us comes from the inside. This over-protective mind of ours has been tricking us and pushing our buttons for many years. We must learn the value of silence so we can be invited to its inner workings. So we can take a seat at the board of our life and put forward our plan. Even when we seem tested, and the mind is asking us by tough circumstances 'are you sure you want this'. We will know the answer – we will pause when we need to, we will yield when we need to, but we will never stop moving towards something that holds real value for us.

It is the process that delivers us, not one day of effort, but that we know the effect of many days moving in a single unified direction. It is the process that concentrates our efforts into a single meaningful 'bang'. It all seems so easy when we trust that it is the process that takes us there, not one single day or set back. We walk across those very fires of hell by each intentional action. By what we do every day. It is never getting to the goal that saves us, but the small everyday actions we take towards our success. It is the clarity of our intentions that allows us to know at all times that we are moving in the direction of meaning and choice.

Conditioning is our only true enemy and the one we are always at battle with. It is in recognising the form it takes that we prepare ourselves for an exponentially better life. It is the things we do and believe without question or thought – that we do automatically and unconsciously that is the unseen enemy of satisfaction. What we do without thinking about it, is the same as saying we didn't know we were doing it, or didn't feel like we had a choice. When we reflect on what's important, and move with intention towards what has meaning, it is the opposite to living unconsciously and without any consideration. Nothing desirable can come from an unconsidered life. An automatic life.

How much choice do you have over what's happening in your life? Very little, if you don't realise conditions, and 'reality' as an unconscious reflection of state, or of our emotionally created expectations.

Anyone who can buffer themselves from the normal and automatic pattern of reacting to the external conditions of the world, in so doing also inherits more power to mould the world to their will – to turn it into what they would prefer to see.

Our conditioning is also armed with that unstoppable force we call momentum. It has been running our life for millions of moments leading up to this one, and it can certainly blindside us if we try and take it head-on. If we are at war with how we feel and hate what's happening in our life, the battle lines have been drawn just to get a foot hold into what we want to do. If it is peace that we want then we must start from peace. If the way we get there is ever able to reveal itself we have to be able to imagine the feeling first. Much like someone who designs something as complex as an aeroplane never starts with the wheels and works up. They must start with a vision of the final product so they can see where everything fits and what is missing, and what is the next step that needs to occur. I believe that we only need imagine and feel the end as if we already have it and don't need to worry about 'how' or the next steps to get there. If we know the feeling the 'road will rise up to meet us'.

We have to both imagine how it would feel and remind yourself it is never other people that are stopping you. Even if it may seem that way, whatever we blame someone else for we also forgo the power to change. If we are unable to feel the way we want to in this moment, we can at least take a breath until we can console ourselves. While we don't feel the way we want to we can never be shown the way to get there. Conditioning and beliefs are always the obstacle at the heart of our displeasure, but another of the ways we can expose them is by understanding the framework or mental models that we think from. The emotional platform that supports our way of thinking. If we can't feel good, then our way of thinking is the very thing blocking the solution. We have not provided the mental framework necessary for us to think in terms of a solution if we're mad as hell about the problem. We can never imagine anything outside of this mental framework that is formed by our emotional state. To build the building we have to erect the scaffolding in the form of an emotional blueprint. We have to entertain what is possible if we are ever to see the way we will get there.

When we can independently shift how we feel we get a true idea of what a 'house of cards' these mental models really are. How the entire framework of what we were told we can be, can be dismantled and reassembled in hours if not minutes. We have all had those experiences of our whole outlook shifting from the smallest of events. That close friend that we thought had an issue with us calling to say they'd been away, or that one person who noticed something that we did, just lifts our whole game. Shifts our whole perspective on life and people. If only we understood how we could make those moments from within ourselves when we had nothing better to do than dwell on what someone said about us, and restore the scaffolding around our inspirations.

Instead the majority of the time we live unconsciously by the notions of who and what we can be, handed to us by someone who never even knew us, or knew what they were doing at the time. Before we ever knew we had a choice, we were told what we were worth, and consequences persist to this day. Have ever since been playing out in how much joy comes into our lives, and how much faith and confidence we have in ourselves. Bloody shame I reckon.

What we can do about it.

Can we do, be, and have all the things we ever wanted? I've heard this promise from every guru I've ever read but this is my attempt at 'oversimplifying' how we get it.

- Why do I want it and what will this allow me?
- Mindfulness and going deep into our centre cleanse' us of conditioned energy patterns, and instils in us the deep sense of peace the subconscious knows as its normal state. Gives us a new perspective on our dramas and who we thought we had to remain.
- Thinking sideways, or laterally about our obstacle or problem. There is usually an easier way around them that hasn't occurred to us because of our frame of thinking.

We are the most informed and mentally nourished our species has ever been but at the same time live with pandemic levels of sadness. We are worse off emotionally for a variety of complex reasons which can't exclude the looming fate of humanity. But it is also because of this gap between the conscious and subconscious minds that we have been conditioned over time to be much more lineal thinkers. To not think intuitively about our issues or easier ways to get to our goals. We tend to stare at our obstacles and cling to this one single way we imagine is the only way this can unfold. The way we go about solving everything in our life, just can't apply to everything. As a consequence we get wild and judge things to have gone so terribly wrong, when in fact we were being delivered to a better starting point. We were being taken to an improved vantage point, or learn something that was going to save us lots of time and heartache when the time comes. We aren't able to think like our forefathers did, and trust in the intuitions that led them to water, or navigated them across great spans of ocean without even having a compass. The intuitive and instinctual minds they managed to navigate early life on earth with has been bred out of us and we are not better off for it.

I believe we have been progressively coaxed out of trusting in our own instincts. Convinced that intelligence is external to us and someone smart is taking care of it, so don't worry your pretty little mind. We are extremely intelligent beings, every single one of us, but they've convinced us we are basically stupid. Society at large has reduced that main core of our intelligence (our instincts.) to be little more than an unhelpful superstitious mind.

Yet at the very same time women are beginning to dominate the business world because of how highly skilled they are at reading people, situations, and relationships. So I have digressed, but I have to think it is worth remembering just how many of our big problems could be solved, and how much easier we could take perspective on our setbacks if we just learned to return some faith in our own great source of answers – our own great source of intelligence, and to think a little more 'sideways'. We don't have to hold back the tidal wave that is the momentum of our dominant emotional state – we have to learn to surf.

If we are enslaved to the opinions of others and results being a certain way as a condition of our worth and happiness, we open ourselves to the manipulation of the world and people.

The Devil Wears a clever disguise.

> *"The whole universe is summed up in the human being. Devil is not a monster. Devil is a monster waiting to trap us. He is a voice inside. Look for the devil in yourself, not in others. Don't forget that the one who knows his devil, knows his God."*
> **Shams Tabrizi**

Our conditioning is the only true devil in disguise. If we saw it for what it was. If we saw it as those ill-founded and illogical suggestions, made to us many years before we ever had a choice in it, they would be pulled out like a weed to dry up and die. The problem being of course that we don't recognise the form these suggestions can take. We don't see the enemy in the things we do and believe without question – that we do unconsciously. We don't recognise that 'harmless' habit, or the voice of reason that talks us out of what we want to do, as the face of evil. If we saw these beliefs in action, or if we understood the trickery and what's happening in our life unconsciously as our foe, it would be a far easier demon to do battle with. If we realised the subconscious patterns that jailed us, and screwed us over, as a beast, we would kill it quickly and decisively. The real problem is in recognising our foe. How can we be free of what we don't even sense has us in its clutches?

Someone put those beliefs in us, and we never got the chance to play a part in how these conclusions have tampered with our lives ever since. We never had a choice in how we were conditioned, and it has wreaked havoc in our lives ever since. We were never clued into the main aim of our reality maker. But in my way of seeing it, what is happening in our life subconsciously and automatically, is quite often happening in contradiction to our conscious will, and without us knowing it. It has us at war with ourselves – a war that most people have just given up on.

Recognising the enemy

"We were convinced a long time before it was a choice for us of what we can do, what we deserve, and those suggestions have unconsciously tortured our life and what we will attempt ever since."

This 'enemy' has itself so deeply buried and well disguised in our psyche that we can never tell the difference in tone between our inspired muse, and an overactive drama queen. They both seem to be making an equal amount of sense, and they sound the same to us. We struggle to tell if it is our angel or the devil on our shoulder speaking. It is near impossible for us to sense how our patterns of thinking can make nonsense seem to make perfect sense. That it is our vibrational pattern, or the force of our habits doing the talking when we don't do what we should or that we said we were going to do. Our enemy doesn't come all dressed in battle gear and face us like a fierce warrior. You can be certain that if it did, we would stand a much better chance in this fight. It is not because we lack courage that we aren't doing the things that we'd love to – it is that we don't see the enemy for what it is, when it shows up.

If I told most people that it was that wild beast over there that represents every single thing that has gone wrong in their lives, almost everyone I know would run at that thing without fear. **It is not courage that we lack – it is that we do not see the enemy for what it is.** It is that we don't recognise what is at stake in that moment we yield to an unreasonable voice. And it is not that we are lazy or scared. Our way of thinking can't entertain the fact that this action could lead to a real result. We don't think it can actually happen so there can be no effort. We aren't able to care enough about the result to take action. We don't realise **who else we are doing it for** or who else will benefit from us becoming the person we might like more. Even if that is something as simple as becoming a less bothered and calm person. We can do that so easily, but we don't recognise the enemy, realise the reward, or how far beyond our own personal benefit that reward goes. We are always the primary beneficiary of any effort and undertaking towards a more chosen and conscious life, but the whole world is affected by our choices.

Our enemy is that grudge we can't let go of, and the 2 pointless hours we spent on Facebook last night. It is the emotional energy we wasted complaining about someone who makes zero difference to our life. Only when we consider all of the ways in which we waste our valuable emotional energy can we begin to see the things that subtly stand between us and the things we'd love to have. That we would be devoted to getting if we could sense when we were getting in our own way. We could have these things if we saw what was stopping us for what it is. The conditioned mind itself takes the form of every single distraction, and chunk of our energy that we 'spend' on things that are unimportant, and we have no desire for or ability to change.

I am certainly not what I could consider the most driven person I've ever met. Nor do I care very much for standing out or recognition for that matter. I don't care about much outside of sharing this awareness and connecting on a deeper level with the people who want to be in my life. I am not driven to hell by my ambitions, but our lives would be so much easier if we only did, thought about, and spent our emotional energy on the things we really cared about. If we recognised the true enemy of our lives for what it is – being our unconscious conditioned patterns in the many forms it takes. If we were more conscious of how we felt more of the time we'd stand a much better chance of moving towards the things we want, and living a life of purpose.

Conditioning is our only real enemy. It creates the outside world that pushes our buttons and seemingly forces us to feel in ways that we don't consider we have a choice in.

We can do anything we want in our life if we get clear on what's important to us and why. Anything can be done if we get clear on what's stopping us and implement the systems that will take us there. If we engage in the process and keep moving. If we 'just keep swimming', as Dory says. Our life is about the processes we follow, not the deadlines being reached on time or our goals being reached by the deadline. **We are successful every single day we move in an intentional direction.** When we do the things we want to because we choose to. The trouble with most of our humble ambitions is we don't have an understanding of the power of a system, or step by step plan to take us wherever it is we want to go. It is not what we do for a month that becomes our victory – it is what we do every day because we like to. Then our dreams happen so easily – they happen, dare I say automatically.

> *"Success is the progressive realisation of a worthy ideal."*
>
> Earl Nightingale.

Chapter summary

- What's going on in our life depends on how we feel about it and the meaning we attach. We change the event itself when we change how we feel about it.
- We change the event, its control over us and its meaning when we change how we feel about it. We take back the power to change 'reality' itself – something we might have thought was off limits.
- The essence of Law of Attraction is the world is created from an internal state of mind that reflects back to us the same feeling from which it came. It is how the higher mind automatically sustains our state of mind, and is the most perfectly disguised and convincing feedback loop on the planet.
- It's also why no matter how hard you work and try sometimes you're not able to feel any differently, and tend to downplay any achievements we make very soon after we've done them.
- The outside world we see can only support evidence that reflects how we feel. When we feel differently, we are in a different situation.
- When we take control by feeling differently and less effected by an event, we don't just change it in that moment, but all moments like it from that point on. We are sending a message to that higher aspect of our consciousness that we are aware of the feedback loop and its play on the conscious mind.
- We only have one true enemy - our conditioning the suggestions of who we are and what we deserve before we ever developed a rational mind that could dispute what we were told.
- Those suggestions went deep into our psyche, and haunt our reality and limit our choices to this day.
- If we are not clear on what is important to us and live our lives intentionally, we hand the steering wheel of our life, and what's happening in it over to an automated process that is

completely out of our control. We don't even sense when this is happening so there is nothing we can do about it. The consequences can be far more devastating than we ever realised. Our life just feels like we didn't chose it and there's nothing we can do about it.

CHAPTER 4
'Reactionality'

"Living your life guarded by God is like flying a plane above the storm clouds. You can see the storm you're just not affected by it."

Author Unknown

Reactionality.

We are all aware now how much our reactions have a tendency to trend - that when we are in a downwards spiral, we tend to notice more evidence that supports that mood. How we feel skews our filter, or perception of the world. A bad day can get progressively worse, but we also know how irrationally fickle we humans can be - that one tiny new piece of evidence can completely change what we think is happening and our outlook. In nipping small reactions in the bud, or 'conjuring' up a better feeling by bringing to mind a desire we have, or a fond memory, we can cut ourselves off from that down trending cycle getting out of control.

But what we often don't realise is that **we are always reacting.** Always subtly vibrating to every micro event that's occurring out there. Every song we hear, or sunrise we stare at – every small gesture, or insinuation. We are always in a constant state of flux – of emotional stirring. And as we have learnt, it is those subtle reactions that the mind is using to stabilize our reality. To keep in check that we are in a familiar seeming world. But we never realise that by this process of our 'trending' reactions, how those seemingly inconsequential and 'unchecked' reactions can, without us knowing, snowball into what become the larger events of our life.

We are always 'vibrating'/ reacting, as a means of maintaining the state of mind 'bandwidth' that we occupy or refer to as normal. If we get too low, in that frequency range, we will subconsciously remind ourselves of things that jolt us out of that frame of mind. If we are getting overzealous in our ambitions, dreams, or expectations, we'll usually get brought back down to earth. Although it's not always the case, and many people have lived to contradict both ends of the spectrum, reality generally has a framework that keeps us inside a framework where expectations are met with precision. We don't get what we want, we get what we subconsciously believe is true. Even though some people have gone beyond what they ever dreamed possible, and some have found all the faith they had ripped from beneath them, these are both exceptions to the rule.

Do we have any control over this? And I accept that many won't ever be able to believe that we can influence the universe and things ordinarily resigned to 'fate' but that is not my experience. Nor it reflect anything that I have learned about our ability to not just impact the subconscious aspects of our life, but to move those 'sliding doors' of reality in our favour. That by our shifting our energy we can witness the miraculous, and influence meaningful chance to our favour. As the world turns, we can get it to turn in our favour by our energy and expectation.

> *"You can't always have a good day. But you can always face a bad day with a good attitude."*
>
> **Author unknown**

Does a good attitude have a real time effect on what we see? Do we change what we look at by what we look for? Can we influence the outcomes we experience by the energy we project and our expectation? These are all relative to that same question we asked ourselves in the beginning – does your state of mind have an effect on how the world seems? On the evidence that becomes most apparent to you? Does your mood have an effect on the type of things you see, and what's 'going on' for you? I really do hope that you ask and find and are able answer these questions, so you find the proof in your own way. I hope it becomes as undeniable for you as it has me.

Because it's absolutely possible to raise the energy levels that typifies our mood without reason. No matter what might seem to be going on around us, we live in a psychological experience. We live in what's going on in our minds at the time. We are the ones that make it either a magical and fun time, or it can become a dull and boring day. The difference lives in us.

Our reactions have less to do with the events that we imagined caused them, and more to do with our own mind working away to persuade us that things are ticking along as normal. What's going on can't happen without our participation and presence. The events aren't as 'real' as we imagine. They are a cog in the wheel of maintaining our typical outlook and characteristic mood. **Anything that comes on our radar.** Whether it be something annoying that we notice, or an act of kindness, what comes to mind is because of us. And I know we'd all like to see more of what pleases us. We've got more of a hand in it than we ever imagined. Everything we see are markers, or props used to secure our reality and the sense of normality. Anything that gets our attention grows into a permanent fixture. So we can't dwell on anything that we wouldn't want to keep experiencing. **All reactions have the potential to become a permanent part of our experience** – with us as the unconscious passengers.

What we refer to as our life amounts to little more than a pattern of reacting.

The state of mind we hold actually precedes the event itself. And while we all see the same world, no two people will experience it in the same way. When we start to see this plot of the mind, then the 'jig is up' as they say. We have become privy to the 'trickery' of our minds. When we wake the reactive cycle we're in, a few strange things begin to happen.

We start to become **far less reactive to what we thought was 'going on'**. We naturally become far more aware or sensitive to how we are 'vibrating' in each moment. Because we realise how a lot of the more dramatic events of our life are the culmination, or build up coming from the smaller, and seemingly unnoticeable things happening. We start to get the picture that it is in becoming more careful and aware of all of our reactions that we are actually learning how much choice we have in controlling reality itself. Because we remember that once you change how you feel about something, you have effectively changed the nature, drama and meaning of the situation. It is often the things we hardly notice that build towards those events that completely bowl us over.

That's why I've called this chapter **'reactionality'** because reality itself is made up of a series of seemingly random and inconsequential events, all designed to keep our reality humming along in perpetual motion. Isaac Newton said "That a mass will continue to move in the same direction, until an outside force acts upon it." **Our conscious mind is that outside force,** and from this perspective we can see that all of what we might have seen as our 'ordinary' reactions can be seen as opportunities. Opportunities by which we can consciously alter reality itself. From the subtle to the extreme, it is our reactions that make up the world according to us, and how the subconscious mind maintains the status quo of our vibration. All of our reactions can be used to counter swing the mind out of its autonomous cycles. To get in behind the work of our conditioning - or the undesirable life that is going on without us. We can use the smallest of inconsequential reactions and subtle feelings in shaping the world to be more to our liking.

You see, when we alter a 'normal' and 'knee-jerk' reaction we've been having, (sometimes for years.) we don't just feel slightly better in that moment - we also send a message to higher part of the mind that **we are waking up to the game,** or 'tricks' it has been playing on us. We claw back some of the control we had unwittingly been giving up through our lack of awareness, or our unwillingness to participate in the reactionary process itself. We're no longer by-standers in what is going on robotically and automatically. We don't just feel slightly better in that moment, but for every moment like it from that point on. This is that 2 degree shift that radically alters where our life ends up. From this 'observer' position that we hold, we have more choice in anything similar to what caused the reaction from this point forward. And not only in the particular type of circumstance we just reacted to – we start to realise that **this is a life, and reality hacking skill that can be applied to every type of emotion we encounter.** In developing the pattern of becoming more and more conscious of how we are reacting, we gain the ascendency over how we feel and what's going on in our lives in the process.

We've all heard of the scenarios where we only need to alter the course of a cruise ship or an aeroplane by 2 degrees and by the completion of its journey it will end up in a completely different destination. It is these small changes in our reactions when multiplied over time, create exponentially different results for us. This is our two-degree shift, and it is available in every moment. What is regarded as the definition of insanity? Doing the same thing over and over again and expecting a different result.

The message of emotions.

Much of what has developed and been diagnosed as mental illnesses in our society stems from our inability to understand the **message of emotions**. To be able to tell why we feel the way we do, or what the emotions we are having are actually signalling to us. We just don't like the way we feel and often conclude that we are somehow flawed because of the body chemistry bomb that just went off in us. Did you know the same neurochemical that is released in us to evoke fear is the same one we get for excitement. That same butterfly's in your stomach feeling we get when we're going to engage in an event that holds some importance for us such as giving a presentation to a group, or even just speaking up at work sometimes, is the very same chemical that floods our bloodstream if we're doing an extreme sport or experiencing a sudden fright. In all of these different occasions, our body gets dosed with adrenaline – the fight or flight chemical that is used to narrow our focus, heighten our senses, and sharpen our reflexes.

To be anxious and afraid is to experience the same chemical dump as would happen if you were sky diving or in a boxing match. It is nervous energy designed to help us out. It is that 'high ranking general' of our mind saying, "Look sharp son – this is important." But these two different applications of it force us to have two very different experiences, and come to very different conclusions about ourselves. One of which most people hate and the other, lots of crazy people can't get enough of. The tragedy of it all is when we get up to speak or take on that formidable task where the fear begins to take us over, that people start to believe that because of this they are somehow personally flawed. It is not something we are used to doing, so the body wants us at our sharpest. And the more often we do it, the less fearful we became or the more accustomed we become to the feeling.

We sadly push against or resist the feeling and end up double dosing on the chemical. We get angry because we're scared, and the psychology of the experience leaves us feeling completely vulnerable and disabled. And leaves us feeling like we are permanently incapable. We turn the event into something that is way more than it really should be. And I'm not suggesting that people should have an aim to be constantly uncomfortable in their lives, but if something keeps presenting itself as a fear we'd like to overcome, then we owe it to ourselves to take the baby steps. To come up with a plan to dip our toes in the water more and more. Remember the arachnophobes who in the space of a few hours had spiders crawling on their skin.

Most of what we fear is irrational and can be proven wrong if we take it in bite size chunks and become practiced at it. Or as cognitive behaviour therapy (CBT) results would suggest, normalising experiences that used to scare us in small incremental steps - or 'putting our toes in the water' can have us doing things that used to scare the pants off us. We can go from putting our toes in the water to swimming the length of the pool, without any fear of drowning. We might actually start to wonder why we were ever fearful, and see our fears to be as weird or strange. 'Why was I ever scared of that'?

But we tend to dive into things and get a double shot of the 'sharp drug', making us feel 'sick' and incapacitated. We interpret what's happening to us as a life-limiting character flaw, and thus we should avoid any situations that would 'corner' us in such a way. The natural and free hit of 'excitement' gets translated by us as our foe and we back pedal from all events like it. But the obstacle is the way. What we think is stopping us highlights the very thing that would mean a great deal for us to overcome. That which forces us to grow and develop strength is what enables us to navigate life with ease. As Marcus Aurelius put it: *The impediment to action advances action. What stands in the way becomes the way.*

> "God gives his hardest battles to his strongest soldiers."
>
> **DeMarcus Cousins.**

We tend to put a black mark against anything that might rise this 'negative' emotion in us – marking it to be avoided at all costs. We shy away from any such events, and never entertain the idea of what we might get or become on the other side of this fear. We mark ourselves as emotionally flawed, and unstable because we've not reflected on what could be gained in taking it on one chunk at a time.

And I think the same can be said of anger. It always has an underlying issue or need that is trying to be communicated to us. We don't feel capable of meeting the need, or we don't understand the value we think is being compromised so we lash out. This is what happens when you back a scared snake into a corner. When we get to the bottom of what the issue is, and actually work towards solving it in a healthy way, it is often what has us soaring like an eagle. When we nut out what the problem is and overcome it, we usually feel better than we ever thought we could, and we're not angry anymore. As is often the case with depression.

People often have an underlying purpose for their lives that is not being met by the way they've been going about things. And the subconscious is limited to one way to get in contact with us. One way to tell us, and often this is to make us so ill that we start reflecting on where we are going and the direction of our lives. Depression is often a symptom of us having a strong sense of empathy and social conscience. That we don't like something and think we can do something about it. When we meet that need we are filled with energy rather than sadness.

The poor old mind has only one way to try and get our attention. And that is to make us feel terrible – sometimes it is to bring us to our knees. Sometimes it only has one way to get us to slow down and realise that what we are doing isn't congruent with our values. If we find ourselves on buckled up in the foetal position crying – we're getting some message about our lives that something needs to change and drastically. We're getting a profound message in the only means the mind has at its disposal. Sometimes it's the only way we will listen and start paying attention. The subconscious mind is limited in the ways it able to get in contact with us. Our feelings are all it has, but sometimes we don't get the meaning, or we misinterpret fear for excitement. Sometimes it has no way to wake up to its presence and what it can actually do for us than bring us to our knees so we start to look up and ask.

> *"There is no coming to consciousness without pain. People will do anything no matter how absurd, in order to avoid facing their own soul. One does not become enlightened by imagining figures of light, but by making the darkness conscious."*
>
> **Carl Jung**

I think a lot of people get all mixed up in the grandeur of the idea that we need to be making scientific breakthroughs, or building shelters in third world countries to consider we are living our life's purpose. But if we are no longer 'happy' to be doing what we are doing, it is usually a sign that it's not our purpose, not some reminder that we are emotionally and personally flawed. It means we have character and a social conscience that just won't shut up. And I don't say this so that we get all admirable about ourselves. I only say it in the context of this topic – that sometimes what we interpret horrible emotional episodes as a chink in our armour, or something wrong with us is a bloody crying shame. Our soul is crying out to us and trying to direct us to a higher calling, but so often it gets interpreted as our personal judgement of being hopeless. What's even more of a shame is that many people remain there. They get medicated out of being able to feel much at all and silence the inner voice reminding them that there is so much more to us than we are seeing.

Many are so bogged down in their programming or the sense of family responsibilities that to hear this inner voice would be too much for them to handle. But that doesn't mean that it will stop. If we can't think outside the box of what we are doing, or what we think we must do for now, it doesn't mean we can't start to incorporate some of what holds real meaning for us into our lives. For some living a life of meaning (helping) can't even come on their radar, because they are just too busy. Feels so distant from where they are now that they have resigned themselves to the sadness. A sadness masked by a few purchases and holidays, but with all of the family stuff they've got going on, they just couldn't possibly entertain the idea of change.

Most people have little to no idea of the driving forces behind why they feel the way they do. And the answer is universal – to become more conscious of mind. More present in our minds, which includes becoming increasingly more aware of our reactions, and sensitive to how we are reacting in each moment. Sounds easy but it is an ongoing process that will progressively lead us to a place we maybe never thought we could be. Peace of mind that is unconditional. That is not coming in the future, or needing anything in our position to change. The outside world will matter less when we become reactionality hackers.

And the next time those butterflies come to your stomach, you foam at the mouth with anger, or you wonder why you are so deeply dissatisfied, I'm hoping you won't take it as a personal flaw, and you'll reflect on what matters to you, and how it might be related to how you are feeling. The next time we get those butterflies doing loops all the way up to our throat, it might help to realise there is a very good reason we are getting this fix of adrenaline. We might not say 'thanks' for the free 'dope flood' the first time, but it certainly might help us use and understand the emotion, rather than consider ourselves hopeless. We might stand back from it a bit more and consider how normal it really is. might be the observer and start to love how deep we are breathing. We might even open ourselves to ways we can get smaller doses and get to the bottom of how irrational our fears really are.

Reactions as opportunities

The only point I wanted to make in this chapter is how our reactions can be utilised as simple and easy to take opportunities to alter our programming, experience, and lives. When seen in this light, we are quite often looking forward to that next time we lose our minds. Because the next time, we know we can get back to control and back to 'zero' faster than last time. We understand that there is something meaningful at stake. Our peace of mind is far too valuable, and we certainly don't want to be eternally repeating this event. We get reflective on what caused the reaction and **naturally (without any effort whatsoever) become more patient, tolerant, and resilient people**. We know what we are losing, and what is at stake when we lose our shit. So, if and when we do we want to know it is for good reason, and remind ourselves that we have the power to change it.

We naturally become better moderators of our emotions. But being more aware and more sensitive doesn't mean that we walk around like snowflakes that are going to melt at the first sign of heat. To the contrary, we are far more capable and willing to put ourselves into harder to deal with situations. We have naturally, without any effort, expanded our emotional bandwidth as a consequence of **frequently exercising our reactionality skillset**. In being more sensitive, we notice when those little things that build into bigger ones try to sneak by, unnoticed. When things are 'mildly' not right, they will arrive at the roadblock we've created that only lets happiness and satisfaction past. More sensitive means we are joy seeking missiles and waste no time correcting the slightest skew off course.

When we practice our reactionality skills, we don't allow any emotion that we couldn't say was chosen to make a permanent nest in our bodies. We only want light, so we repel anything that resembles darkness. It always comes down to answering these very simple questions...

- *How am I reacting right now?*
- *What outcomes am I attracting in reacting this way?*

- *Would I feel this way if I had a choice?*
- *Do I want this reaction/emotion to make a permanent nest in my body and experience?*

Because we know anything that is not wanted, any reaction that comes on our radar has the potential to become a permanent part of our lives, until we say, "Stop, I don't want this in my experience anymore."

What we consider our lives is little more than a pattern of reacting that we have little choice in if we don't get an idea of what's going on at a higher level of consciousness. Change the little things – become more sensitive and we change the entire world around us.

Reality is the true face of evil.

The suggestions made to us long before we were ever able to realise we had a choice (or our conditioning) still shape, and often ruin our would-be best moments. Our conditioning steps on the things we'd love to do and go after. And sometimes other people squash our ideas and the things we are passionate about for their own reasons. But it's just a feeling. A feeling that we often don't think we can do anything about, but this is the form that our conditioning takes. That this shape-shifting enemy cunningly warps itself into beliefs disguised as the truth about who we are – it just feels like a reality that we can do nothing about. Conditioning is an enemy so well disguised that we never suspect the part our beliefs play in creating both the event, and the way it makes us feel. And our lack of awareness is what ensures it can go on indefinitely.

"Why do you look to reality to advise you of what is going on? Knowing what you know, is it not wiser to act upon your desire with more fervour and truth than this idea of reality? Would it not be more to your duties to yourself to be mindful – to be imagining how you want to feel more of the time, and let this 'reality' thing go on fooling itself? Do you want to be the victim to that same face of evil who first convinced you of your lack of worth? Do you even think you have a choice?"

Our oppressors

Our oppressors are the suggestions made to us of what we could do and what we were worth that we live by like they were the truth. We float on in support of this BS story about ourselves every time we quelch our desires as something meaningless. Our oppressors aren't other people, but the dumb stories we became convinced of long ago by someone who had no idea who we were. They didn't even know who they were. These suggestions made to us have ruined so many moments of our life since. Those times when we got nervous, took the easy way or we acted in any way contrary to the way we would have loved to. In not becoming the person we'd love to be, we allow those narrow-minded lies about who we are to rule over our lives. It doesn't seem fair to us, or to the people we share our lives with.

Our reactions are our oppressors – the parts of our life we imagine we have no choice in. Any way we feel that we'd rather not if we had a choice. We become so certain that the sources of the aggravation were external, and that we couldn't do anything about it. And the reaction just simmers in us and becomes part of our routine. We might come across some very annoying people, but who is to say we don't have the same effect on people sometimes? The point of this chapter was to remind us of the link between this and the last chapter. If it comes to our attention and we dwell on it, it will be repeated – will become a permanent part of our experience. And to not be aware of this is to sentence ourselves to suffering for a crime we never even committed.

Break the reactive feedback loop and its game changed forever.

Our torturer

Our true torturer is those parts of our life we think we have no choice in because of how deeply automatic those patterns have become embedded. If we don't realise who's sticking the knife in, we'll just keep doing it to ourselves. Our true torturers are hellish in nature because we don't even sense who's hurting us, or that we can do anything about it. If we saw ourselves as the culprit who's sticking knives in our back we would stop, but we don't think that it's us. And that kind of defines torture in my way of thinking. We just keep stabbing ourselves thinking 'where is that awful pain coming from – I wish it would stop'. In becoming aware, it is not as if it will immediately cease, but we can at least have some form of defence - and as we will see later in the mindfulness chapter, we will at least have a place we can go to heal and stop the stabbing.

To win the war within ourselves, do we have to lay down our arms? Yes – but we also have to become aware of who's doing the name calling and why. How do we win that battle over ourselves? One tiny reaction at a time. We win it by that time when some arrogant 'so and so' cuts in front of us in traffic, or pushes their way to the front of the que. And we start to remember in that moment that our peace is way too precious. This person is not going to get one moment of my emotional time/ space. We are all going to have reactions – some small and some very dramatic - how much of our time we spend in the aftermath is up to us. And the sooner we get to a place of thinking the way we want to the better. We are not becoming pushovers – to the contrary, we are becoming more willing to speak up because we can control ourselves. How much difference that person who just pushed in front of you really makes to your life and character is more and more in your hands. And I've got a feeling they're not going to spoil your life.

Increasing our ability to 'buffer' ourselves from the outside world – to become less reactive, and less under the influence of any habit we'd rather not have, equates to reducing the effect of conditioning. Is as synonymous with consciousness as the word choice is.

Chapter summary

- Our reactions are not what we think and far less to do with the external antagonist than we might think.
- What we consider our lives, amounts to little more than a reactive pattern that we are passengers of. But the more conscious we become of this, the more power we have to alter the pattern of, not just how we feel, but the very circumstances of our lives.
- Become more sensitive/aware of the little reactions and the big ones will take care of themselves.
- The more we are able to buffer ourselves from the effect of the world (conditioning), the more we are able to feel the way we want to and impose our will on the world – because the world is an extension off how we feel.

CHAPTER 5
Memory Implants.

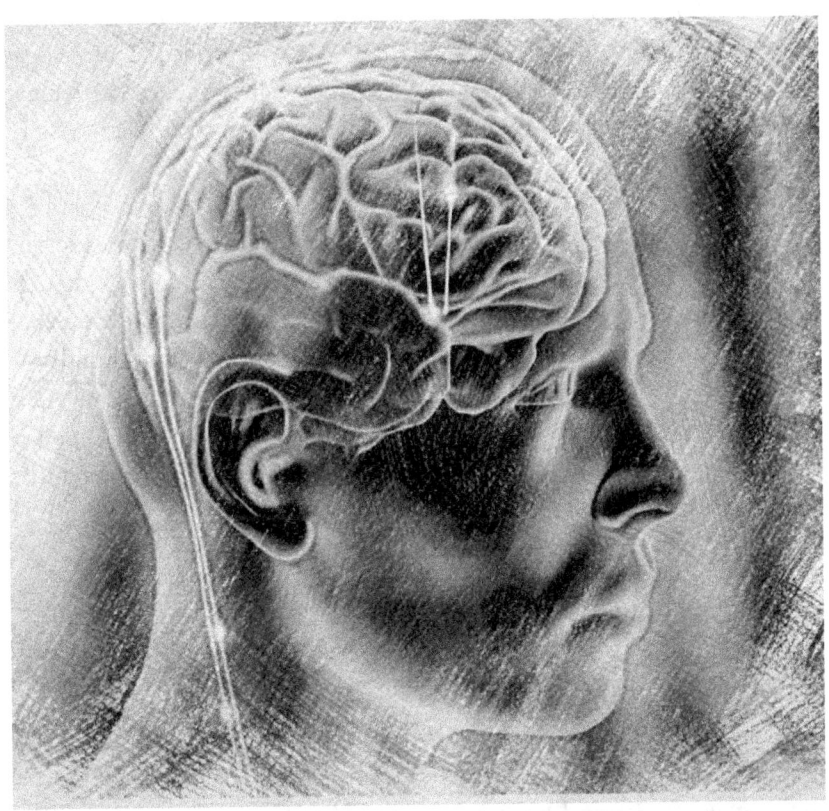

"There is nothing more profound in this world than the unrealised, and under-utilised power of imagined emotional states."

Simon

Memory Implants.

While I believe that mindfulness, and deep relaxations to be the most powerful keys to accessing and reprogramming the subconscious mind, the power of **imagined emotional states** comes very close behind them. As in the above quote, I believe imagined emotional states to be the most underestimated force on earth. The created feeling is what reassembles the world as we know it, so being clear on what we want is the determinant of how quickly we will see it in our reality. Mindfulness cleans the slate of how we feel, clarity makes the feeling as real as it can be, and that feeling in turn changes what we notice in the world outside of us.

It is the feeling that determines the type of evidence that comes to our attention by the subconscious perceptive processes'. It is the feeling that projects what we know of as our experience. The feeling reflects what has come from its source – that has come from us. Imagining how it would feel, or creating emotional states without reason, (without evidence.) is the greatest return on effort we can engage in. If we are not utilising imagined states of mind, we are shooting ourselves in the foot in attempting to create more satisfied lives.

There is no other way of securing the futures we desire than to imagine how it would feel to have them. If we've managed to bring anything we like into the real world, this is the reason why. Even if we weren't conscious of the process, what we have now is the result of what we imagined we could one day have. We believed it was possible and could imagine that feeling as real. We created a subconscious expectation that it was very likely. Daydreaming and visualisation 'work' may seem to most people to be an 'airy' and fruitless pursuit – something at the bottom of our priorities and 'if we get time'. But being able to already feel like we have the things we want, and re-running those scenes in our mind, is the most effective 'work' we can partake in.

What the hell am I talking about by Memory Implants? As we have already discovered about the nature of our subconscious, world creating mind, it has no idea if the pictures in our mind are grounded in fact or are fictitious. This part of our mind only portrays a world that reflects and reproduces the feeling that has come from us. Change the feeling and you change the reality. Every event, or visual image that is seen in our subconscious minds is viewed in the same context as if it has already occurred. No matter where the feeling comes from, it has an equal effect on the reality we perceive. And it is for this reason that visualising a desire is no different implanting them as if they are memories of what has already happened in our life. Our visualisations are no different to implanting events in our memory that have never happened. We can make things that may have seemed impossible, seem to the reality creating mind that they are part of our normal experience. Like we have done them before – like they are just another day in our life – another walk in the park. What we may have always considered difficult and stressful can become, easy, simple, and fun to our gullible mind.

This is not a play on words but on the mind that is permanently creating a familiar seeming experience. Whether the images in our mind come from past memories, worries of the future, or specific desires we have they have an identical effect on our state, and consequently our reality. Every thought we have in our mind has at its heart a related image. The deep mind thinks in pictures and has done long before we even had words and language. Every word in our head is translated into an image in this deeper part of our mind. The subconscious mind speaks in images – it is the language of the deep mind. The images we have in mind elicit the same response in us regardless of where they come from in time.

Making it more real than reality.

There is no greater influence we can have over the subconscious mind and subsequently the reality we experience, than sensory rich visualisations done in the deeply relaxed state.

Of course, our real memories carry the advantage of being rich with detail, and certainty in our belief. But even when we change the meaning of an event and its effect on us, we are changing the actual details. Of course, the mind knows when we don't feel like something is real in our heart, but that is why we add all of the details of the senses. The world reflects who we are, not who we want to be. It reflects what we think is already true. We need to be as convincing in our visualisations as we are in our real memories, or the mind will sniff us out. How badly do you want this thing? Do you think it is actually possible? Are you willing to feel like it has happened already, knowing the real-time effect those emotions have? This thing you want is hard for you to believe? This is as hard as your work will actually get.

This is the biggest 'bang for buck' work we can engage in. It honestly seems ironic that we are so encouraged to do the 'grinding' – to work ourselves to a standstill, and sacrifice our sleep, peace, and health to get the things we want. We're smothered with the advice to "wake up and GRIND if you ever want to see your dreams come true". I think this advice is a tragic overstatement and misuse of what are our greatest assets. I have to believe that the 'hardest' work we can engage in is imagining pictures in your mind – imagine them like they are a real and familiar part of your life. And while I understand that this aspect of our mind demands a certain level of concentration to picture these visualisations with some level of believability, it is hardly what anyone could consider 'grinding'. This is the most effective work we can do both in eliciting desired states and bringing about the consequential realities.

This is effortless or we have forgone one of the most crucial ingredients to the mix. That we remain calm and expectant – that we are in a deeply relaxed and expectant state. We don't claw for this prize – or even fight or try for that matter – it is already ours. We see what we think is already there. And to think we have to grind is to come from the place where 'I don't have this yet'. We are up against no more than ourselves on this one. If this thing we want is ever to be ours we have to know that in our heart. Is that hard? As hard as you want to make it.

To imagine our dreams are going to be a slog to get to, is to forgo that ancient part of the secret that will save us all the heartache. Yeh, this is the same idea that was presented in that over-simplified book 'The Secret', but 'The Secret' left the most crucial aspects out. It doesn't explain how automated our state of mind is, and the gravity we have in repeating the past. We have to know exactly what we are up against, or we will naturally drift back into old patterns, and we'll be deeply back into them before we even realise. We see what reflects vibration. This idea is alive and well in our consciousness – we just have to move to the next aspect of using it. We've already got the gist of how when we change how we feel we change what we start seeing in the world. The 'hard part' we are faced with is not doing it but validating it as an effective tool. If we don't, we won't bother using it very often.

The clearer we are on the details, the sooner it will come before us in the 'flesh.' Make the visualisation as real and believable as a past event, and the feeling created will soon begin to reflect in our world. The feeling is what opens the gateway to alternate realties and dimensions that are just as real but have remained invisible to us before we had the desire. The only reason we have a goal, or want to acquire any possession is for the feeling we assume will be ours once we have it. But we don't have to wait for feelings – we can create them. And the truth is when we have the feeling that we think we will get, we no longer have the need for the thing. We don't want it – we already feel like it is there. And it is surprisingly that when we no longer want for something that it just appears. It is that feeling that brings the goal, possession, or highlights the how we get there for us. It is the feeling that lights the path of the clearest and most direct route. Emotion is the currency the universe deals in.

We don't have to wait for the feeling. And the only things we will see in our reality are those which we feel like we already have. It's why Neville Goddard would often refer to this not as the Law of Attraction, but the **Law of Assumption.** We see what we feel is already there and rightfully ours. We don't need what we think we already have, it just 'shows up' there as a normal and familiar part of our experience. This

'Law' is in reality more about understanding the difference in the feelings of having and wanting. What we already have we attract, but what we want we subconsciously push away. To want is to assume that we don't already have it, and that remains our reality.

We want the car, for how it makes us feel. We want the job, the house, the partner, and the body, for 'how it makes us feel. We don't want the 'thing' as much as we want the feeling we associate with having it. You are already in possession of this thing – it is right beside you, if you would just turn to see it. It is behind that wafer thin veil of our belief in its absence. If you can define the feeling, and spend all of your time living in that feeling it must appear. If you have the feeling it doesn't matter if you have the thing. You have faith in whatever time it takes to be a part of the natural order. The flower must come before the fruit. And a sapling never doubts that it will soon be a tree. When we have the feeling, we just trust that it will be here in the proper space of time.

If any of this seems unbelievable, and a stretch for you to imagination, then start by asking for small things. Ask the mind to prove something small to you. I'd be astounded if we earnestly kept our eyes open that we wouldn't be shown something of this truth. But to think it's all a bunch of BS is to ensure we'll never get even a small result. Is to rob yourself of the very gift they have been trying to communicate to us for thousands of years. It won't just handicap your results, it is also to shun what the seers, prophets and wise men have tried to communicate to us for thousands of years.

We can feel like we have it now – and from 'the forest of everything' it will come forth. It will emerge from the landscape of the infinite – from the haze of all possibility. Like an image emerging out of ten trillion multi-coloured dots, our desire becomes visible. All the supporting evidence comes to us piece by piece. The way is revealed, the shortcut, the mentor, the chance meeting, all to bring about what we once couldn't believe was possible. All the supporting evidence presents itself until we have those keys in our hand, are sitting in our new office, or we are waking up next to that partner that just blows our mind. All of reality has at its core a frequency - a way of feeling. We are little more than tuning forks, with a heart and hair. Or antennae tuning into a particular station.

Which is why I've likened visualisations to implanting new memories in our mind. Like they are things that have already happened. Like we have changed the past by the single convincing moment that we felt like this thing had already come true. We are using the higher part of our minds to implant imaginings just as if they are memories. I think it is how we should be thinking of it, if we are to come to the perspective of just how effective visualisation work really is. The desire we have chose us. It came to rest in us because we know the feeling already – because we've had a taste and we want more. It would never have come to our mind in the first place if it did not already exist in some place in our future. What we are doing by our imaginings is skipping time. We are arriving at this future place without all of the steps the conscious mind is so convinced is our only way of getting there.

We would not have had the desire if it hadn't already happened on some plane of existence. How would you think, act, and speak if these things were already true? What are you going to do with the money, health, free time that is already yours. Or as Neville Goddard suggests, "*After you've experienced that shift and are certain that it is already complete and yours, you'll attract people and circumstances that are perfectly suited to assist you in achieving your goal.*"

It has already been completed - all we need do shift our expectations. We see what we already assume to be true. So what do you imagine is not just possible for you, but are willing to already assume is true? Would you be happier? Be it now – however it is you think the feeling you are wanting is. What do you assume has already happened, for that is the only limit to what we can see in our futures?

NLP – Eliciting states without reason.

> "Since most problems are created by our imagination and are thus imaginary, all we need are imaginary solutions."
>
> Richard Bandler

There are a lot of commonalities and shared principles between Law of Attraction work and the practice of NLP, or neuro linguistic programming. NLP techniques come from the understanding the language patterns and internal filters we use interpreting the world and communicating with ourselves. It is designed to expose any flaws in our perception or how our way of thinking is creating undesirable results for us. As we understand, our problems and blockages are created by our way of thinking, but we can't see this from the inside. Very common to NLP are techniques that place us in the position of being an external observer of our lives – looking as though we were watching our lives from the seat of a movie theatre, or from the outside looking in. Just like we've been exploring in the 'reactionality' chapter, we're less reactive when we see the situation from a higher perspective.

Also common to NLP principles is defining the results we want to see happen in our lives. We must become clear on the sensory evidence that defines the desirable outcomes as real, and reminds us that what we wanted has happened. Describing the scenes in detail - what are we doing, and with whom and when. For things to become true for us, our results have to be measurable, and defined. We have to know when we have arrived so we can give a little cheer for ourselves, and keep the process in motion. If we overlook important milestones it is more difficult to keep the momentum going. If we don't celebrate our successes, big and small, and acknowledge when we have arrived at specified places in our journey, or minds don't have the check-points with which to navigate a way forward.

Another of the NLP practices encourages us to 'act as if' this goal has already been reached – what will you be doing, feeling and have when this goal has been realised. NLP reminds just how effective the creation of states is towards altering the reality we are living in, and how states effect our performance. How an 'artificially' conjured up state of confidence, calm, and worthiness before important events can benefit real-time results for us. Putting ourselves into worthy and expectant states alters what happens in the real world. This isn't hocus pocus – we all know it works and it is one of the foundations of NLP work.

The four pillars of NLP work are.

- <u>Outcome orientation</u> – setting clearly defined and measurable goals.
- <u>Rapport building</u> – getting in sync with clients, or customers.
- <u>Flexibility</u> – being able to change our tact quickly when necessary so that setbacks can be learned from, and strategies can be altered.
- <u>Sensory acuity</u> – Being able to pick up on the subtleties of voice tone, body language, eye movement and gestures, so you can hear between the lines so to speak and communicate more effectively. Make quick use of any change in strategy that might be more effective.

But of course a great deal of NLP work and techniques focus around being able to elicit desirable states of mind at will. Putting ourselves in the frame of mind as though everything has already happened to our liking. It is our ability to create states of mind without reason – no matter what is 'seemingly' going on around us that will most effect the quality of our life and results. To be able to prepare ourselves for important presentations, or job interviews, by building up our confidence with body language, recalling times when things had gone well, or visualising ourselves post event as being happy and satisfied.

Social psychologist Amy Cuddy has proved that 'Power Poses' actually reduce cortisol levels and increase feelings of confidence. She is famous for the 'Wonder Woman' pose – which known to increase personal power and confidence levels. So even when we are not feeling 'powerful' we can literally lie to our minds with our bodies – these confident postures send a message to the mind that we are in fact feeling better than we thought we were. The mind has no options but to respond to the bodies lead. The mind has no option but to respond with feelings of confidence. The act of forcing a smile, even we feel mad or depressed has been proven to alter our mood. How 'dumb' is this mind thing. We can trick and lie to it just by our posture and gestures.

Call it a 'Simon' fact, but of everything I have ever read, or experienced in my own life points to this single truth. The single greatest gift we have is our ability to create states of mind from will. Even when we have no reason to, we can conjure up and elevate our emotions with our imaginations, and these have a corresponding effect on the realities we experience. Without reason we can change how we feel, and this practice lies at the heart of NLP philosophy. Being able to elicit states of mind without any need for physical evidence. Without having the support of 'reality' to make us feel the way we do – we can create the state of mind for no better reason than we want to. And we indulge ourselves in this work/practice because we understand how much state of mind effects our results. Because we understand that our results come from a state of mind. **Our results are a state of mind.**

What is NLP?

NLP is a system of understanding our internal language patterns, and the filters through which we interpret the world. When we know the language we to communicate with ourselves, we can use the same language patterns for the things we find easy to do, and apply them to the things we find more challenging. It is getting to the bottom of how we are creating situations in our head, or how our skew on reality is preventing us from seeing the solution. In what way is our way of thinking, deleting, distorting, or making a generalisation about the situation that is skewing the facts of what is really going on. What lies at the core of the problem that is making it seem unsolvable? How is it that we might be lying to ourselves about our part in what we are finding difficult? How have our experiences led us to a conclusion that may not be as set in stone as we're making it? What have we tackled that is similar that we might be able to put into the context of this challenge? Or what are some of the resources we have at our disposal (colleagues, skills, achievements.) that we might not have considered could help us out with this problem?

NLP was developed in the 1970s by Richard Bandler and John Grinder, as a tool for breaking down the traits of human excellence into a learnable and repeatable set of behaviours. A way to be able to map and follow the characteristics of success so we can short-cut desired results for ourselves as quickly and painlessly as possible. To help us become more conscious of the filters we use to frame our experience, and how these perspectives may be skewing our view of what is going on for us. How our point of view might be getting in the way without us realising it. We can't see from the inside that our way of seeing is the problem. Because our way of seeing is what got us this far, and solved all of our problems to date, it's very difficult to see how it might be creating problems for us now. Our resolution is able to discreetly disguise itself where we can't see and wouldn't ever care to look or think of. We often need the help of a sleuth to investigate what might be wrong with how we are looking at things, because the solution just doesn't seem to be jumping out at us. And as simple as this might seem from the outside to change 'the way we're looking at it', sometimes these issues can be disable people. They can't go outside, or feed themselves without thinking there is something in the food. And sometimes these skews can be so subtle, and have become entrenched in how we go about our lives that we are the last to know when these issues have developed into a physical illness.

So sometimes we need a 'Sherlock Holmes' to do some investigating and pull back the curtain of what's going on beneath the surface to find that our solution is maybe not as difficult as we were making it. It's hard to admit some things to ourselves, particularly if we've been doing them for a very long time. We need the help of an outsider to ask the questions we'd never think to ask ourselves, and see alternate ways of looking at things that leave the culprits of our anguish no place to hide. The very thing that was causing us so much grief is often far easier to resolve than we could ever consider on our own. A new angle of attack, or a change of heart can often occur in a casual conversation - by the flick of a very simple switch.

NLP helps us bring to the surface new ways of thinking and resources we have that our habit mind had somehow not considered. It helps us think laterally about the problem and find that 'easier way' that we might not have ever thought of. We tend to stare at the problem and not look past it. When we consider what our lives might look like one the other side of the problem. Think about why we want to get past this issue and what it will mean for us, the solution often begins to reveal itself - and in ways we never expected. 'We just didn't think about it' and this is because of the mental models, or platforms from which we think are scaffolded by our current state of mind. We have to be in the state of mind that the problem is solved in order for the solution to come to us. Or as Einstein said it, "We cannot *solve our problems with the same thinking we used when we created them.*"

The world may be a deeply enchanted place with boundless opportunity, or a haunted house that is 'out to get us' and either way we are right. The difference is not in the environment but in our filters. NLP is designed to help us fix those filters, or see how they might be skewed. See how we might be getting in our own way without knowing it. They help us to understand that the things our experiences have taught us to avoid may well be turning shadows into monsters. What a relief it must be to change our mindset from not wanting to do something, to looking forward to doing it more than anything. And when we understand what the 'dragon' (thing we were worried about) might actually be keeping us from, then we start to understand that even dragons have weak spots. It starts to feel like 'bring it on you flying freak'. We can't wait to reclaim that thing that has always been ours, but some 'imaginary' scary thing had prevented us taking action.

I became a huge fan of NLP philosophy and practices because I had witnessed firsthand how quickly and permanently it could correct those irrational skews in our perception. But also love it because it shows us just how much our state of mind and way we look at things can change, both a situation and how we go about attacking a problem. There is nearly always another way, and an easier way. And, of course, I love it because I think that the power of imagined emotional states is the most underutilised, reality hacking tool we have at our disposal. And NLP makes good use of these in its approach to moving mountains in our life. Imagined states are a world altering resource. NLP initiates states of mind beyond what we have real reasons for because it understands just how much these change what is real in our mind. Acting as if we are already the person we want to be, goes a step beyond the old 'fake it till you make it'. It goes right to the heart of realising we are all pretending – we are all mimicking the traits and behaviours of the people we admire. We are whoever we pretend to be – the only one we need convince is us.

How would it feel if we already were that person – how would we walk, talk, think, and feel? What would we be doing? What kind of problems would we be pondering.

Probably not all that dissimilar to that old practice of, 'what would… Dirty Harry do'? Or whoever's mindset we mean to emulate. I've been an advocate and practitioner of NLP for a number of years for that reason. It just appeals to my best judgement and fits with the Law of Attraction principles that I think are so fundamental in bringing about a more conscious and mentally well world. Yes, I am a dreamer, but imagine if more people felt the way they wanted to most of the time. There wouldn't just be less people lining up for their counselling appointments – maybe we'd all be a little more empathetic and tolerant. Enough so that people were able to live the way the wanted to, without offending the 'minority' that carry on like they stand for the opinion of the whole world. And just maybe the power hungry might be able to feed themselves on smaller portions.

Most importantly though, is understanding that eliciting states of mind doesn't take time, any special learning (can be understood in a very short space of time.) – we don't have to get to the physical evidence of the result we were chasing, to experience and live in the spoils. State of mind is a non-conditional choice that we can make right now that will vastly improve the conditions of our life.

Many of NLP practices use very similar tools to hypnotherapy – and indeed any work designed to effect more permanent changes, or reengineer from deeper levels of mind will utilise deep relaxation techniques. If we are talking about altering long conditioned programming, we have to go into deeper levels of consciousness. To access the subconscious levels of mind we have to get the conscious mind to stand down. That's when the subconscious mind wakes up and becomes extremely receptive to suggestion. The use of sensory rich mental imagery done in the deeply relaxed state is the most effective means of imprinting desired results directly onto the subconscious mind – in my humble opinion.

When the conscious mind is progressively calmed and permitted to 'stand down' so too do the belief filters that frame our experience. Our beliefs are the over-protective parents of our life, and we won't ordinarily permit any ideas that question those beliefs. We are never looking to prove ourselves wrong. Any idea will just be subconsciously ignored if it questions what we know in our experience, and our hearts to be true. So, it is kind of a big guard to get past, and can create a lot of angst in our life if the belief we are trying to change is the one stopping us getting what we want. The belief has subconscious ways of protecting itself, or better said, convincing us in the conscious mind, that it is not a belief at all, it is just how we are - how reality has always been. But when we enter the deeply relaxed state those subconscious beliefs put down their defences a bit. We can at least reason with them in getting them to stand down and consider this new idea we'd like to have about ourselves. Dare I say our own mind becomes more approachable and receptive to new ideas.

NLP is designed to open us to new ways of looking at our problem and unearthing resources we have that we may not have considered. Reminds us of things that we have already overcome that could very easily be transposed onto this issue. Some things are simple for us, while other things seem difficult, only because we haven't applied our problem-solving approach and life experience to solving what is in front of us. Some things that we can do other people would be petrified of and vice-versa. We have faced many obstacles, but what we are stumped with is applying our problem-solving skills with overcoming this one.

Can you imagine a UFC fighter who was afraid of cats? What could a cat possibly do to harm a high-performance martial artist? But such is the irrational nature of anything we fear. It is rooted in an experience where we once thought we were in danger, and our fear is what saved us – what protected us. So the conclusion remains and haunts much of what might otherwise happen as a fruitful and enjoyable experience. Much like 'Truman' wouldn't row across the water that surrounded the movie set, because they had implanted a make-believe trauma in him associated with boats and the water. And when our 'sea' is found to be nothing to really fear – freedom awaits. If we can apply the analogy to the UFC fighter who was afraid of cats – when we discover the roots of our fears – when we see them for the irrational and blown out conclusions we came to over one stupid event, the fear can become something truly laughable to us.

How horrid to think we could actually laugh at something that held us back for many years because we couldn't see the root of the problem. We can't solve something if we don't know how the problem started. And such is the case with most of what we find challenging – it's for a dumb and irrational reason. But thankfully it is not always a case of having to face every one of our fears to know how irrational they are. Sometimes we just outgrow the need to even bother doing the thing that worried us. We don't have to 'conquer' everything just to prove to ourselves that we can. Sometimes what once seemed like a challenge just seems unimportant – that it's not actually getting in the way of anything we think matters to us. As our priorities mature so too does the need to live in fear of anything that doesn't expand us. We know longer fear it because it just doesn't matter to us.

I think it is better to outgrow a fear than remain stuck trying to prove something to ourselves that doesn't mean anything.

NLP works though because if we can manipulate and 'play' with a picture in our minds, we begin to understand how pliable a memory's meaning and effect on us. If we can manipulate the size and shape of a picture in our minds, we are at the same time changing how it makes it feel. We are changing the meaning of the event and what it symbolised for us. By adjusting the mental imagery we see just how pliable the event becomes in our memory. If we can manipulate a picture in our mind - make it smaller, turn it from colour to black and white, or go blurry, we can also manipulate how those memories are stored in our minds. We are altering the effect they have over our lives. It's like we just had a loose wire up there somewhere. We just needed the circuitry welded and off we go to a life that is less bothered by unreasonable conclusions and events that we didn't even know were still affecting us.

How often have you pushed towards a goal, only to get there and find that the feeling you expected never quite matches what you'd been striving for – it's not how you thought it would feel? and the reason this happens is because the dominant vibration that pushed you there still exists in you. The one that was seeking the prize hasn't changed. We get the prize, but we are still locked in the 'seek' mode that got us there. We want the next thing – we don't want this anymore. And that one fleeting moment of victory could never satisfy the 'doer' we've become in getting there. It is who we are now – forever full of an unquenchable ambition. We have been the seeker for a very long time, but that is what we should embrace in ourselves sometimes. It is more of a reason to like us than be dissatisfied. Because the thrill of getting where we'd been striving to isn't going to change when we get what we want – we'd be foolish to expect that it would.

Do you suspect the point I'm going to make here. *Imagined emotional states are hardly in the same class as that fleeting feeling of victory.* We are always victorious if we can feel the way we'd choose to. And those feelings aren't dependent on people, events, or anything so fickle as 'reality' – that bloody thing changes like the wind of our mood. Better to be firm in our choice to feel, or be in mindfulness and a freedom from conclusions. We don't need the world to approve of us – we don't need permission - we only need connection. Connection to the source of the only thing that is sacred in us – our ability to imagine – our ability to appreciate the creative aspect of our own mind and perceptions. What more is there to this world than what we ourselves are able to make it into. My question to you is could the created feeling actually be better than the 'real' thing? The one that makes demands of us, and requires the validation of others? I mean do we know and value what it is that we are able to do on the inside that changes everything?

Chapter 5 Summary.

- It is possible to alter our past and implant a new memory of our life because the pictures we hold in mind are seen as the same by the subconscious mind. The subconscious mind has no concept of time, so it cannot tell the difference between what are desires and what are real life memories.
- They are the same in the way they make us feel and the subsequent effect on our perceived reality.
- Of course the real-life memories have the benefit of being very believable and defined. So this is how real we need to make our desires feel. Rich in sensory detail – like they have already happened. A very adventurous task but the single most effective work we can engage in in arriving at our desired reality.
- Being able to create the emotion of already having something and therefore no longer wanting it that lies at the heart of short-cutting our results. The most subconscious and effective 'work' we can engage in.
- This is a cornerstone of NLP practices – being able to put ourselves in winning frames of mind even if we may have never experienced those outcomes in real life.
- Making our dreams just as real as the reality we experience may be for some a stretch of the imagination, but we will always live in a reality that we think is there already. Everything exists in our imagination, so your ability to command yours is the sole determinant of the joy you will experience in your life.

CHAPTER 6
Light and Dark Emotions

"The universe doesn't speak English. It speaks frequency."

Mayuri Rana

Light and Dark Emotions.

Heaven is a state of mind - a feeling we create. A psychological experience we don't have to wait for. A benefit of our newly formed habit of appreciation. When we live in complete acceptance of the way things are we form a union with the higher level of mind that has created it so. We enjoy the level of peace that this aspect of mind knows as 'normal'. We are one with the creative source. But on the other hand, 'Hell' can be just as believable - the way the world, circumstances or conditioning seemingly force us to feel. One way of feeling comes from darkness, and a lie suggested to us about who we that happened a long before we had a choice. The other comes from purity and the truth of who we really are. The truth that is born in the heavenly realm, where all that comes forth from the field of potentiality begins its life.

One type of feeling is internally created, and one is forced upon us by that all too familiar enemy we are becoming acquainted with – the conditioned mind itself. That inward villain that has us falsely convinced of the danger we are in, and how limited our response options really are. That limits the choices we have in how we feel, what we believe and what we imagine we are allowed to do with our lives. Limits that have much less to do with our governments, partners, peers, and bosses than we might think. All that is required for us to move towards peace and having more control of our lives is to identify in the moment which one of these types of emotions has taken up residence in our Mindspace.

We need only recognise that one emotion is light, and is born in pure creation and truth and the other, in contrast comes from darkness, a lie, and is the unseen face of true evil. **Making a clear distinction between the two is the beginning of a process that will sky-rocket our growth, success and transform our reality.**

First, we must draw the line and recognise the clear difference between the two and see how different these emotions truly are. Because however real the emotion might seem, one is forced upon us, and the other comes from our internal power. One is created deliberately, and the other is part of the automated processes of the mind. Making a clear distinction is our only challenge because it makes the second part of the process so easy, and hardly even a choice for us to make.

If we recognise these two emotions for what they are - how vastly different they are, both in how they are born, or where they come from, then what they create for us will become obvious. We either get a continuation of an unwanted cycle that we didn't even know we were creating, or specifically designing our life experience by choice. Our only challenge is getting the gist of where the emotion is born, we will naturally gravitate towards the light. As difficult as this may seem – let's make it simple. One emotion we like, want, and would be happy to continue, and the other we don't. one we would have by choice, and the other we'd be happy to never feel again if it were a choice for us.

One emotion is light in nature, and one is darkness. If we recognise which one we are experiencing, and where they come from, we will naturally move towards the light. As this process evolves, it will change the game forever.

Any feeling has been generated by something on the outside of us, or seems forced on us is darkness, or part of the unconscious illusion. It is our conditioning taken form and the continuation of what other people told you about who you are, what you are worth, and how you deserve to feel. We have no choice in reactions if we are not present enough in our own minds, to sense these as old, outdated beliefs.

We have become somewhat numb to the difference between what has come from inside us and what circumstances seem to be forcing on us. Most people aren't in the habit of creating emotional states, or understand the difference they make to our lives. Partly because of the immense competition, where our eyeballs have become the product of this world. But there seems to be so much going on around us that we have almost had to become obsessive with the outside world, and our inner world – well who would care to look there? Maybe our ill health (mental and physical) is just as much a symptom of the times we live in as it is us being medicated out of our minds. Many people are also happier to ignore or deny that we in fact run from a program – think it's all a bunch of BS, and therefore remain unable to have an impact on it.

Most of what we do, and of what 'happens' in our life happens by the 'will' of the subconscious mind, and not by our conscious will. By way of a mind that quite literally has no will, or desire of its own. As we've learnt it is more like a robot or machine, churning out a repeated story. It just plays on repeat past experiences and behaviours. When we believe that we're in charge and not the automated programme, we'll live with less ability to change what's happening for us. But if we understand the natural dominance and how subconsciously most of our life happens, we tend to ask 'why' a lot more of the time. We live with a sense of curiosity, and willingness to learn, rather than a sense of judgement, and staying in fixed conditions. This is not to say that we act like whining victims asking, 'why did this happen to me?'- but if we don't like what's happened then we try and get the lesson and avoid a repeat. How can I learn the lesson so I can move on, to something else I might like to understand? We are coming from the mindset of wanting to learn, rather than remain in judgement.

In questioning we evoke a higher level of awareness – we think from a higher perspective and actually stand a chance of understanding why this might be happening, and how we can change it, permanently.

When we engage our curiosity, or learner mind, change happens much faster than if we were to stay in everything's f#$d and that's just the way it is. Without succumbing, or yielding to what is happening subconsciously and seemingly beyond our 'reach' or control, we stand little to no chance of altering our experience. To 'go it alone' or by our will alone is like clawing our way up a slippery slope. We're literally staring at a world that mirrors old feelings and working our butts off to feel better. This is the heart of all frustrations. We really do need to enlist the assistance of that higher part of ourselves that is 'running the show' and all the reality altering resources at its disposal.

It is only in reflection that we can get a clear insight on the values that are not being met if we feel lousy, or keep experiencing the same unwanted scenarios. In contrast if we know the reason we do, or want anything, we've already done most of the work necessary for change. Once we have a good enough reason, all we need is a plan. Once we have the plan or map, it is the reason that gets us there – even when times get tough. And if that reason matters to us, then you better not get in our way.

> "People don't buy what you do, they buy why you do it."
>
> Simon Sinek.

We have to have insight if we are to understand the unmet need our current behaviour (or sense of fear.) serves if we are ever going to outgrow it. We don't do anything for dumb reasons, the reasons have often become entangled in our reasoning. We aren't conscious of the web of conclusions that are behind why we feel the way we do, or find a habit hard to take on. We're stuck with old behaviour patterns, because they are embedded in our flesh – old behavioural patterns that are overshadowing our evolving values. When it comes to our habit forming, a small amount of effort, and a little bit of insight can go a long way.

Big Mind Cannot tell light from darkness.

I didn't want to mention it in the 'Big Dumb Mind' chapter because I needed to add this to the framework before I could explain the whole picture. We now know there are ways and means by which we can play tricks on the subconscious, just as easily as it has seemed to be playing on us. As in the earlier chapter the subconscious has no means (or doesn't sort of care) if the pictures in our mind have come from experiences or dreams. Nor can it tell if those pictures have come from our assumptions and conclusions about reality, or we've generated them because they are something we desire. It can't tell if the image-based emotions we have are light or dark in nature – can't tell if they come from conditioning, or desire. If we in our conscious minds are able to make this distinction, we are one step ahead of the subconscious mind. And most of the way towards a life by design. We are in the game that we didn't even think we could get on the field for. By the simple question – would I feel this way if I had a choice?

What something 'means' is not a decision we make but part of the instant and unconscious processes of the automatic mind. If we walked around trying to deduce the meaning of everything all the time, we'd probably get hit by a bus just as we realised it was something we need to get out of the way of. What things mean isn't a guess or hit and miss, it is 'assumed' and inferred instantly. Of course we can reflect in the conscious mind, take perspective, and reinterpret the meaning of an event after the fact. But state of mind comes from the automatic part of us that 'knows' – not the part that thinks. And as we've learnt, this part of the mind 'knows' what's going on, because it is the thing that made it so. We don't partake in what things mean, supplied by the fast mind, but we can reflect on it in the slow one.

In that moment when things are happening, the meaning and our reaction is implied and unconscious. But that doesn't mean we can't manipulate that meaning if we don't like how it went. And when we do, we don't just change it in that moment but from that moment on. We can become the skilled in the manipulation of that initial meaning. Dark emotions are ones that we don't have any initial choice in. They happen suddenly and automatically, but when we change our mind about what we think happened, we change the meaning, and the event turns from black to dark grey. The emotion gets a little bit lighter because of the choice we made to be less affected. We may not have direct access to the subconscious, but we can certainly send it telegrams. Just as we can make dark and unwanted events have a 'lighter' impact on us.

And this is why I wanted to make the connection here – to add this distinction between what is forced on us by reality and what is created inside. This adds another reality bending skill to our repertoire. In deciphering is this comes from force (outside) or our power (inside) we are able to recognise and make a decision that is far more profound than we could ever imagine.

Dark emotions are instant and automatic reactions, and comes on quick and strong as a result of what is happening - but it has its roots in conditioning. It is a part of the ongoing lie we were told about who we are. 'Big mind' can't tell the difference between light or dark emotions, but we can, and the sooner we name it the faster we can get to a more conscious life. Where we have some say and choice in how things go for us. Big mind might not care where our feelings are generated, but we do – don't we? Just like we can tell big mind lies about who we are, we can make chosen feelings more convincing, and prominent than so called real ones. Big mind is impartial to what we feel or why, so we have to move into the office space where we can create our own realities.

Whatever is seen on the screen of our minds has an identical effect on our state, and what we experience as reality is the consequence.

Visualising an event sets up the same neural pathways that our memories do. If we see something often enough in our minds it will happen just like Déjà vu. The more present we are in our minds, the more we are able to sense the difference between what are chosen emotions and what are conditioned reactions to the world. If we want to become more conscious we only need to define how much of our time we are plagued by the lie of reality, and how much of our time we actually feel the way we'd like to. Our aim should always be to feel in a way that we wouldn't mind feeling if the feeling became indefinite.

Complaining about anything only serves to validate the reason for the complaint. Ensures whatever we complain about we'll experience again.

The mind isn't doing this to screw us over, its role is to recreate a familiar seeming experience. And it's why some men and women continue to 'choose' people that are wrong for them. The real problem being that we equate choice with consciousness. Most of what we do and choose happens subconsciously, so we are attracted to things that are a vibrational match – we are attracted to people that carry that similar vibe to the one we've known since we were kids. Until we change who we are – what we value and what we want to do – our vibration is the thing doing the choosing for us. So people who aren't right for us, seem at first to be very attractive. The only real way out is to become more conscious of the patterns and why unwanted stuff keeps happening. Do the work that changes that inner picture of what we deserve. This part of the mind is not trying to do a number on us, it is just matching the energy we know of as home. Recreating a familiar experience – that's all this part of our minds can do. And it is powerless without us making a choice to participate in our lives if we no longer find things tolerable.

The subconscious is not able to think and adjudicate as we do in the conscious mind. But it kind of thinks that we must know what we are in charge of. It assumes we know what we are driving. That we're sending instructions of the type of lives we want to live. That we know of the consequences of our thoughts, behaviours, and habits. The subconscious isn't privy to what we like and don't – it supplies emotion, but reproduces them like a machine. We have to play the role in our own lives of captaining this great ship. The subconscious doesn't operate to spite us, or purposely go against our will and desires. It is not something that is aside from us - it is us. And consequently carries an even greater affection for our desires to be met than we do. It is as fond of us as we would be our own children, but it doesn't have the 'hands' – doesn't have the ability to act of its own accord to save us. It is designed to normalise, regurgitate, and present the world just as we think it is for the sake of our own continued survival.

3The force of habit has a tidal wave of unchanging and unrelenting power on its side. It is how we have felt for many years. You will continue to see the old evidence, even with all of the effort you are putting in. but with vigilance and persistence that massive tide will turn to our favour. Often when you maybe just about to give up hope and think what's the point – this is all a bunch of BS. A crack will appear and the light of all of our combined efforts will pay off in ways we could have only 'imagined'.

Old patterns will persist if we keep giving them our attention. But every time we acknowledge any small piece of desired evidence, we are giving it permission to get bigger and become more prominent part of our experience. **'Thank you'** might seem like two simple and powerless words we use to show we have manners, but there is magic in them. They are how the universe hears what we want and enables it to continue to show up in our lives. Gratitude is magic and affects reality in ways that defy our conscious knowing. Thank you is just another way we control the outcomes we may have imagined beyond our control.

Imagine for a moment that this 'big' mind – our over-protective guardian, was tricking you as to your abilities, what really was 'dangerous' and who your real enemy was. Now imagine this 'big' mind resembled a big, dumb boxer who had no arms (means to defend itself) and was scared of being found out for who it really was. Just like the wizard in 'The wizard of Oz'. So, it devised a way that it could 'hide out' in our minds undetected. Managed to convince us that - 'Nah mate, you're making all of these decisions – I'm not even really here.' That the subconscious is so different in how it functions from the conscious mind is how it is able to convince us we had nothing to do with what is 'going on'.

That we think it is not even there means it can run amok with our emotional triggers, and go nuts on the control panel of our emotions. It is not playing a game with our feelings – just wants us to wake up to its presence. Sometimes the only way to get through to us is force our hand by putting us through complete agony. Those times when we find ourselves on our knees we are actually opening ourselves to there being something beyond us. Sometimes the only tool in the box for the subconscious is to knock us off our feet – so that it might remind us to 'Please, please look up and employ my help. Engage me for what

I can show you of how I can help – how I can cross oceans of time in a single day.

It is this gap in the difference of how the two aspects of mind function that makes us feel like we are getting screwed over, in the way we feel. it might seem like the subconscious is creating a completely undesirable experience, but it really wants us to have the best life. But it is often scratching its head as to why we don't choose that – it can't even think for itself. We have to do the thinking for it. We have to start thinking, and feeling, like something world creating is eaves dropping on our minds and bodies. Start telling it what we expect to see, and what is easy for us. The stuff that we used to consider hard.

This part of the mind can't argue with us. It is carried and delivers by the momentum of our existing vibration, and this will for a long time colour our thinking and experience. But it is time, good people, for us to get our own back. This is not us pumping ourselves up, 'winning' or tricking the mind back, it's just us starting to get an understanding of how it works and working with it.

Final word

Maybe I had built this chapter up and you might be thinking when is he going to tell us about the key he'd promised. But I already have, and it is a very simple idea.

There are two types of emotions we experience in this world. One is forced upon us from the outside world, or how circumstances seem to demand we respond, and the other comes from inside us – comes from anyway we'd choose to feel, if we had a choice in it. Whether those feelings are the product of fond memories or imaginings of how we'd love things to go, they are the opposite of the former. Light feelings are ones we would have by choice and dark ones are not.

One is born of conditioning, and the other from desire or choice. Learning to tell the difference and understand just how underqualified our conditioned responses are in advising us as to what is real and important holds the key to transforming our lives. It is vital to our emotional health and personal growth that we make this distinction and become appropriately distrusting of conditioned and unconscious reactions and their causes. Dark emotions, and the conditioned mind they come from, have been thwarting our growth for all the years of our life. It is the only demon we face, but it has no means to harm us if we recognise unwanted emotions for what they represent. But the light emotions – well they are birthed in the heavenly ether and represent what we absolutely would want for our lives. These emotions are cataclysmic poles apart. One born from the lie we were told to believe and the other, in contrast, flows directly from the source. From our truth and who in our hearts we know ourselves to be, and deserve to feel.

It is a very simple idea, so I won't complicate it any further with even more words. But the feelings that come from inside us – be they from our visualisations, fond memories, and any way we'd choose to feel, come from the light. Come from the truth of how we want to feel, and the purity of desire. And the others – those ones that are an automatic and instant response to a world gone mad, come from the darkness. They are not only undesirable, and have no grounding in truth or reality - they stem from the ill-intended suggestions made to us before we ever had a choice in it – a.k.a. our conditioning. Our conditioning, and the reality it creates **is an untruth**. The suggestions made to us about who we are, what we are worth and what we are capable of, is not true – it came from someone else's ill-informed and awareness deprived opinion that was passed on to them when they were too young to choose for themselves. Their despondent energy got projected onto us – the poor unsuspecting kid who knew no better. And so has been the cycle for thousands of years. Nip that shit in the bud, for all of our sakes.

There is no thought of 'maybe' or doubt in our mind if those light emotions are what we want. It is a given. We might always have reservations of how possible those desired scenes and images might be. Might question the likelihood of them coming true, but what comes *from the ether of our dream scape*, and our aspirations is the complete polar opposite of our conditioned responses to the apparent world. Nearly all of what goes on in our life is our attempts to prove the conclusions of conditioning wrong. Conditioning is what we are trying to push through, in moving closer to a life by design, or of our dreams. Everything about that feeling the world seems to have forced on us, since the beginning of our conditioned patterns, reminds me of the idea about 'original sin'. An unwanted emotional state that became embedded in our experience that wasn't our fault or doing, but we've all been sentenced to pay the price ever since.

The two steps to turning the tables on this conundrum are, first to recognise if this feeling comes from a truth or lie and then secondly to realise how profoundly different our life becomes when we spend more of our time in feeling states that have come from inside us. Recognise what are dark and untrue emotions (that they are born of an ill-conceived idea), and how much our life will genuinely change when we come to value emotional states we create and have by choice. The more we come to validate the power inherent in chosen emotions and recognise those dark ones for what they are, the sooner we can get to feeling the way we want to more of the time. And I don't believe I'm being overly romantic in equating this to also represent our transcendence of the human condition itself.

We may not be living the life of our dreams straight away, but I reckon to feel the way we want to no matter what is going on 'out there' is damned close. And we may well be up against a mountain of our past negative ways of feeling, and reacting to our environment, but at least we are a foot in the game in distinguishing what these two emotions really are. Recognising what's going on inside us is what I believe, the first giant leap towards the healing of our kind. Once our mind is open to distinguishing between these two types of emotion – once we become alert and sensitive to them and how very different in their natures and consequences they are, we are almost certainly on our way to a better experience of the present.

I've tried to present these two types of emotions in a way that we can understand how different they truly are – how 'evil' and unwanted the effect of conditioning is to make this an easy and clear choice for us. To try and keep us alert to dark emotions as a source of something way south of desirable. Because they tend to 'creep in', they quietly invade our lives and peace when we least expect it. When we are 'switched off' or on autopilot. Those feelings that are not there by our choice, are the very enemy that has managed to infiltrate our system, and go by unnoticed. They contain the seed of all those occasions that we were not able to be at our desired best, and the things we still find so challenging that we'd rather avoid.

These are the small insignificant moments when our choices and control become inadvertently eroded. There is far more at stake in allowing these dark forces to survive. This is giving those false conclusions of our conditioning air to breath. This is the evil that wrecks our life and erodes our confidence. Little by little evil manages to sneak in and make these demands of us that just seem like normal life – reactions that seem unimportant. They go by unnoticed, but these are the very opportunities we have to take back our lives and destinies.

Chapter summary

- There is a stark difference in the two types of emotions we have, and if we can differentiate between them, we will set our souls on a course towards always feeling the way we want to.
- When we recognise them and understand the difference in where they come from it won't even be a choice for us anymore.
- One type of emotion is forced upon us by reality or the outside world. Be that from people or circumstances that are seemingly 'making' us feel the way we do. These emotions are born in conditioning and are the lie that has hampered our ability to experience joy since the earliest years of our life.
- The other type of emotion is created internally by our wishes, dreams, and imagination. It is the truth of how we want to feel, and is born in the purity of desire. There is nothing more truthful on earth than that which reflects how we would choose to feel. It fills us with light, energy and connects us with our higher selves.
- It is not always a simple task to sense the difference, but one happens by the instant and automatic reactions we have, and the other comes from our conscious imaginings.
- It is understood in its simplest form as – would I feel this way if I had a choice? Do I want to continue to feel this way? Yes or no will tell us for certain if it has come from the lie that was forced upon us, or come from the truth and purity of how we want to feel.
- The all-powerful subconscious mind cannot tell the difference of where these emotions come from. They have an identical effect over our reality.
- As this becomes our habit, we are actually inheriting the ability to transcend the human condition itself, and bring an end to the cycle of passing unwanted causes to an innocent generation. We live in the time that can break the cycle of evil that has existed in this world by unconsciousness.
- If we allow the robot mind to drive our experience exclusively, we unknowingly commit the steering wheel to darkness.

CHAPTER 7
The Portal

"The white space of a free day seems unfathomable because we have become hypnotised by a false but compelling need to respond to all of the needs of others".

Brendon Burchard

The Portal.

There's been a lot of talk about Mindfulness in the last few years. It has become the 'darling' of the therapy room, as well as being widely used in the corporate sector to help employees deal with the stresses of the workplace, as well as think more creatively. So what actually is this 'weird' practice – it's supposedly thousands of years old but seems to be making something of a comeback. And is broadly being used in everything from the treatment of mental illnesses to creating synergy and encouraging free thinking in the workplace. Kind of opposite ends of the spectrum really, but it is nevertheless obviously very effective, so warrants closer inspection. If the same simple tool is being used in our approach to mental health therapy, and fortune 500 environments, then it's a pretty broad application of this 'medicine'?

Mindfulness is the buzz word of this era – the 'go to' for everything from healing to high performance, but it doesn't cost anything beyond our attention. It is a phenomena in itself that something that is as old a practice as mindfulness is could have been overlooked for so much of our history. It began all those years ago, but then hardly raised an eyebrow until about 25 years ago. I've heard Neuroscientist Joe Dispenza regard mindfulness as the single most important practice in aiding us to rewire our minds and reconnect with our supernatural abilities. So how could this weird thing possibly help towards making our minds more elastic, raising our consciousness, and cleaning us from the effects of conditioning?

I was first introduced to the idea of mindfulness by the now famous Ekhart Tolle book 'The Power of Now', but ever since its release in 1997 my interest has never waned. To the contrary, I've watched as the world has embraced the idea from every possible angle. Tolle suggested that Mindfulness was not only a common founding principle of every religion, but also holds the key to the evolution of human consciousness itself. Seemingly 'all of a sudden' mindfulness has become the centre of the world's attention - something that is childishly simple to do, so how could it possibly be the miracle worker it's glorified as? We talk about things going 'viral' – well mindfulness thing is infecting human interest from its roots. So I have to think it is warranted in trying to understand it further. And here in this chapter I'm going to through in my 'intuitive two cents worth' as to what it is, and why it works.

There must be something in it, right. But I think it needs to be simplified, both in what the practice actually is and what it does for us. We wouldn't have any time to practice anything if we weren't clear of its benefit. And I think much as in meditation, the benefits aren't things that are privy to the logic of the conscious mind. It just doesn't make sense to us – which is why for a great number of people it falls way down in our list of priorities.

But mindfulness and meditation are most definitely our most direct pathway to the reality forming aspect of our minds. To our subconscious minds. To the level of mind where our circumstances are actually formed, and where we can find it much easier to make deeper choices about how we feel, rather than be blown about by apparent conditions. I like to refer to mindfulness the **doing nothing that changes everything**. Because as far as the conscious mind is concerned we aren't doing anything. We don't have any conscious recollection that we are moving towards a higher plateau of mind. And we certainly aren't doing anything that might go towards elevating our status, or putting any money in our bank.

Why would we bother with such nonsense? Because as Timothy Leary so eloquently put it 'To come to our senses we have to go out of our minds'. Meaning of course that to access those aspects of mind where reality is born, we have to take ourselves beyond the conscious mind. beyond those running stories about who we are where the conscious mind lives in a permanent state of illusion. To change reality we have to go to the place that is beyond our current one. We have to leave the shores of reality, in order to see from a distance just how 'mind made' and changeable our circumstances really are. But the benefits are indeed 'nonsense' – as in, they make no sense to the reality loving conscious mind. You really do have to feel it for yourself to believe it.

To get to a place of understanding the benefit, I really think you have to ask yourself – does reflecting on our life have any value? Does desiring something bring it closer to us? Does writing our goals down get them done? All of these activities must be considered pointless and mindless if we didn't know better, and in my opinion mindfulness trumps them all. But if we can't imagine there are any the mind-altering benefits of such a practice we are never going to indulge in it. Something that has been highly regarded as the single most effective cure of mental illness on our planet – doesn't flicker on our radar. If our failing mental health stems from unconsciousness, and consciousness is the cure then mindfulness is the purest and strongest antidote. As Ekhart Tolle has put it – "By living aligned with the present moment, you also align your will with the universal will, which you could call the will of God". Or in more common language – "The only reason we can ever feel like shit is because we lack presence of mind." Because mind creates all things.

How do we do it?

The practice itself is simple in the extreme. Immersing ourselves so deeply into the physical senses in this moment that we become oblivious to the minds habit of making up stories. We temporarily lose touch with that normal chattering of mind, and story we keep retelling ourselves. We are so filled with the information of the senses that we limit all space for the mind to do its thing of telling us who we are and how we should be reacting. "I'm tough, or smart, or classy, or whatever – so I should say or do this." The pretence we have to keep up of knowing how we should be affected, and what someone like us should say. We're so engrossed in the senses that we lose all sense of who we think we are. We're so grounded in the physical that all else falls to the background. Even if only for that brief moment that we can hold our concentration – we've kept reality at bay. Kept the illusion from the spotlight of our minds.

In that brief moment there is nothing outside of this moment that we're in. No past – no future, just one tiny moment expanded into a lifetime. We are so profoundly connected to the present by our attention to it – by attention only the senses that everything else gets pushed to the background of our awareness. We have temporarily suspended judgement of 'what's going on' – of identity, situations, filters, and the story we have running in our head. There are no situations going on, no relationships, deadlines, regrets, problems, or flaws in our character. For one fleeting moment we have managed to suspend all of the 'scaffolding' of reality itself. And at the same time connected ourselves with that core, primal, creative part of ourselves. We have entered the subconscious mind itself. Become one with that aspect of our minds that knows no concept of time, situations, or self-image.

The subconscious mind just mirrors the world as we feel it. It is unable to care if we like it or not – its only job is to sustain vibration. To make the outside reflect the inside and keep the feeling alive inside us going. And in mindfulness all we 'feel' is the sensations of the senses – the sensations from the source itself. In mindfulness we have poked our head up into the ethereal realm where reality itself originates. Where even our identities themselves are fluid and pliable. Where the idea can enter our mind that I don't have to stay the way I am – I don't have to react, or think, apologize, or be approved of. However long our concentration will allow that moment to be, we have broken the surface of consciousness, and moved towards a 'pre-conditioned' state. Moved towards that state of innocence to all of those false conclusions we had 'served' on us, like subpoenas for crimes we didn't commit. In mindfulness we touch the void of creation itself and are, for that moment, joined with the subconscious mind.

I have heard experienced monks proclaim that we if we were always mindful we wouldn't need to meditate. Mindfulness is a moving and waken meditation. Immersion in the senses and clear of all mental chatter. We will always be dragged back into the mind's stories because our ego, or self-image, despises the mindful state. It needs to be able to push our buttons to survive. So the ego doesn't like us venturing off into those parts of mind where we are the witness to the 'truth' being constructed into the fiction we call reality. In the egos desire to keep itself alive in our body, it needs to be able to push our buttons.

Or what Ekhart Tolle refers to as the 'pain body' – it is a living entity just like a slug or an amoeba that feeds off our situational pain and dissatisfaction. Our body is playing host to a vibrational ghost that is addicted to its own suffering. An addiction that is facilitated by a mind that is so much more powerful than the one we use that we do not stand a chance to change how we feel, unless we become aware of what is actually happening when those buttons get pushed.

All sounding similar to everything we have heard already right – of the reactive pattern we refer to as our life – as the feedback loop the Law of Attraction uses to support itself. We need to understand what we are up against if we are to stand a chance in this battle to win territory of our own minds, and freedom over how we feel. Mindfulness is not some blasé practice that we should 'spare' some of our time and attention for we have nothing better to do. it is entering the zero point of our consciousness – it is merging with that eternal and sacred source within us – and every time we do, we cleanse our body of the habit energy that is feeding off our pain. Mindfulness is a 'portal' to higher dimensions. Free from time, illusion, suffering, and any form of control you thought anything in the outside world had over you. People talk of the escapism of drug induced states – mindfulness is the ultimate escapism. Escape from situations, guilt, obligations, and any false sense of who we are.

The more we go there the less hold this 'reality' thing has over us. And every time we come back to the 'real' world our situation has changed a bit. Maybe it hasn't been all fixed, and everything is great now, but we at least get the sense that we can see it in a new way. We have visited where reality was created, and that deep sense of peace we temporarily experienced has cast a little spell over how much the situation can control us. So, *it is a temporary hiatus from our mind made situations that cleanses us of the effect of conditioning, helps entertain the idea of how pliable our identities are, and instils in us a deep sense of peace.* Think that about covers it? Wait no, it also allows us to see clues in our world that are evidence of where we have just visited. Allows us to see the residue of a dimension the ego had been hoping we would never find. That's why I refer to mindfulness as the 'Portal'.

The Portal.

> *"His disciples said to him, "When will the kingdom come?"*
>
> *Jesus said, "It will not come by you waiting for it. It will not be a matter of saying 'Here it is', or 'There it is.' Rather, the kingdom of the Father is spread out upon the earth, and men do not see it."*
>
> **Gospel of Thomas.**

By the very things we've been conditioned to value, we've been lured away from the celestial, and ideas of a 'magical' nature that have been shared throughout centuries of storytelling. The stuff of adventure, myth, and legend. When people believed in dragons, and sorcery – and the supernatural forces of nature that could not be seen by the naked eye. And to its detriment, our society, as 'smart' as we are now, has become sterilised of all sense of enchantment – of the magic and the mystery of the celestial, and the 'heavenly.' Of the stuff that goes on in the higher dimensions of awareness of those subtle but magical forces of nature that control all of this.

We think our beloved science can 'explain away' our futures, even though it fails to agree on or make sense of ancient ruins that seem to contradict the evolutionary theory itself. That seems ok with casting a huge anomaly stamp over the very things that defiantly prove that we didn't evolve from the animals, and there had to be some extra-terrestrial intervention. What science can't prove, or come to terms with shouldn't equate to unimportant. There was once something supernatural and sacred about the prophetic that has been suffocated by the accepted cultural presumption that we now know everything. We have all but killed the prophetic and with it our supernatural heritage that is surely only dormant in our imaginations.

Those sacred and forgotten aspects of ourselves that can open our consciousness to things that have been somewhat rationalised from our sight. Or are the prophecies that have existed since the dawn of time that mapped the first and last chapters of our existence, now just too farfetched to be considered plausible guidance? Those imaginary friends we used to play with that may well be far less imaginary than we even thought at the time. The ones we were told were not real and then lost the ability to see or feel them altogether.

And I totally get it that this is maybe not why you picked this book up. To be given some history lesson on religious garbage and prophesies and stuff, but what I am rather referring to is the very parts of our mind that can see things that go beyond the ordinary, and it is the ordinary that we are truly entombed in. These are the very same ideas that allow us to enter newly imagined situations as if they are real. We should never do ourselves the dishonour of underestimating the magical, the miraculous, or the majesty of mind. What it can do for us relies on what we ourselves are willing to entertain, and if there is a portal within our own minds that can take us to voids where the unimaginable is possible – imagine what just a sprinkle could do to our ordinary seeming life.

Has the glitter of technology managed to murder the wonder in us, or that part of our minds that can think way outside of the 'box'? I bet if you offered a group of teenagers the choice between a long trek through some cold and mountainous region, to explore the proof of a living dragon, or a trip to time zone with some soft drinks that the first choice wouldn't get too many 'thumbs up'. It reminds me how George Orwell had tried to warn us that 'they' were in the process of censoring everything we read. Whereas Aldous Huxley rebutted that, they won't even have to bother, because soon we won't even be curious enough to read. We are in the process of becoming almost completely blinded by consumerism and entertainment that all we are interested in is immediate gratification. Instant dopamine hits. It seems we have become content, and secure in the knowledge that someone smart is taking care of it all. "If it is not on my phone, it's not true or important".

And while that might all seem a little off topic from trying to present people with simple and easy to use methods of personal transformation, I think it has everything to do with what might get in our way and why transformation might seem so far from us or hard to entertain. We have lost access to the 'dimensions' where transformation is just an everyday thing we can do. It's too hard for us to believe because our attention span has become compressed by environmental pressure, and our belief structures have been highjacked by those who are manipulating our attention. What we need to see is right in front of us, but they manage to keep us to looking elsewhere. It's right on our table, but... wait, 'look over here'. It might be an easy and simple enough sleight of hand to control where our attention becomes diverted. And indeed many have already warned us, but we fail to believe them, because our 'imagination land' has been boarded up. We traded our backstage 'pass' to reality for a ticket to the 'Willy Wonka' factory.

We have been 'kicked out' of heaven, so to speak. But not by any kind of evil ploy or noble power, but by how the social culture has sterilised our imaginations. How it has shut the doors to the existence of dimensions that can and do transform an 'ordinary' seeming world. We have been blinkered by how our society has evolved to ever be able to see the magic in the simple things, or see anything that would actually surprise us for that matter. Much like the Easter Bunny started to disappear in the movie "Legend of the Guardians", because people stopped believing in him, we have sealed up the doorway to a dimension within our own minds that could see the life in a tree, or the miraculous beauty in a dancing school of fish. And we are none the wiser to what we are missing out on because there is only one form of gold that glitters to us – and that's the shiny stuff. Only money speaks the language we can understand.

But these very realms of the mind that I speak of are the same that can reveal new opportunities, or become fearless towards things that had bothered us for years. Could a wizard just cast a spell on you that turned you from wimp to warrior, without ever learning to fight? Is there a spell cast on us already but we have no awareness of its effect.

I fear we are not open to the idea that it's possible, because all we are interested in is immediate gratification to take away our pain for a short time, and meaningless toys to console us for what we don't like about ourselves. We don't believe in the idea of healing, or expanding our imaginations to see the phenomenal world that we might have been blind to – we'll settle for a cruise or something, because from the position we are in, where our imaginations have been taken hostage, it is just too hard to imagine.

Would you be interested in visiting a realm that could wipe the slate of your conditioning clean? Make you feel like you were someone different, because you were no longer under the influence of the unknown subtle side-effects of the beliefs we never chose? Cast a better spell on us than the one we've been living under? What if this very same place opened our eyes, to an innocent creative mind space where we were free to imagine our dreams as convincingly as if they were real things? Imagine there were no constraints as to what you could create in that place because feelings instantly became real things before our eyes. Think of this place as a land of magic clay, where even thoughts begin to take form from an invisible ether and solidify right before our eyes. That by the power of our concentration they became solid and real. The more we focused our energy on an idea, the more it began to materialise from the subatomic swirl of particles, moving into shape. Everything just started to become drawn to our idea – to our vision as it moved from mind into matter.

> *"The bible reveals the keys by which man enters a dimensionally larger world – for the purpose of changing the conditions of the lesser world in which he lives."*
>
> **Neville Goddard.**

Have I gone too far? Because I'm only just beginning to try and entertain your senses as to **how very real this place is.** It is the dimension through which everything that is on this earth must begin its journey into matter. The spiritual realm of thought and emotion is the blueprint of the world we know as real. How fast this happens is never how hard we grind, or the result of working ourselves into the ground, but our imagining. It has little to nothing to do with the hours we put in – but how clear we are on the details of what we'd love to see - how convincing the feeling we create of having those things – how much of our time we spend in that emotion. That we are able to validate imagined emotional states enough to do it more of the time. It has less to do with our 'linear plan of how to get there, and everything to do with spending our time between the mindful and an imagined state. And mindfulness is the very best thing we can do to encourage us to dream, imagine, and come to the realisation of the power of emotion.

How real we can make it in our minds. If we felt exactly like we had it now, we would be surrounded by the evidence in real-time – that is attraction 101 – a law as certain as gravity itself. It is never a matter of time, but clarity of the feeling, our commitment, and concentration to it.

This is a realm where we can wash away the effects of our conditioning and create our new life from a blank canvass? You'll have to follow me over the mountains to the dragon's lair – lol. Only joking… well, kind of. You see, you will have to open yourself to the realms of possibility a little, to be able to see the things you have unconsciously put up a guard against and found difficult to imagine. We have to put some merit in the power of emotion and this realm of creation to be a real and tangible place if we are to unlock what it keeps for us. If we don't think it is real or imagine that it has any real power that belief becomes our 'self-fulfilling' prophecy. If we don't understand the science behind this idea, we are hardly going to practice it. But once we start to prove the effects of mindfulness, combined with the imagination of attraction we'll be experiencing it more of the time than we do 'reality'. We first have to validate it in order to practice it and begin witnessing the results in real time.

So, are you ready to enter '**The Portal'?** The doorway to higher **dimensional creating?** It is pretty tricky but take a deep breath now, and…that's it, you're in. Not even kidding - it is that easy. This Portal is no more complicated than having more presence of mind. More present in the very mind that is doing all the creating. Present in the mind that is responsible for who we are, the situation we are in, and what we think are our options about it. This state of being mindful never goes anywhere – we are the ones who remove ourselves from the peace of this moment with the story in our heads of what is apparently happening. A story that is hardly favourable and regurgitated from yesterday. But in mindfulness that can all begin to change rapidly if you want it to. We are so busy trying to keep up this false façade of who we are that we are never present in our minds. Never realising the 'paradise' we are being pulled from by those forces of past and future. Being torn from both sides out of the one and only place where the truth of who we want to be can happen.

Welcome to the true garden of Eden.

> *"We meditate to enter the operating system of the subconscious mind."*
>
> Joe Dispenza

Our ability to see colour where others can only see grey – to find peace in the midst of a crisis, or relief in the middle of our suffering — is not dependent on any miraculous event, but by something so childishly simple and easy to do that it hardly occurs to us. It is the free ride to transcend our situations and see through the darkness of how unnecessary our stories and suffering truly are. These are the parts of our mind that I believe have lain dormant in many people because of how technologically dazzling this world has become. I mean they are trying to convince us now our futures will be in a completely virtual world, because it will be so much more sensational to the senses. Are we kidding, how lazy have we become that we cannot shift the very senses we were born with, and prefer to see some techno created fallacy that seems more amazing? They try and tell us that we will all live and do business in the 'Meta-verse'? A simulation of what is real because we have all but collapsed the abilities we were born with to make the small things more amazing than they are in our minds. Is our species worth preserving? Or should we all just head over to the Meta-verse where it is supposed that 'they' will do all of our thinking for us, and make 'things' so amazing. Just plug us into that machine for our periodic dopamine hit and we'll never have to think again. We have literally given over our will and never even noticed when we were doing it. We've entered the Matrix – and have just realised the container we're in.

We aren't able to see the magic in the normal and everyday things because of a combination of being over stimulated, and because of the competition for our attention our concentration spans have shrunk. For something to grab our attention it has to be covered in neon lights and look like something we've never seen before. Normal things seem so boring that they are painful, that we plug back into the matrix for the short-term pleasures it promises. But we possess something far more powerful and profound than just having to be entertained all of the time. We are the ones who can 'cool' situations, or create humour from the simplest of things – create light when there wasn't any, and just when a situation so desperately needed it. We are the ones who can remind a friend of something truly breathtaking about themselves they had forgotten - right at the point when they most desperately need to hear it. We are the magicians of this world, and we call ourselves 'ordinary'??

What is mindfulness?

> *"Mindfulness isn't difficult. We just need to remember to do it."*
>
> Sharon Saltzberg

Mindfulness is emptying the mind of all thought and judgment, by flooding our attention with the sensory and physical information we are constantly surrounded by. That's all mindfulness truly is -

immersion in the sensory data of the present. Becoming so engrossed in the senses that we block all available space for the psychological blackmail we refer to as our life. Well, maybe it is not that bad all of the time, but the point is that when we take a time-out from our apparent situations — or 'escape' them temporarily, the change in us changes everything on the outside like a little magic spell.

Mindfulness provides a passageway to another dimension, where all is well and can be created without the trappings of the conditioned mind.

We may not refer to any of this stuff as 'magic', but how much easier does our life go when we are more present in our minds? How, when we discover that painting that a friend had hidden under their bed turns into a work of art to us when we look at it properly. When we have nothing else on our mind and take that 1 minute out of our lives to be fully present, we actually see that picture. We appreciate something about it that even its creator had overlooked. Most people are so unaccustomed to being heard that it will usually stop them in their tracks too.

We are the ones that make that 'dad joke' funny and see something more than was actually in each moment when we are present – most people are always just trying to get to the next moment, while entertaining this little story of who they are in their head, and how to keep up their appearances. How easy could it really be to make someone's day if we are present enough? And does that really mean nothing to us? That doesn't do anything for how we feel, to make someone's day? We have become so time poor that we seem 'forced' to disregard most of the moments we walk through as being completely void of value. We are the ones who provide any value to any moment – just by being a little more present.

We get so busy rushing from one moment to the next like we are missing something, or getting to somewhere that is so much more important than this moment, that we miss the magic right in front of us. That's waiting to be brought to life by just our noticing it.

"Maybe that famous 'rainmaker' was simply a 'day maker' – someone who could make your day and that could so easily be any of us."

Living in the subconscious

"I live in the Subconscious."
                                    Jim Morrison

Over time, we have been sterilised, and the magic has been bleached from each moment. We've been so indoctrinated by our traditions and social conformity that we're now unable to even imagine magic and miracles exist or have any grounding in reality. We never look for or, expect them - never even raise our suspicions about this world of wonder that lies just beneath the cracks in our awareness. We are just less able to be surprised because of how 'smart' we've become. Everything is indeed built from our expectations, and magic is the last thing we'd ever expect to see – and so we don't. We never noticed as we gave our faith over to science or what we were sacrificing. The magic, abilities, and healing power of this 'background' mind. And we have traded what was on offer for… I can't really answer that? The certainty of our futures – a stable, comfortable, and less labour-intensive living standard. We have all of the time saving devices one can imagine. Our lives and homes have become full-automated, but we have far less time, less peace, and less wonder.

That is what we have lost in our technologically enhanced lives – we've lost the wonder and enchantment that had a place in our minds and hearts when we weren't so… *clever, connected, in touch*. I'm really not sure which of these is the best thing that we've gained as we have evolved from our ignorance. We're not too concerned with the tricks the mind might be playing on us, because we seem to have everything we need right in front of us. And consequently we live at the mercy of that mind because we don't feel like we really need to be present in it. But we could very easily live a life that is not so seemingly opposed to our will, by the very simple and easy act of becoming more conscious of the subconscious. **And that is the essence of what mindfulness does.** It connects us with the subconscious mind. For those fleeting moments when we are completely immersed in the senses, we are the subconscious/ non-thinking mind.

Mindfulness is our exclusive access to those outer regions of the subconscious, reality creating mind. It is childishly simple to do yet for us, ego driven devotees, there is no more difficult a practice to regularly engage in. How could we be disciplined with something that doesn't seem to do anything at all? Mindfulness makes no sense to the ego because there is nothing — no 'thing' in it. It doesn't elevate our status or buy us a new pair of shoes – we're the ones who have to go out and do that. And 'oh I'm sorry – I really don't have time for that stuff – I'm on my way to the shoe store'. Even though this mindfulness thing, and forming a union with the parts of our mind we aren't conscious of, may well hold the keys to not just our contentment and control, but the evolution of the human condition itself.

It has long been theorised that this more evolved version of our earth home is here already – we just lack the presence of mind to be able to see it. Imagine that? That it is here already – right beside us, but we can't look it in the eye. We lack the presence of mind to be able to see this 'something more' in our environment that would light the way to the glory of the human mind. Remember at the beginning of this book I said that it was surmised that the Buddha had 'entered' a world where he was surrounded by beauty. And quite obviously a beauty that wasn't in his environment, but in his looking. It was in his appreciation, and his willingness to see what others remained blind to. And this is what we have been saying all along through this book isn't it. That we change the nature of the physical environment by how we are. Maybe there is more to the mindfulness stuff than just being able to 'shape-shift' our situations.

> *"We cannot create a new future by holding onto the emotions of the past."*
>
> Joe Dispenza

I think it should occur to us that taking some time out from the mind that is 'full-time' employed in selling us this irreverent story of who we are, could be good for our souls. That temporarily removing ourselves from the ego driven filter that provides the framework for our reality, has to make it easier for us to think straight, and view our situations more objectively. I mean this is the place where children live their lives. Little wonder we stare at babies – how we must envy those young minds that are still so full of the innocence and wonder that we have replaced with the far more important stuff. Our flaws, situations, bad memories, and family feuds. All of that 'important' stuff. We let it fester there in our minds and think nothing of how our life might be if we were to just let it all go for a short while. Doesn't mean that it will disappear, but it might grant us the space we need to look at it from a better perspective – one that might actually look towards a solution.

We can't change reality at will every time we enter the portal, but we can at least get the idea of what is pulling the strings. And that thing that is pulling the strings becomes less like a separate and foreign entity – we realise that it's a part of us. We realise how at some level of our own mind - we are the ones making everything the way it seems. We have, in effect, 'crossed over' to that reality making part of us and returned with the knowing that this 'string puller' takes its instructions from us. We start to hear our own thoughts and understand how they might get turned into what we are getting. I mean you can't argue with reality right? If this is what we have, and these are the thoughts/ feelings and instructions I'm sending, then they must be inextricably linked. If my thoughts are like this, and I'm getting that, this might be what I need to change. Our thoughts have become 'louder' in a sense. We get the idea of what we are instructing and how. How from the way we think, this world might be built into the form it has taken.

The subconscious is the thing that beats our own heart so we get a very real sense that it could hardly be considered 'far' from us – just deep and quiet, with very big ears with which to hear our instructions.

Mindfulness is the ultimate escapism, without the need for alcohol or illicit drugs we enter the only true place of freedom. Freedom from our stories and who we think we must remain. It's the most health efficient escape on earth because it not only helps us let go of the unnecessary, and eases our mind a bit - in connecting us with the subconscious, it gets all of our cells connected and communicating with each other. It cleanses us of habit or conditioned energy - making us feel less strangled by any part of our experience that we find displeasing. There is truly nothing healthier that we can do, than clear the body's tissues and organs of the pent-up frustrations, and constrictive limitations that ordinarily exist in us unnoticed.

Mindfulness lets us behind the curtain of reality's creation before it hits the stage. Cleanses our body of the unease that can lead to physical illness and weakens the structure of the beliefs that are doing us more harm than we know. Mindfulness makes them less solid, in the same way it brings form to the things that we do want. It brings to life our inner magician, making it free to 'spin gold' from the 'wool' of otherwise ordinary moments. Mindfulness is our hall pass into the ether of unbridled and unrestricted creation. Mindfulness allows us to enter the portal of the infinite of possibilities' where anything imagined can become as real as that rock you dropped on your foot.

In this realm of mind there are no stars or universe, just a picture that begins in our mind so freely, and begins to take form, with the added sense that we are almost certainly creating something real. Here we are not taunted by any frivolous ideas of what is possible. Out here ideas can be entertained that breech the impossible. We go where only 'Buzz Lightyear' has been – to infinity and beyond. The very same place that every great composer visited to let his mind off the leash. Where every great artist, thinker and inspired leader went, and returned with the great forms that have graced, and energized our species since its beginnings.

It is the realm where every single thing that you see here on earth was given life and come through the portal into matter. From the realms of deep creative thought, what you see here was born in the higher realms of the immaterial mind. Is this place real? Can it be measured? Does it have form? No, no and no. It is light waves – it is a vision, and an emotion. But if it is also the birthplace of all that has been created here on earth, then it has far more substance than a car, or a mountain even. To consider if it is real is to question the very nature of reality itself. Do we believe this inner world is a place of substance? Is it real? Can we actually visit this place in our minds? That place indeed exists and waits only for us to be open and willing to let ourselves in. Only for us to surrender to the depths of our own being and only then be permitted past the gates.

There is no 'price' of entry – only our willingness to surrender our conscious armoury. It is a very real place, where there is more to us than we are conscious of, ruled by a form of magic and order beyond what we can know. How do spells work? It is only on this level that is beyond our scope of understanding that the power of spells can be known. And despite how it may sometimes seem, this higher order always has our best interests at heart. And sometimes it has to break us into pieces so we can be re-built to go beyond our old trajectory and ideas. Sometimes we need to be spun at 180 degrees so we can see what we never considered as our best way forward. So that what we thought was better left behind us, really needs to be out in front of us. Sometimes our only way home is to be crushed so our small pieces can make sense again. Maybe what is most valuable about us never even occurred to us, and the only way we can be shown this has to begin as something we never wished had happened. It is only when we are mindful that even in an apparent defeat, what's greatest about us remains and reveals the shortcut we thought could never come.

Mindfulness is the only thing that can 'clean our lens', allowing us to see a world that waits patiently to be noticed. For us to finally see a world that we have long been convinced was no more real than Santa Claus. We have been hoodwinked by the values of this world in the hope that we would forget our power and value. There is a place of profound beauty and opportunity right in front of us – right beside us - but it is just as invisible as that car you never started seeing until you bought one yourself. The one that starts to show up everywhere now. We are so naturally predisposed towards looking into our environment for the threats and danger that we don't see what else might be there – that we can't see because we aren't looking. We have an evolutionary predisposition that has us turning the world into something substantially more undesirable than it need be. This is still the 'jungle' but it is so much more laden with beauty than we noticed, because beauty is not on our radar. And that is a tragedy.

We would never have come this far if it weren't for our shared and inherent core value of compassion - if we didn't care about each other.

But our predisposition to keep one eye out for danger has made us fragile and overly dramatic about the reality of what now really threatens us. We think we must remain on guard because this life thing might end at any moment, and possibly violently. And it would seem that the 'powers that be' have exploited this natural tendency and have us dialled in to the horror – to the dramatic. What's that old saying in the media – 'If it bleeds it leads'. We gravitate to the dramatic, and painful because it reminds us how temporary, unjust, and unholy this place really is. We don't want that very real danger to creep up on us because we were staring at a rainbow or that butterfly that landed on us. But if we keep staring at the gore, we will not only remain as fearful, panic stricken and controllable as our overlords want us to be.

We'll miss the doorway. We won't see the way out. We'll miss those everyday experiences that may well remind us that this place is far more like heaven than we might have realised. Indeed, we are the ones who turn it into a better place by our looking. If this book gives you nothing else then I hope that it is at least that. *The knowing that we change the world by how we are* – we see things that are only there by our intent to look for them.

They may have managed to get us to turn and look away from the other side of life – the hope, the beauty, and the power of a love when it stands against hate. There is another world out there we don't see because we lack the presence of mind to value what it may offer us. Our energy contagiously infects the world around us – we affect matter. Our light is what drives and makes the world what it is. But are we conscious of where we are driving it and how quickly we could get there if we had a common goal? Because I think we all do want very similar things at heart. To love and be loved. To be heard, and the freedom to live the way we want to – not convinced of how wrong it is to live the way we want to. That we've offended some make-believe image of a judging almighty spirit by how we choose to live. They may have managed to divide us on so many things – they may be trying to scare us and have us looking at everything but the beauty - but compassion will always lay at the heart of our being. Something we all have in common.

> *"The rule is you have to dance a little bit in the morning before you leave the house because it changes the way you walk out into the world."*
> **Sandra Bullock**

Chapter 7 Summary – The Portal

- There is a reason Mindfulness has come back into vogue, and being used in everything from psychotherapy and counselling sessions to large fortune 500 companies.
- A 3000+ year old practice that science is just starting to realise its potential for being able to clear distortions in our cognitive biases as well as calm the mind from all forms of emotional disturbance.
- If the cause of mental illness is unconsciousness then mindfulness is the universal cure. The most direct means of connecting with the subconscious aspects of mind where reality itself is created, and feelings can be created and chosen from a more detached perspective.
- It is so simple a child could do it – in fact children and animals alike live their lives there. Deeply immersed in the physical senses in the moment.
- It is an expansion of the present moment where we are able to temporarily suspend our judgement of what we imagined our life situations are, and are momentarily free to breath and be ourselves.
- But mindfulness is more than that – it also provides us a doorway to a dimension that goes beyond our imagination. A dimension of the mind that has been lost, sealed, and forgotten. A magical realm that has been all but bleached from our culture. A culture that 'knows better' but has lost the true mystery, potential, and sacredness of mind. A realm that exists beyond what science can measure, touch, or guide us towards.
- There is a magnificence waiting for us to just notice it – if we can break free from the intoxicating overtone that we are so smart that we humans now know everything worth knowing – and have dissected it down to a defined level of importance.

- Mindfulness is not just the universal cure to mental illness - it is the doorway to a dimension that will surely blow our minds — if we can only justify what appears to be of little value to us.
- **Mindfulness is the doing nothing that changes everything.**

CHAPTER 8
The Accelerator

"Those who focus best are relatively immune to emotional turbulence."

Daniel Goleman
(Focus: The Hidden Driver of Excellence)

7 The Accelerator

> *"Focus is more important than genius."*
>   - **Greg McKeown**

In my humble opinion, I believe that all emotional turbulence and mental illness related issues stem from **an inability to concentrate our minds on meaningful goals.** It is what we focus on that leaves no room for all of the other crap to take up space in our minds. It is what we ignore and what we give our attention to that determines our state of mind and tells the story of where we think we are in our life. What we focus on determines our sense of worth, and the perception of value we hold of ourselves.

If we don't understand our own goals and purpose we tend to look to world for an external sense of validation, which discounts our value, and puts our mood in the hands of other people. It is the willingness to focus our sustained attention on a goal that we consider meaningful that not only keeps our demons at bay, but builds our sense of confidence. That determines our discipline and fades false perceptions we might hold of ourselves. Our focus is the laser beam that we can point at obstacles, and when we've built our energy up because the reason we're doing it matters to us, we'll blast through solid rock to get to where we want to be.

Giving our attention to what we want and what we are grateful for, and ignoring those aspects of our lives that don't contribute to our peace lies at the heart of controlling our mental health. It is in those inconsequential moments when we allow the mind wander 'off the leash' and into complaining, gossiping, criticizing others that we form undesirable patterns in our life. And those very same patterns become what we know of as our life if we have nothing better to do. We don't really notice how deflating and habit forming these behaviours are. They destroy our sense of worth and purpose, and distract us from the things that elevate our spirit, and confidence.

And for most people they don't even notice as these patterns become deeply ingrained into their character. They would never even consider change, or sense that the dissatisfaction they experience lies squarely with them. For many people we've just wander aimlessly into the patterns that have become our lives – we don't know how we got there, or imagine there is anything we can do about it. As Winston Churchill said – *"You will never reach your destination if you stop and throw stones at every dog that barks."*

The foremost key to solving every one of our problems is to resolve to build our ability to concentrate. And to notice what it is we are giving our attention to. To put our sustained efforts into achieving something that has meaning, and doing our very best to delete all of the rest.

> *"If you don't pay appropriate attention to what has your attention, it will take more of it than it deserves."*
>
> Dave Allen.

Time to push the accelerator.

> *"The successful warrior is the average man, with laser like focus."*
>
> Bruce Lee.

So, we have our 'car' now – that vehicle that we want to travel in. In the form of the image of who we want to become and what we stand for. We have our navigation set because we know what's important to us, and who we are doing it for. We know our why and who else benefits from what we vow to do. Even if we break down, have setbacks, detours, or even what may seem like accidents, we can't be stopped because this matters too much to us. We might go slow sometimes but this engine will never stop because it represents the heart of what holds meaning for us.

We have a tank full of 'super-clean' fuel, because that is what imagined feeling states represent – pure unadulterated energy. We live in the feeling of having already done what we wanted – we have moved from the feeling of wanting to the feeling of having. We are on the lookout and expect to see this evidence in our world. We are powered by and running on 'light' emotions. We don't have any need for external validation, or approval, or to be 'seeing' signs of the evidence all of the time – the outside often being an illusion. We can't be dismayed by apparent setbacks, and we certainly don't need any form of sedative. If it is the way we want to feel why would we want to mask it. If we occasionally don't like the way we feel, we know we can 'escape' to mindfulness, and live in an innocence of how we are feeling altogether. The only escapism we need is the occasional detachment, or unplugging from the illusion of conditioned situations. But if we don't like the way we feel, we now see it for what it is.

But there is an old saying that **the universe loves speed** and it's time to put the pedal down.

And how exactly do we do that? Not just by the clarity of the feeling we want to live in, frequent reflection on where we are going and any needed directional changes but also by concentrating our efforts. By building our ability to concentrate. By engaging in activities that require our full and undivided attention. Otherwise we will only have short sharp bursts of energy that are fired in no particular direction. When effort is meaningless it has very little substance and neither do we. If we are unable to concentrate our efforts and energy we will be lucky if we could blow a toy sailboat across the bathtub. We have to be able to clear the clutter form our minds. Have to be clear on what parts need to be eliminated. Our confidence in who we are only comes from our ability to concentrate, and communicate how we feel. Our ability to articulate what we mean comes from our ability and willingness to narrow down to a single-minded thought and idea.

> *"Success demands singleness of purpose."*
> \- **Vince Lombardi**

Meditation is not just a means of quieting the mind but building our ability to concentrate. In meditation we are both stilling the mind's tendency to speak randomly and incessantly, and practicing our control of the mind. We are observing the mind so that it doesn't unconsciously control us. Meditation doesn't just clear the mind from rubbish thoughts, it allows thoughts to pass through our mind without being drawn into the dramatic emotional judgement. Through meditation we have less thoughts, but more intentional ones. We can hear each of our thoughts and have a direct experience of what we are asking for in that thought. Of how the thought is making us feel, and the consequential effect it will have on the reality we are projecting. To meditate is to draw in all inconsequential and wasted energy into a single-minded purpose. Peace of mind comes from concentration, and concentration comes from peace. To meditate is to think 'subconsciously' – meaning to understand exactly what instructions we are sending to the reality producing aspect of our minds.

Through meditation our thoughts become increasingly louder and clearer in their meaning. By improving our willingness and ability to concentrate we are granted a greater control over the realities we experience and the confidence that comes doing, and communicating the things we want to. our life and goals become increasingly important to us, relative to our ability to concentrate and focus the mind.

Reality is checked.

> *"Effectiveness begins with elimination. Choose your ignorance's as carefully as your interests."*
> The Stoic Emperor

We'll no longer tolerate reflex reactions to exist in us unchecked, or allow their lingering mood to spoil any more of our life than necessary. We know what are dark emotions and what are light, so we'll never be so easily fooled again. What does our accelerator pedal look like? How do we enter this reality in the fastest way possible? **The three C's – Clarity, Concentration, and commitment.** Remember we have already arrived by our defining of the feeling. But we can race to our success, by ritualising all of the things that facilitate the manifestation in the best ways we know how. By increasing our powers of concentration, and keeping the goal, and goal infused feeling at the forefront of our minds. By keeping our list of goals on a small piece of cardboard where they can be sited throughout the day. Confirming what we want to ourselves each morning and each night. Going to sleep at night with the feeling that it has happened, and waking up the same way. And by anchoring this whole story into one powerful symbol that can be easily called to mind.

Three Positive Rules of accomplishment from 'It Works' by RHJ

- *Read the list of what you want three times each day: morning, noon, and night.*
- *Think of what you want as often as possible.*
- *Do not talk to anyone about your plan except the great power within you which will unfold to your Objective Mind the method of your accomplishment.*

From 'It Works' by RHJ – The famous little red book that makes your dreams come true.

Focus is not a dirty word.

> *"Concentrate all your thoughts upon the work at hand. The sun's rays do not burn until brought to a focus."*
>
> **Alexander Graham Bell**

We are naturally predisposed to the easy way. To leaving the largest chunks of our life to the program, and floating down this stream without a paddle or rudder in our hand. To chilling. And for many people, those things that force us to concentrate on something (anything) or over-extend ourselves, represent a feeling akin to 'pain'. But 'au contraire' – it is only when the mind is focused on something that it loves to do that we enter the zone or get in the 'flow' that accelerates our joy and removes us from that foe we considered effort. Flow brings what happens easily, sharply, and naturally. It takes concentration, but not effort, and the results happen all by themselves. It is the one place where all the distractions and dark places we might wander in the mind become, by default, 'out of bounds.' It is only in our focused state that all of the BS has no place to nestle in our minds. The mind becomes leased by a meaningful goal, and leaves no room for squatters.

We have been gifted this accelerator pedal – the way in which we can make all of the manifestations of mind become a reality before us even sooner. We have a way to 'hatch' the egg, faster than brooding on our nest. An accelerator we can now push to increase the speed at which the things we want come into form. It is only by the clarity with which we describe our desires, and our willingness to keep them in mind that we increase the speed at which those desires become flesh. For us to be that person now is one and the same as clearly describing it as if it is real. For us to describe what that person is like, and in any way that the person we have been until now might differ from our hero. How does this new version differ from who we have been? To act as if we already have those character traits, is all that is needed to move from pretence to reality.

> *"The difference between success and failure lies in your ability to control your wandering mind".*
> **Daniel Goleman**

Like all muscles our ability to concentrate needs to be practiced and stretched in order to become stronger. Concentration is very much like the pair of hands we were given with which to mould the 'clay' of our reality. The greater our powers of concentration, the more we are able to stay on point with mindfulness, our created feeling, and keeping up appearances of how our new character differs from the way we used to behave. Concentration keeps out the distractions and helps us clearly identify the 'way' – what is taking us closer and what is a diversion. With 'focus' we can keep any displeasing element of our reality from ever becoming a blimp on our radar of concern. With focus we control our attention better. The more we keep the thing we want in mind, and the clearer we are, the sooner it will arrive. It is no more complicated than that.

And while we have this moment of clarity I ask you to remember that as much as I may have taken several thousand words to communicate this message, it is no more complicated than answering these four questions.

- **Do you want change?** Are you fed up enough with how things are to be open to change?
- **Into what?** What do you want to change into? What do you want to change, or what are the details of what would be better than this? You will never be able to see it if you don't know what it looks like. Unless you are looking for something it could walk straight past you in the street completely undetected.
- **What's stopping you?** What are the obstacles or the first steps towards this change? What is your best idea of a 'plan' of actions you need to take?
- **How will you know when you have got there?** For a plan to come to fruition it must be measurable – you must have a finish line, or there is only a constant, messy push forwards without reward, achievement, or an appropriate level of celebration.

This simplification is without any explanation of the tools provided in this book that ensure our best return on effort, but getting what we want is no more complicated than this pathway. And if we don't know what we want we will never see it. We remain blind to it. What we want is what we turn the world into, and there is nothing more debilitating – dare I say, there is not a worse squandering of our greatest gifts than to not want anything specific. No matter how 'small' and insignificant you might think that thing is to other people. But of this simplified formula above, it is our ability to hold our concentration that brings desire into being. That adds matter to a formless idea. Concentration is the hands that mould the clay of reality, so why wouldn't we want big strong ones.

The real trouble with most humans is that they are half-on and half-off most of the time, and they struggle to tell the difference. And look, I'm aware this is not really accurate and a little unfair. We were never designed for life as it is lived in this age. Our biochemical structure was designed to have us in one of two modes – fight or flight, or rest and digest. On or off. Either hunting/ warring, or getting ourselves out of harm's way - or kicking back, relaxing, and letting our food go down. 10% of the time we were adrenaline charged machines, and the other 90% of the time we were able to replenish those adrenal reserves, calm our minds, and live with some degree in an unthreatened peace. If we are to compare that to our current way of life, I think we get the idea that we are never really able to 'switch off'. We are always on display – on show. We are either in situations where we feel like we have to live up to the perceptions we think others have of us – we have to live up to our expectations, or go one step beyond them.

> *"All life's difficulties are caused by mankind's refusal to sit calm and be relaxed."*
> Mark Stuart – Selfhelpnirvana.com

There is no relaxing in this culture, or it is certainly not something that we are consciously getting better at. We rarely allot an appropriate amount of time to really 'unwind' from the constant state of tension that we refer to as normality in this age. We don't get 'better' at concentrating firstly because we don't internalise its value, and secondly because… In truth I don't know all of the reasons? Because we have to be 'grinding', the fear of missing out, or we just feel plain old guilty if we're taking some time out? And there are other reasons why we don't relax well. We don't know how to do it properly, and because we have no real comprehension of its value. Don't factor it in as a necessary part of building our concentration muscles. We don't have periods of 'flexing' those muscles, followed by periods of recovery, like we do with our physical muscles. We don't allot time to replenish. (Without the use of external tonics.) We are either 'flat out', or we are drugged up, sick, or exhausted. We are always as 'on' as we can be, and it is not the best means of strengthening those concentration muscles so vital to the conscious materialisation of our desires.

I am not going to give some list of what I consider the best ways to flex this concentration muscle. I'm far from an expert on anything, and my ways are obviously relative to the things I like doing and concentrating on. What are the things that we like to do that require a measure of focus, but we wouldn't consider work? That is not to say that it is not hard for us to do, but things like playing a social sport that we like as our form of exercise. (If we hate going to the gym.) I'm of course an advocate of meditation and the periodic quieting of the mind for the added benefit it gives us of calming and becoming more aware of thought. Outside of mindfulness and meditation, I can only advise people about the benefits that focus has as a catalyst of change – it is up to us what we should be focused on.

Concentration is the firewood – the coal we shovel into our furnace that fuels the heat of desire. Fuels our inner fire. Is the thing that keeps us on course when we are unsure of our options. The thing that prevents us bouncing around like a firefly inside a bottle, going from one desire to an opposing one, in the blinking of an eye - without ever realising the energy we're wasting. In this former analogy, if we are the firefly inside a bottle, then our ability to focus is the determinant of how bright we shine, while being clear on what matters to us is what keeps us going in one direction. This will be covered more in the next chapter. But it is those moments when we lose our focus that we fall prey to sabotaging and undoing a lot of the effort we put in.

We should aim to know ourselves well enough to take our own 'time-outs' and avoid those dog-tired states when we start looking for our usual 'crutches' to lean on. When we take ten steps forward, but then slipping back 4 steps because we got past the point of exhaustion. We have to know when to slow down a bit. It is just so easy and natural to slot back into our deep rut, and old way of being that we should try to foresee these danger zones. Should factor them in and take precautions. Because there is nothing worse than seeing all our best efforts going to waste for no good reason.

Focus and intention prevents the mind drifting off into falsely created scenarios – those waste of our time worries that will probably never happen. And those scenes that we replay in our head of the things we wished never happened. Stops us giving up the ground we have won in feeling the way we want to, by letting self-defined 'dumb stuff' take up the real estate of our minds. Letting situations that don't make us feel good and aren't as real as we're making them, be traded for our time here on earth. Be traded for our life. Our ability to concentrate is not just the accelerator of our desires coming into focus faster, it is our only path to peace.

> *"It's not that I'm so smart it's that I stay with problems longer."*
>
> **Albert Einstein.**

A mind 'off the leash' is not capable of guiding us to a sense of peace. It is only in flexing those powers of concentration that we become able to string longer more powerful and effective thoughts, and broader ideas into the culmination of a larger context. To see the 'bigger' picture we don't just have to stand back, or see it from above, we have to be able to concentrate enough to understand how different ideas can be connected in a such a way that they lead to a new and better idea for us. So that the sum of our ideas can become greater than its parts. To bring larger ideas together we need to be able to concentrate. And it is only by deliberate intention that we can go deeper into our own minds. That we can know ourselves well enough to cast out any idea of who we are that is not born in sound reasoning. To eradicate any notion of self-images that seem like they are contrary to who we know ourselves to be.

The power of each thought is measurable in its effect by the intensity of the feeling – by how much it makes us feel. Intensity that is characterised by focus. Any ideas effectiveness can be known by its frequency, or how often we have it in mind, and it's intensity, or how focused the energy of that thought. Is our thought wave a torch or a laser beam in its intensity? How much do we want it, and why? Or what Esther Hicks refers to as 'rockets of desire'. The fuel that rocket fly's on, is both our ability to concentrate, and our willingness to keep it in mind.

> *"He who controls others may be powerful, but he who has mastered himself is mightier still".*
> **Lao Tzu**

Our ability to focus and exercise control over ourselves is the accelerator pedal of our manifesting ability. And if we want to put the foot down we only need to increase our powers of concentration and practice discipline of what we take in both of food and thought. And incorporate defined periods of relaxation. To be disciplined and more conscious of not just of our reactions, but all physical impulses. To realise our dreams we don't just have to keep them in mind and feel like they have happened, we also have to keep the 'gunk' out of our minds. Keep our body and mind clean, and free from anything that might threaten to disturb our peace. The strength of our focus is what blots out the distractions, frustrations and, of course, any part of the 'reality' illusion we want to shrink down to size.

> *"Without selective interests, experience would be utter chaos".*
> **Daniel Goleman**

Without looking for something specific in our environment the world outside becomes fuzzy and 'out of focus'. The mind turns the infinite that surrounds us into the familiar, but the more conscious we become of mind and what we want, the more we are able to turn the outside into something that resembles our choice. By the strength of our desire we bring that picture into focus – we bring the specific trees forth from the forest of all possibility. We turn more possible outcomes than we could ever understand into the single one that we want. By the strength of our desire we bring the 'fuzzy' to come into focus.

We see something that didn't exist before or wasn't visible to us before we had the desire to see it. Being clear on what we want is how we take the power back from what's happening in our life automatically – which can be translated as, without our consent. This is not just for many people – but all people run from the autopilot. Life is happening without our consent, and the very best we can do is to minimise by how much, is by being clear on what we want. By our ability to concentrate or keep that feeling of what we want alive in our hearts and minds. If we want some degree of choice in what's happening in our life, there is but one way. We really do have far more control over the results we experience than we exercise our will over. Because we don't recognise the world as a consequence of emotion, and consequently don't make the choices available to us in every moment that we can to improve how we feel. But it all gets better with awareness and our accelerator pedal. Both our ability to concentrate, and its marriage partner taking time-out to relax properly.

> *"In a world deluged by irrelevant information, clarity is power."*
> **Yuval Noah Harari**

Chapter 8 – Summary

- Our ability to focus is the main determinant of our ability to manifest the things we want into our lives with optimal speed.
- But it is also what grants us the peace and confidence to do all of the things we want to and understand our value without the need for validation.
- Meditation is not just a tool for bring peace to the mind and hearing the messages from our soul, but also for sharpening the minds ability to focus.
- Our life comes down to the things we ignore and the things we give our attention to. The more focused we are the better the chance that the things on our mind have a reason and purpose for being there.
- Our future vision is a hologram in our mind – we add matter to that vision in proportion to our ability to provide a sustained focus towards it. Our focus is the hands that mould the 'clay' of our reality.
- Our reality is determined by the strength of our focus.
- We have everything else at the ready. We have our vision of how we want our life to look. We have the vehicle that we want to travel in that is full of pure clean fuel in the way of 'light' emotions. It's time to push the accelerator by becoming more focused. By concentrating our energy, and efforts.

CHAPTER 9
Intentionality

"If you don't know where you are going, any road will get you there."

Lewis Carroll.

We did it on purpose

Did it ever happen that you were in the playground as a young kid, and you accidently bumped one of your playmates off the slide, and they said, "You did that on purpose"? Now I don't really know if it was an accident in your case, but what they meant was - we did it intentionally. We meant to - but how much of our lives do we do because we 'meant' to, and how much of it happens unconsciously? The implication of this, as we've learnt, is that much of our lives have happened, by accident, automatically and to an extent against our will. How much of our lives do we do, 'on purpose'. And how much do we unintentionally leave to that uncaring monster we call fate? Or the overwhelming portion of our lives we have now come to understand is handballed to the robot.

Once we learn any skill it is handed over with faith to the robot mind and added to our 'systems' for operation. And we trust in those systems to respond appropriately, and know the necessary motor skills to perform the learned task. But it is not just these physical tasks that are entrusted to the robot, but also how we related to other people, and the strategies we use to go about our lives. Our vision of 'what's going on'. We trust in those learnings and memories that are handed over to the robot to be our guide to circumstances and how we should behave. How easily the small things we accept can grow into a life that has become off the leash. And it always seems as if we are the last to know. We just wake up one day and are shocked to find ourselves in a completely unchosen and foreign seeming environment. We wake up as if from a hangover, and wonder how we got there. It is like we were the last to know of this joke that was being played on us.

Sometimes the robot gets the 'what's going on' part wrong. We experience this as pain. Our old way of being doesn't suit our newly evolved desires.

> *"Your aim sets up the world around you, and organises all of your perceptions. It organises what you see and don't see."*
>
> **Jordan Petersen.**

Any part of our lives that we willingly leave up to the 'unplanned' programming running in the background of our lives we have limited control over. By our lack of conscious choice over where we are going (out goals), we literally but unknowingly are allowing our lives to happen by accident. By that same incidental thing that we didn't do on purpose. A life lived by accident is void of meaning. If we don't make any attempt to influence or enact our will on the programming, we literally have a 'nut' loose at the wheel.

It's kind of scary to think how much of our lives is going on that we don't even give a thought to. That without even thinking about it we attach the same level of importance to the job we do, to routine tasks that we do just as robotically as brushing our teeth or tying up our shoes. And we spend huge chunks of our life and abilities doing jobs we don't hate enough to quit. We do them for no better reason than they pay for the bills that keep us alive.

How much joy do you think we can get out of a life that we had a very limited say in? Or even worse, didn't think we played any part in it – never realised we had a choice? Some people were never told that we had to have a plan in order to actually influence the world around us. That we could change the world around us if we had a plan, but it would all look like a blur of meaningless and uncontrollable events if we did not. For some people it just never occurred to them that we can only feel good in relation to what we offer other people. We were never warned that the things we believed in and standing our ground, should and would change. So we'd have to be prepared to move the very ground we stood on. No one ever told us so we never got the chance to feel as good as we could. How happy do you think we can be if most of what is happening in our life doesn't seem of our choosing? We have the opportunity to be like anyone in the world, simply by mimicking their actions and characteristics, but we never even make a choice.

What's our life going to look like if we don't have a plan? The eye is a highly specialised device, designed to spot even the most miniscule difference in our environment, but we have to assign it a task. We have to tell it what we would like to see more of. Have to tell it what we are looking for – aka, what we are turning the world into. What's the difference you're looking for? Because it is there – I guarantee it, because it does not come from the world but from within your own mind.

How very different a life lived intentionally is from a life lived as a passenger. That life where we hand over the steering wheel of what's happening in our lives to a someone who looks remarkably like that adult who first 'kicked us out of heaven', or the playground in our minds. Kind of makes you want to do as much as you possibly can 'on purpose'. To make a choice in what's happening in our life, because it's simple to do so, and the alternative is by definition, hellish. Who would willingly sacrifice that level of control if they knew the choice they had? Particularly in light of understanding that it all boils down to feeling a certain way? To understanding our choice to imagine a feeling. Why do we think we couldn't do that? Is it that someone is stopping us feeling the way we want to, or that we still aren't convinced 'feelings' do anything to reality.

The meaning is relative.

> *"If a man knows not to which port he sails, no wind is favourable."*
> **Seneca**

We can only know what anything means by relating it to our agenda. The meaning of anything that happens is relative to what we are trying to achieve and what we value. Is the event taking us closer, a setback, or something we could learn from, can only be known by how it affects and relates to our goals. Therefore, the more intentional our lives are, the more we are able to not just be clear on what things mean, and how they make us feel as a consequence, but *bend that meaning to suit our agenda*. If we are driven towards something that matters more to us than anything, then everything else matters less as a consequence. And a setback can never devastate us if our eyes remain firmly on the prize. Imagine you desperately want to open a new fruit shop in your area, and just as you have secured the lease of an appropriate venue, someone else beats you to it. Your plans are in ruins, and you fall to your knees thinking 'why me'?

And 'why' indeed. You are forced to go back to your 'why', and ask yourself why did I want to start this business in the first place? To provide my community with a fresher, cheaper alternative to the produce the big supermarkets were providing. So instead of collapsing in despair and thinking how can I compete – how am I going to pay this lease when this guy has just beat me to the punch, you pick yourself up with an open mind and an entrepreneurial spirit – you have a new approach to how you might use this competition to your advantage.

And as it happens, this new fruitier plans on supplying quite a different line to the one you were going to – more exotic type fruits and vegetables used in Asian cooking. You find that while you do have some cross-over supply items, you are actually able to exchange better suppliers, and garner bulk discounts. You find that some customers come to you because of who you are and what you offer them aside from their produce. And you get the idea to devote a section of your store to a health food market. You are now offering advice to some people trying to lose weight and cater for specific dietary requirements. You are now offering so much more than you originally set out to, because of this seemingly forced diversification. And your community has so much more knowledge, expertise, and choice available to them because of your competitor.

None of this could have happened if you'd folded in a heap or tried to start undercutting your new competition in a local produce war. None of this could have happened if you didn't have a strong 'why' – a good intention for what you wanted to provide for the community. You could have lost your temper, packed up shop and started elsewhere. Only to find you didn't know enough people in this area and had already lost too much on the existing lease to cover your smaller profits. When we have something we want badly enough, and are clear on the reason that matters to us, we can turn the meaning of any event to see the 'silver lining', as they say. The clearer we are on what matters to us the more control we have, not just on how we feel, but to altering the meaning of what is occurring in our lives. The more intentionally we live our lives, the more we can bend the meaning of what's happening, and reality with it.

When we do our life 'on purpose' there is an inherent ability to feel the way we want to and manipulate the meaning of any event – to be better able to mould the world to fit our needs. We can turn things to our favour and provide something of real value if we aren't pouting and complaining. By our concentration and strong intention we bend whatever happens to our will. When we act like this was meant to happen the way it did, we are forced to see the lesson and make good of our fates. If it happened it is part of the plan, so how do I make this work for me. What is the lesson here – how can I take some advantage. The Stoic philosophy coins a phrase '*Amore Fati*' – or to love what happens. When we love or at least are accepting of what happens as if it were chosen we can use it. We understand that it was woven into our destinies somehow and meant to be. We have to look for the higher purpose of this event, because it didn't happen for no reason. And there is every chance it happened for a better reason than the one that seems to be staring at us laughing. Our problems are custom built as our personal means of salvation.

We are always looking for what can be gained when we are living with intention. When we have something we want to do, and the reason matters enough to us. By intention, we take the world in our hands, and bend fate to our will. We can make whatever happens relative to the plan if we have a flexible and well-reasoned plan. If the result of the plan matters to us more than the way we thought we were going to get there. Whatever happens can help us, even if it is by knowing what we definitely wouldn't do again? But if we aren't moving towards a meaningful goal, we can never 'bend' the meaning or get whatever lesson we were supposed to. And so much of our lives seems to become 'shit we never asked for' because it doesn't seem to relate to anything meaningful for us.

Without a clear intention we can never be sure the effort we are putting in is towards something of value – something that we are building towards, no matter how slow our 'progress' might seem. Progress isn't made by speed but certainty of direction. If what we do doesn't matter to us, then we could do anything at all, and it wouldn't matter. When what we do is devoid of meaning then all effort becomes pointless. And I think that everyone could appreciate that this is what defines depressing. When we don't care about what we do. In contrast, the more something means to us, the more durable we become in its pursuit. The more we are willing to look for the good and shoulder the apparent 'setbacks'. We will always go the extra mile for anything of sufficient importance. We don't avoid things because they scare us or are too hard, but because they don't matter enough to us – yet.

There is always another hill to climb.

Our life is one long learning journey. And while we may meet goals and checkpoints along the way, there will always be another hill to climb. There will always be another milestone and a bigger challenge on the other side of the one in front of us. I think it's important to remember this before we get all too tied up in our results. Like any of them can 'mean' enough to bring us to our knees. That missed opportunities will come around again in time – or they won't and something even better will. What could possibly make us quit our 'game' if our goal has for a very long time held meaning for us? We can never take a step in the right direction until we take stock of where it is that we actually are.

We are never playing 'catch up' – are never behind on the score board. We are only playing against ourselves, and only judged by ourselves. Why is it we feel like we've lost the game so much of the time – that this isn't good enough, or that we need to be doing more than we are. We can't do any more than we are, until we set down some plan of execution and are doing it. But once we are, we have to have some faith in that plan and the actions we're taking. And while we can do our best, most of it is left to the will of a much greater system of underlying intelligence than we can fathom. We are where we are supposed to be – doing what we are supposed to – trying as hard as we always have – marching up a mountain that we will never summit.

We will never be finished, or complete – and I think that it's essential to remember this as a form of consolation for all that we have become already. Yeah we have goals that matter to us – that matter a lot, but they should never matter more than our peace does. We do them for peace's sake, so it would be the ultimate irony if we were to allow them to 'break' us. What is 'our life', refers to the ever-evolving process of our direction becoming clearer, and our efforts being more 'funnelled' by what matters to us. As what matters becomes clearer, so too does our life become richer and our energy and effort less wasted. And as it does then what is 'meaning-less' gets pushed further from our sight and attention.

When we understand this, we become more committed to the process of change and clarity, more so than any one particular goal. In this realisation we understand how foolish it becomes to be so 'goal oriented'. To spend 99% of our lives clawing towards something we don't yet have, for that brief luxury of time where we think that we have 'got there'. Most of our lives are spent short of our goal (or 'failing') for that very brief encounter we have with 'success' that happens just before we start climbing again – towards something that we once again 'don't have'. We see that most of our lives are spent in this 'purgatory of desire', and so little of our life and time where we are actually satisfied and have some sense of completion. And we have it in mind that it is our ambitions that lead us to peace? It is better for us to think that every day that we're working towards something meaningful to us becomes the reward in itself.

It is about trusting our 'systems' to deliver us to where we want to be. That in the work that we do every day for the pleasure in itself we become 'successful'. What was Earl Nightingales definition of success? *'The progressive realisation of a worthy ideal'*. Success is the person who is doing the thing that he loves because he loves doing it. We never get to the goal – the getting there is the goal. Or as Thich Nan Hat refers to this – **"The path is the goal."** We can accomplish anything we keep moving towards and breaking into small enough steps. And cherish anything that help us get there as being as desirable as the goal itself. If we've placed just one piece of the jigsaw puzzle in place on this day, we are a bit closer – we can see it starting to come together. Every step towards the goal, we have to receive some joy from the 'process'. In this light the process is just as valuable to us as the goal – the process is the goal – 'The goal is the path'. When we realise the system that gets us there is the goal itself, every day becomes a cause for celebration. How could we ever get to the goal if we aren't as invested in the doing as much as the arriving itself.

The value in caring less.

Anything that doesn't matter to us no longer even raises an eyebrow. And a lot of the angst we may have suffered through due to delays, setbacks, and impatience, now gets brought into perspective. Anything that may have been bringing us down, becomes replaced by our faith in the system that's getting us to where we want to go. We know we will have the product, the proficiency, or whatever the perceived prize of our efforts, when we just trust in the system and do everything we can every day that we're able. Anything that stands between us doing what matters most to us, will almost certainly drive us mad or worse.

Whether what is in the way of us living a purposeful life is circumstances or people, or our perceived obligations, it will either destroys us, or crumble. Even if that thing holding us back is our own lack of personal intention, it will kill us if we don't do something about it. As human beings we crave purpose, and the feeling that we've helped someone, or had a positive effect on the world, more than we do fame or money. If it is our own stubbornness, or arrogance, or self-pity that keeps this from our sight, we will convulse from the inside out until this inner tension is resolved. And I think many people harbor 'unknown' causes of physical illness because of a failure to address what matters most to them, and the pursuit of a meaningful life. If we feel like we are somehow forbidden from this thing we must do, nothing in our life will matter.

The unconsidered benefits of a purposeful life.

I think a lot of people regard a purpose driven life as something reserved for the 'do gooders' and the saints among us. That it consists of an unshakable passion and almost certainly a monetary form of sacrifice. That it's something like starting an orphanage, or feeding the hungry in the third world. And while these are very noble, selfless, and inspiring pursuits that's certainly not the extent of purpose. Purpose is quite simply defined as to make ourselves useful. To have purpose is to help. To provide a solution to a problem people are struggling with. And that can be the pain of buying a new car. Selling is helping, and I personally find no distinction between selling solutions and having a sense of purpose. If we are earnestly trying to do people a favour with what we are offering, our offer is our purpose. To have purpose is to help someone do something. I think a lot of people don't imagine this great 'purpose' thing can apply to them because it is routinely overcomplicated. But there is an even sadder reason why people don't engage in a life of purpose, or think it applies to them. Because there are some amazing benefits of becoming clearer on our purpose that I think don't get considered.

Imagine living a life where we weren't in two minds about everything as much of the time. Almost no second guessing, indecision, or doing stuff we didn't really want to, but we thought we should. That we didn't do anything out of a sense of obligation, guilt, or fear of missing out. We never questioned ourselves because, we had something better to do. We only did things that were important to us, or we just didn't do them. So, there is no more time wasting, wallowing in what could have been, or being in one place and wishing you were somewhere else. Imagine a life where everything we do has meaning for us. We know why, and for whom we do it, and the result or outcome it is towards. How much easier would it make our lives, if everything was done with a sense of certainty – even the time we'd set aside for play and relaxation. It is a life that is clearly juxtaposed to a life lived purely out of habit, or because it is what everyone else is doing.

This is what I believe is the unconsidered 'glory' living a life on purpose stands to offer us. And I don't use 'glory' in some exaggerated sense – a life lived intentionally gives us power over what is happening and brings every element of our experience into perspective. Enables us to bend the meaning of what happened, or manipulate it to be favourable to our outcome. When we don't do anything for 'no good reason', we do everything we do like it matters. We don't just feel better about ourselves and what we bring and give us more control over what's happening, it elevates us to parts of the mind where we understand ourselves in the context of the greater scheme of the world around us. It allows us to consider and remember that we affect everything, and everything affects us. We couldn't think that we could possibly know all of the consequences of how what we add reverberates and bumps into the lives of others until it is brought into the context of a greater meaning. If it means something to us, then it means something to the world, and way more than we know. When we are on purpose then we know how, by everything we do, we are dropping a pebble in the big pond, so to speak.

What many people like to refer to as chance, luck, or 'strange coincidences' are anything but coincidences. It is how the universal intelligence works to wake our minds to the order beneath what might sometimes seem random, or disorder. To live with intention is to enlist that 'outside' help that has as much interest as we do in getting our form of help to the people that most need it. When we have a sense of purpose we are aligning ourselves with something quite beyond the ordinary to help us. Even things that might first seem like a roadblock or detour, are quickly accepted as the universe at work, and probably taking us on a short-cut. The more we do our lives deliberately, and on purpose, the more meaningful and chosen everything that 'happens' seems.

When 'intelligence' gives us a little reminder, or nudges us in a particular direction, we know it's because it hears our intention, and says, 'Follow me'. And when that nudge feels like a setback, or a kick in the teeth, we trust that the universal intelligence works in mysterious ways but knows what it is doing. We trust in the process and live with an expanded sense of faith in everything that happens. We accept that maybe that thing we were aiming at was for the wrong reasons, and we're being opened to a new direction. We never fight it when the guidance is clear. A life lived on purpose means we have more time, things are more important to us, so our lives are richer in meaning. We are always being prepared for something even more meaningful.

When we live with our lives with intention we accept whatever is in this moment. And it is that acceptance which allows us to not only use the lesson, but to remain the masters of our energy. To merge and be one with that reality creating energy itself – where non-resistance clears the way. When we live with intention we can boldly step out on a limb, and trust in the 'intelligence' to be our wings. Because the reality is our life is more like a **game of snakes and ladders.** And what at first might appear to be a snake, or a fast downhill slide, puts us two steps away from a very tall and helpful ladder. We can be delivered at speed, but we have to be willing to trust the process, and remain open and present, with our purpose in mind.

Want a better life? Describe it in more detail.

So how does this look when we piece it all together. Living with intention and doing our life 'on purpose' not only gives us a sense of contribution and deeper meaning, but it allows us to be more calm, faithful, and poised. We don't jump to the first conclusion when things go 'wrong' - instead, we trust that there is something at work that wants us to see this and is probably either re-directing us or taking us on a weird shortcut. When we live our life intentionally, we are sending instructions to the program that we would otherwise be an unconscious passengers of.

When we are a bystander to that life happening on autopilot, nothing that happens seems chosen, meaningful, nor do we have any power to integrate its meaning into our lives. We can't bend it to suit our needs. We didn't choose it, and there is nothing we can do about it. But when we have a clear agenda we can manipulate the meaning, or at least appreciate something about even disasters that might otherwise destroy our faith. If we didn't have some belief in the higher order of 'planning', we'd never see the 'way'. We can only know the meaning of anything in relation to our agenda. We see the world through the filter of what we want to do. The clearer we are on our goals, the easier it becomes to decipher, and bend those meanings. We can quickly shift our response from a conditioned to a more considered and useful one.

We never do things out of a sense of guilt or obligation, and become more decisive, determined, and fuelled by meaning. We are less distracted, reactive and time poor - everything we do has a level of personal importance to us. We don't mind personal criticisms, because we are open to understanding new perspectives we hadn't considered, and we aren't doing what we do for the people who don't understand or get anything out of it. While we are not doing what we do for the people who don't like or understand it, they might be the ones who help us to improve what we do and make it appeal to an even broader audience. How much easier does that life sound, regardless of how 'noble' we have judged our intentions to be?

Why wouldn't we want to get clearer on what matters, and holds a level of meaning for us? Just like our state of mind and filters alter what we see in the world, we change the world relative to our intentions. The clearer we become, and the more focused our drive, the more we are able to manipulate meanings, and bend reality. We change the world by our intentions – we program our mind by our intentions – the clearer we are the more we can bend the world to our will – or even bend ourselves when that seems a more suitable course of action. **We can turn the world into something that is more of our choosing when we are clear what we'd prefer to turn it into.** We don't need fame, the approval of others, or wasting our money on buying flashy stuff that we don't need or value. I hope these are enough reasons for you to live your life more intentionally. Surely this apparently mysterious 'meaning' of our lives, was to get clearer on what has meaning for us. To know thyself, or what it is we care about enough to want to change. The meaning of life was surely to know what has meaning for us. And I don't think it takes too much imagination to realise that meaningful things are less relevant to purchases or status than we've been led to believe in, or been conditioned to value.

What's the chance of great things showing up in your life if you're not looking for them?

If we haven't defined who we want to become or don't believe it's even possible, we will never lift a finger towards it. We will only ever see what we have defined as wanted and better, and are actively looking for the evidence of it. And of course it is our gratitude for seeing this evidence that 'permits' it to keep showing up, and becoming a more prominent part of our experience. What we give our attention to, be they things, people or situations will repeat with alarming consistency.

Do our expectations affect what happens?

All of what comes to our attention in the material world comes via our unconscious expectations. It is why we first tried, and are still trying, to improve our understanding of the world. To predict foreseeable outcomes resulting from our actions. We always want to improve our survival and status, and be sure we are putting our efforts towards what will bring us the greatest return from our efforts. By our nature we want to pick the low hanging fruit. We are always trying to prophesize what will happen if I do this – or the expected consequence of our actions. So, we can get some picture of 'if I do this – that will probably happen'. But where we fall down is in the understanding that are the ones who create the actual event in the process of our prediction. And while we aren't privy to the regions of our mind that are doing all of the creating at a higher level, in awareness we can at least start to reason with ourselves as how we might be able to alter those expectations and what we are seeing.

If we can at least begin to get the lesson in anything undesirable that is being unconsciously expected, we have some chance of changing what's happening from a subconscious level. When we get that 'we should have seen this coming' because it was created by us at some level, we'll be able to better deal with it, become more accepting of it, and use our god given perspective to alter what happened to suit our needs. It is by becoming more conscious of our created expectations that we change the world.

How we get where we want to be may not always happen in line with our 'plan', but we have to have the plan to know if we've veered off course or need to change our tack. If we are guided by a clear heading of where we want to be it not only makes better use of our time and effort, but makes all of the seeming randomness of it all make more sense. And if it doesn't make sense, something in us needs to shift so that it does. If it all seems too random and unwanted something in the plan needs to change. But it is certainly easier to follow a map to our treasure, than experiencing a world where we imagine we have no control over what we are seeing, and what we do doesn't matter.

By our clearly defined outcome, we turn the world around us into what we've declared desirable. And we take each step on our voyage like it matters to something even larger than us. We can only know what anything means by asking is it moving me closer or further away from what I want. Is it a waste of time, worth learning, or a distraction can only be known by wanting something specific. The more specific we are the easier our life becomes - the more power we have to spot the differences we've been asking for. By how much our intentions matter to us we muster and channel our energy, we see through the obstacles, and turn the world into something it wasn't before. We cannot know the true meaning of an event, or our life for that matter, without knowing it in the context of what matters to us. Without knowing who we are becoming.

We definitely improve the likelihood of what happens being desirable by our expectations, but if what comes to us seems 'hard to take', we are always better equipped to cope with it if we have an overriding and guiding sense of purpose in our lives. Because we understand that we can manipulate what happens, what happens becomes integrated rather than being something we might otherwise be resentful of for the rest of our lives. We are always better off to be expecting the best because this is what we will notice more of in the world – this is what we are changing the world according to us into. And this is far from the 'let's just be positive' BS that we might think doesn't do anything at all. If you expect the world to be a certain way, you'll always be 'right'. This stuff actually works, and if these words haven't inspired you to try and prove this to yourself I'm not sure if it will ever occur to you.

Be expectant of the best and all you have wished for coming true before your eyes - because we change 'what is' by what we are looking for in it.

Chapter 9 Summary.

- Our aim is always the same – to minimise how much of our life is happening unconsciously – on autopilot. Without us imagining we played any part in it or can do anything about it.
- The opposite of automatically and without reason is intentionally. It is by our intentions that we are able to manipulate the meaning of events and reality itself.
- We can only understand the meaning of an event by knowing clearly how it relates to our goal or purpose. It can be either be known as a teacher and an aid, or a hinderance and distraction, by is it moving me closer or further away. Without the goal or target our experience is meaningless and unchangeable.
- Having a clear sense of purpose empowers us to manipulate the meaning of an event to suit our needs. But if we don't get the lesson of unwanted patterns, we doom ourselves to an unending repetitive cycle.
- By knowing our 'why' we no longer waste time, or do things out of a sense of obligation or guilt. It is either important to us or we don't do it. Living intentionally means an end to being coerced into things we don't want to do – to any feeling of shame, or minding if people don't 'get us' and what we do.
- As what matters to us becomes clearer our efforts become more funnelled and our life more meaningful. It is a never ending and ever evolving process.
- Without meaning and purpose in our lives we live in a 'hell' of never being satisfied or able to get the recognition we crave. We never realise that we can't buy our 'stairway to heaven'. We don't get the biological force that reminds us that we only feel better by what we can do for others.
- When we have a sense of purpose we can not only bend reality and meaning, and make some sense of the randomness - all of our life feels imbued and marked by strange coincidences. A.K.A we sense that universal intelligence at work.

CHAPTER 10
The Hardest Work

"The opposite of courage is not cowardice but conformity".

Rollo May

The Hardest Work.

The hardest and most effective work you'll ever do is to sit calmly and imagine vividly, exactly how it would feel if you had whatever it is you wanted right now.

I'm going to define 'hard' as that which has the greatest return for us from our effort. And I am not going to beat around the bush here – the greatest *return on effort work* that we can engage in is 'energy work'. Meaning taking more initiative to choose how we feel, rather than leave this to the automatic cycles of higher levels of consciousness. And when I say energy work, I'm referring to visualisations done in the deeply relaxed state. Or taking any opportunity we have to choose how we feel in that moment. Which of course will include being on guard to our reactions and paying attention to where our attention is going. And visualisation work is hard to do. It takes concentration and imagination, and can seem like a big waste of our time. But only in the sense of us believing that it doesn't change anything. If we had an awareness of how much it actually did to change the world around us we certainly wouldn't consider it 'hard' by any measure of the imagination. We have to start to prove its effects to ourselves if it's ever going to make our 'to do' list. And although we have covered a lot of this stuff already, there are a couple of small reminders I think need to be kept in mind.

How hard is it to be crystal clear about what we want our life to look like 5 years from now? How hard is it when we consider that having that clarity is what really makes our life easy, and gives us a clear sense of direction, channels our energy, and ensures we waste the least amount of time. When that is what permits us to manipulate the meaning of events, trust in the process of what's happening, and turn the world into something it wasn't before – turn us into something we weren't 'before' then how 'hard' is it? When clarity of purpose is what gives us a reason for being here, and be better able to bare the inevitable pains in life, is this really what we would consider hard? And I say that because I know this stuff is hard. It is hard for a countless number of reasons -

if it wasn't everyone would have a plan, and be clear on what they want but so very few are.

If I ask most people what they want, the majority tell me either - 'I don't know, or I just want to be happy'. What are the chances of us being happy if our desires are no more specific than that — if there are no guidelines or defined outcomes for the conditions that would support that happiness? There is nothing stopping you being happy all of the time, and you don't even have to do anything. And I totally understand that it might be none of my business either. I think we should keep our cards close to our chest and *show* people what we're doing rather than *tell* them. But I think very few people know what they want, even though that is what makes our life exponentially easier and more meaningful. Making the plan, writing it down, and doing the relaxed visualisation work is the hardest work to do, because people don't have an awareness of how effective it is in chasing our demons away.

Knowing our purpose gives us the assurance of our own value and belief in what we do. How hard is it, when the alternative is to be almost completely out of control of what's happening without even knowing it. In this state no matter what we do we can't change anything, so what's the point? That is what I call hard — that is what I would consider 'painful'. Being clearer on what we want and think that 'most' of our steps are in the right direction, is what I would call easy.

> *"If everyone is doing the same thing then someone is not paying attention".*
> George S Patton - American president.

How hard is it to separate ourselves from the crowd, if we genuinely believe it's not moving in the right direction? We are very social creatures and are instinctively drawn to finding and depending on our tribe for our emotional sustenance. It is only through relationships and conversations that we both gain perspective and test the rightness of our life's hypotheses. We unconsciously rely on the people in our lives to make sense of everything, so to stand apart from the crowd can be a lot harder than we think. We are up against forces inside us that we can't see or do battle with. But is it harder to go along with something you think is wrong? Even our way of life can be threatened without us even realise it, if we are not on guard, testing and refreshing our principles when necessary. Sometimes the hardest work we have to do is taking a stand for what we think is right, as unpopular as that might seem.

> *"The truth sets you free, but it destroys everything in you that is not worthy as it sets you free. And that is a process of burning, and it is painful because we cling to it – partly out of pride, and partly out of ignorance, and partly out of laziness."*
> **Jordan Peterson.**

The hardest work is looking in the mirror and acknowledging we are staring at someone who let us down. Staring at someone we don't care for – who turned a blind eye or didn't stick to their promises. The hardest work is the respect we lose for ourselves when we don't follow through. Or even worse, let someone mistreat us. The hardest work is not the years of grind we have to do from the day we enter the workforce, it's knowing we have absolutely no investment in the work that we do, and never do anything about it. If we can't be bothered with our life it will happen in the blink of an eye and it won't even feel like we had any say in it. There is a harder work to do than change, and that is to not change. To get to the end and not feel like our life mattered to anyone outside of ourselves – that's hard.

It is almost as if all of the things that were too hard for us to be bothered with are what actually make our life easier. Getting clear, eating healthy, living with some sense of purpose and discipline – that's what makes our life easy. When we stick our neck out, quit that job we have no interest in, or let people go from our lives who are obviously going in a very different direction - it's hard, but not worse than the alternative. We're the ones who have to live with ourselves, so we needn't make it any harder than it should be. Rip the Band-Aid off and do what is right for you as soon as you can. Have those hard conversations and tell people what you want and where you want to go. It gives us such a sense of relief that when it's done we start to wonder why we built these things into being more than they were. We all know how hard it is to have all of the false outcomes running around in our head that might never happen. Is the very worst-case scenario something we can live with? It will probably never happen, and it is far outweighed by the best-case scenario. To die and not know represents years of torture.

I'll get off my soap box now, but just thought it was worth mentioning that often the things we imagine to be hard are what end up making our lives so much easier. It's ironic that the work no one bothers to engage in is what usually uncomplicates our lives and makes it go more smoothly. But what is the best 'bang for buck' work we can engage in? The work that might seem so much like a stupid waste of our time that we never bother with it. What makes it 'hard' to do is the belief that it doesn't do anything. We don't bother with the one thing that is truly effortless but completely alters our mindset, what we see in the world, and desirable things landing in our lap with minimal effort.

The hardest work you will ever engage in is energy work. Breathwork, visualisations, deep relaxations, mindfulness, making a plan, watching our reactions, forward written goals, and staring into the mirror. Of course, you have your own ways of maximising and becoming more conscious of how you feel but these are my best options that I find helpful. knowing who we want to become and keeping it at the forefront of our mind, so we know each and every time we need to redirect. I refer to it as energy work, but you can call it what you want – choosing how we feel as much of the time as possible.

Those small and seemingly insignificant choices we make to choose how we feel in each moment to 'top up' our vibe artificially or without any good reason are the **hard work**. Is the hardest work, because it is the most beneficial towards what we see in the world and the thoughts memories and experiences that will come to our attention. By our mood we change the world around us. We don't need reasons to feel good, it's just what we do. Nor do we have to wait to feel like our dreams have come true right now. Because that emotion you just created is the most underestimated and underutilised, reality altering, power on earth. Don't wait for the evidence, because that is all coming from your reality, or better said, familiarity loving mind, trying to recreate the same world as yesterday. Reality will drive us crazy – and you know what they say – if something is driving you crazy, you need to stop giving it the keys.

The hardest work is distinguishing between what are light and dark emotions -what is created by us and what is being forced on us. Once we distinguish where the feeling is being generated, our work is done. It's being aware just how much of a shit story our conditioning keeps trying to serve up to us and knowing the sly form our enemy can take sometimes. Trying to pass itself off as some kind of 'voice of reason'. The hardest work is picking out the disguises our conditioning hides behind. Our enemy is very hard to spot on a good day, but when we spot it we will know. But if we're too 'busy' ranting about the wrong that was done to us – that old demon has once again snuck in through the back door. Choosing/ creating emotions and a better mood isn't as hard as we make it. We make our lives harder than they need be by the lack of insight into how much our state of mind actually changes things. It is the hardest work that changes everything.

The hardest work is validating the use of our time and effort on our energy, expectancy, and mindset. The hardest work is sitting down to write a plan, and reflecting on how you are going with it frequently. Makes me sad to think how few people ever actually engage in this stuff, when it's what makes our life so much more rewarding. But I think the hardest of all work is having faith in the effect all of this stuff has – putting energy work in front of all of the ways our conscious mind is convinced make our life happen. The hardest work is the accelerator of our manifestations, but how it works doesn't make sense and it isn't logical. We're working with a form of our intelligence that far exceeds our logic. This makes it hard to have the necessary faith. The feeling state we live in will always be reflected in our environment, and I beg of you to prove this to yourself if the reactionality example hasn't explained attraction to you clearly enough.

This stuff is the hardest work for many people to bring themselves to do, but every shift in our energy hacks our reality, and changes what's happening for us subconsciously. If we are not utilising imagined emotional states as part of our daily or even moment to moment routine, we are shooting ourselves in the foot – not utilising our highest form of intelligence.

The hardest work is believing that we can do this – trying to counter all of the years we've been telling ourselves that we can't. Believing you can be more than you have been or understanding we are defined not by our history but what we do now. The hardest work is believing you can get what you've always wanted – that is work worth investing your soul in. You can earn money doing something more meaningful to you than you have been. You can change your mind about who you are – it just takes you to be more present in your mind than you have been. This is a decision waiting to be made. How hard is that for us – whatever we can define we can be.

The hardest work starts when it finally dawns on us how little of our life was a choice - that our state of mind that does all the creating of our experience is not a choice we make but repeats itself automatically year after year, creating an artificial world we have no escape from. It is hard for us to look at this and know what happened to us, but state of mind becomes more of a choice for us as soon as we do. And we can make those choices to feel better a priority in our lives. It's hard to change our beliefs – particularly if we are unclear who we want to be and why. It's hard for us to be more conscious and make that choice to feel better, but everything changes when you do. When we put energy at the top of our priorities. And it is a lot easier than a life that is happening without us – that we have no control over or say in and can't do anything about it because we don't even realise.

You don't have to do all of the other work you thought you did. You just have to change your mind about who you are. And it is hard but if we know the difference it makes it becomes the easiest work of all.

Chapter 10 Summary.

- The hardest work of all should be considered the work that we get the most results from. But until we understand the effect our state of mind has on the reality we experience, and that it is not a choice we normally make (is the role of the involuntary subconscious mind) we never engage in the **energy work** that will change the life and reality we experience.
- It is not hard work but granting it the credence that it deserves takes faith and insight.
- The hardest work is also setting the plan and being clear on the type of person we want to become. Making certain our efforts are intentional, rather than on autopilot.
- The hardest work is being willing to stand apart from the crowd and do what is right for us – no matter what people say.
- The hardest work is believing that we can do whatever it is we want to regardless of social norms, tradition, and expectations.
- The hardest work begins when it finally dawns on us, we don't have to do or feel in any way we wouldn't choose to. That we wouldn't want to continue to.
- The hardest work is validating Mindfulness, meditation, breathwork, diet, nature, created states and having a clear plan.
- The hardest work is looking in the mirror and acknowledging we are staring at someone who let us down and broke promises we made to ourselves. And forgiving them at the same time.
- **The hardest work is validating the use of our time and effort on our energy, expectancy, and mindset.**

CHAPTER 11
Our North Star

"Without that guiding star in our lives – the farthest light on the darkest night, we are as hopeless as a ship without a captain or a compass".

Simon

We will never be lost or wasting time, when we are guided by that single guiding sense of purpose that matters as much to us as our own life does. That shuffles our priorities, defines meaning, and identifies what is worthy of our attention – if something is either worthy of our pursuit or a distraction. But it goes much deeper than just being able to shuffle our priorities around, and know what things mean. It's in our darkest times, or when we come to a cross-roads of a looming decision – one that we know will take us on two vastly different paths - that the choice can only be brought into perspective by standing back and 'zooming out' to see our lives through a lens of something altogether greater than our own personal goals. That far in the distance guiding light that we navigate the broader journey of our lives by. Our North Star, by which we can always understand the context of where we are that makes those hard decisions at least a little more obvious.

When we are not sure which way to go because both directions mean sacrificing something that we're not sure we can tolerate losing, we can clearly know why one of them matters more. When everything stable in our life seems to have fallen apart, and we are left to make sense of the pieces we have left, it is that guiding light that allows us to at least know which way to swing the helm of our boat. Even when we feel cold, alone and in the middle of the darkest ocean, we can know with confidence we are headed in the right direction, and pieces we are left with will one day make much more sense to us than they do right now.

Whether that means family, truth, justice, or the greater good – what matters most to us will make order out of the chaos when we a clear on that single value that trumps all others. And many will say family – but what is it about family that means the most to us? Is it that we are there for them more or that we are better providers by spending more time at work? It is that we hold strong to our positions when disciplining our children and make parental decisions as one unit. To just say 'family' is a little too blurry to direct the kind of life choices we're referring to here.

But while we have spoken a lot about the power of a clearly defined outcome – about the magic being in the details, it is crucial to remember just how important it is to know those larger, deeper principles that define us. How all of the smaller stuff fits into the bigger picture can't be underestimated. We can often fall into a trap of looking down and getting 'mouse like' with the scrutiny of the details that we forget it is only by looking up and zooming out that those details are brought into an even more important longer-term picture. The details can be more of a hindrance than a help, particularly if we bow too stringently to those outcomes being matched in reality and imagine it all needs to look just as perfect as on our vision-board. Which one is the good road for us, and which has hidden dangers that don't occur to us? The good road often looks like that low hanging fruit or easy-to-get rewards, but it can be fraught with dangers we weren't aware of.

It's times like these that we must cast our gaze beyond the immediate, all the way to the end of our tunnel, and ponder how does this choice measure in the greater scheme of things? We have to be guided by a greater, but blurrier, gut instinct and be comforted only by the intuition that our decision was the right one. Maybe it doesn't feel like it right now – or it doesn't feel like this fate would ever be something we'd wish on anyone. I don't know if you've seen 'City Slickers' – where the old cowboy says something like 'the problem with people is they get all tangled up in their priorities trying to serve too many masters'. We can only know peace when we have that *one thing* that matters to us more than everything else. That thing that brings everything else into perspective. If that thing is ok, then everything else will be fine. When nothing else matters as much as that one thing that we are clear on, it guides our big decisions, and the rest of our life falls in line.

What's that one thing for you? When that is clear for us, all of the shorter-term stuff that seems to be happening right now matters less or at least no more than it ought to. All of the setbacks, and roadblocks (and bridge collapses.) seem more tolerable. When we know which way to turn the bow of our ship, we will at least know we are on our way 'home'. Our family is something most everyone would say we'd give our life for, and yet find ourselves missing birthdays, and dance recitals, so we can buy them the best of everything. We listen to our bosses more than we ever would the hearts of our children. And as an example – Nelson Mandela, one of the strongest, and most committed leaders of our time, turned his back on the opportunity to be the 'at home' family man for his wife and children. No one could ever say that he wasn't a man of great compassion or didn't have a heart. He was a spearhead for human equality whose cause extended well beyond his nation's borders. Most would consider him a great man, but I'm certain there were times that his wife wasn't on board with the sacrifices he was making.

He acted in the service of his 'greater' family – being his fellow countrymen. And when we are guided by that larger sense of responsibility, we are more easily able to defend ourselves from the arrows when they get fired at us. When it might have seemed like missiles are heading straight for us, we are buoyed by that greater good and they become more like annoying flies. Things we might well rather weren't there, but they will never sway us from our course. Our North Star makes our life easier to deal with – hard decisions easier – and disasters into things we can rebuild from. I have no idea the mind and thoughts of Nelson Mandela, but I would wager a guess there were many times in his life that he had wished this wasn't his cross to bear – that he'd instead chosen a simpler life.

Sometimes our fates aren't pretty, or anything we would choose if it we had a choice, but it is only by clinging to that rock of our principles that we can know who we are, and not drown in the sea of it all seeming meaningless. Or crumbling when the chips came down because we weren't certain of what we stood for. When we aren't sure those opportunities to make our stand pass - we wish we acted differently, but we never really understood what was at stake. And maybe it only happened so that we would clear where we draw the line – and next time we would know and act differently. But we can indeed avoid those regretful times by knowing ourselves, and what are the guiding principles of our life, as clearly as we can at every moment. We are always preparing for those moments when we need to know what type of people we are. Those principles are our compass, and even the largest ocean liner won't get out of the harbour without it.

> "I am the master of my fate. I am the captain of my soul."
>
> Invictus - William Ernest Henley.

It is understanding these things about ourselves prior to the event that makes it an easy choice when the time comes. I read a book that directly related to this theme – 'The Little Book of Big Questions', by Sylvia High. Sylvia guides us on a journey of self-reflection and realising how much easier it makes our life to first know what the things are that we feel most deeply about. Which way do we face when our values are brought before the court of our hearts? Not being sure of these principles is like being the captain of a ship with lots of people on board and setting sail without a route. We'll just 'make it up as we go' doesn't really seem like our best option.

Having already made those big decisions before the challenges come, certainly made good sense to me. Where we stand, and what we give voice to becomes an easier decision than it might have otherwise been. But we've also pre-identified some things that might have been hidden about us. We think differently about what the real skills and talents we bring to the table are, when we know what we want to do and the reason it matters to us. We may very well find ourselves to be much more talented and resourceful than our current circumstances were showing us. When we know what drives us, we know why we got that pit in our stomach when we saw someone being mistreated. Or it lights a spark in us because it finally occurs to us that there is something, we can do about the thing we declared was most important to us. We ponder our talents and awaken to the very real possibility that what we're good at can somehow fit this need. Like Cinderella's slipper we find the pastimes we enjoy and come naturally and easily to us to be just what could solve the problem a lot of people have.

Unless we are looking to help, we don't realise how many people are actually challenged by and want to learn about the thing that we find easy. We don't even consider it a skill or talent because it now comes so easily. What we are good at some people find very difficult and would love to overcome. Our first job is to know what matters to us – what are the things we find easy and enjoyable – then find the people who need help with this. Not one of us are as useless as our circumstances might have us believe. **But we can't change our mind without having that 'bigger than us' goal.** And we don't have to prove that we can do every single thing well to be able to hold ourselves as valuable. We don't have to prove we can do things that have no real value for us. When we have that guiding principle of our lives, and know ourselves on a deep level, we'll want to put ourselves in the firing line of criticism so we can find those people we should be helping. Knowing our North Star will teach us things about ourselves that we'll never want to forget.

Chapter 11 – Summary

- We will never be lost or wasting time, when we are guided by that single guiding sense of purpose that matters as much to us as our own life does.
- It is knowing our deepest values prior to any unexpected event or difficult decision that makes our life and choices easier when the time comes.
- We need to 'zoom out' sometimes in order to see why what's in front of us seems blurry, confusing, and unwanted.
- When we are faced with those tough life decisions and are not sure which choice needs to be sacrificed, we need to be guided by that single over-riding principle of our lives. The thing that brings everything into perspective. We have to look to our North Star.
- When that one thing is clear all of the shorter-term stuff right in front of us becomes more tolerable. The setbacks, roadblocks, and even the apparent 'accidents' don't matter as much to us because we still have that one thing that matters most.
- Only we can know what that one thing is for us, but it will guide us home on the darkest of nights, make a heavy load lighter and that fork in the road seem like an obvious choice.
- Always knowing that thing in advance means we make fewer wrong turns. It is our compass, our crutch, and our teddy bear when we need a hug.

CHAPTER 12
We Matter

"But what can I do, I am just one person".

Said 7 billion people.

It was reading "The Little Book of Big Questions" that made me want to write this book. It helped me understand that there was a good reason why particular things bothered me. It wasn't because I was flawed, or just an angry little man – they made me angry because they both challenged my values and pointed towards the type of issues that I was best suited to solve. Those emotions I was having weren't wrong – they were my compass. Those things that were challenging my values, and making me scared, were my direction - were the very things that I was supposed to be doing something about. I thought that it was unfair that people were being punched senseless by their conditioning all the time, and I need to do whatever I can to bring awareness to it. To help people solve this issue for themselves. How well I'm doing that is both up to me to judge and always forever being refined.

It bothered me that there was so much psychological suffering in the world, much of which happened by way of some simple to correct skews in people's perspective. Suffering that was happening for no better reason than not knowing ourselves, and the flow on effect of a lack of connection to both people and to the work we were doing. Because we never understood that larger part of mind that was doing nearly all of the thinking and feeling for us. Because we didn't realise by far the majority of what we felt was not by our choice. And if we don't know then we can never understand what was going wrong. The world outside of us is a mind made projection designed to sustain the feeling from which it came. And although knowing this might not make everything instantly better, it is a damn sight better than existing in its unchangeable ignorance.

But another thing that really 'burst my bubble', so to speak, was what seemed to be an unwritten 'conspiracy' of a sort coercing us into the belief that **what we do doesn't matter.** That who we are, the opinions we hold, and the work that we do is to small and meaningless for us to ever bother putting our whole selves into it. No one is watching and no one is listening.

There is an overriding 'vibe' trying to convince us that we're all too small and insignificant to think we can change anything or warrant having a say. That we aren't 'smart' or educated enough to allow ourselves to think we could contribute to, or have a say in, how this human drama unfolds. In how the future of our species pans out. That anything we believed should come from the mouths and minds of someone else. Anything that mattered to us was only ever going to be important on an individual level. All of the 'big stuff' was being taken care of by our 'leaders' – those clever people who had our backs. And they would almost certainly alert us to any real and immediate danger. That we could rest assured we were in good hands. But what if these very same 'officials' were the ones we really needed to be alarmed about? What if the threats that we were being alerted to were created by them and didn't pose as immediate a threat as we were being led to believe. I mean, if you're the one paying for the research you could nearly insist on what could be proven as true. You could even make falsehoods to be perceived as true. Who has the gold makes the rules – and who wins the war writes our histories.

It seems that we live with a perception of there is this huge group, or community of 'smart' scientists that are all in agreement over what's going on, what's important, and they will not only lead us into the future but tell us of anything we should be alarmed about. But that is just not the case. For instance, in 1910 the two wealthiest men in America, Andrew Carnegie and John D Rockefeller teamed up to finance what was known as the Flexner report. In which Abraham Flexner, who was not even a physician himself, produced a book that led to the eradication of all practice of homeopathy and use of natural medicines from the U.S. medical curriculum. Some doctors were even jailed for practising homeopathy, and all forms of natural remedies were removed from educational facilities and replaced with the use of patented pharmaceutical products for medical treatments. Patents that of course belonged to none other than Rockefeller, who monopolised the pharmaceutical industry that has today grown into the trillion-dollar machine we see today that offers physicians huge bonuses for prescribing their products. You think they want us to be well and healthy.

The beloved 'science' that brought us out of the dark ages of our ignorance, is starting to look like nothing more than a marketing tool that can 'prove' anything you can afford.

> *"Scientists fall in line with the dominant power structure. They have to because the power structure pays the bills. You don't play with the power structure, you don't get money for research, you don't get an appointment, you don't get published, in short you don't count anymore. You're out. You may as well be dead."*
>
> Michael Crichton

The days of being able to recognise what is the truth have become unreasonably subjective. It depends on how we feel, which has become more and more swayed by the influence of mass, and social media than most people are aware. We gravitate to the majority opinion more than we could ever know. But what the truth about anything will always eventually float to the surface. It prevails because it never has to make up a new story to conceal the first lie. Lies can't hold water, but the truth always will. What is untruthful will always eventually fall apart. Any attempt to deceive anyone of anything has a limited life span. The truth will always be revealed, but unfortunately, I think not until we move to start trusting in ourselves. Trust in the instincts, and greater intelligence, that we all house in our hearts. We have been subjected to a form of indoctrination that leads us to turning off our greater instincts in favour of what we are told by authority figures as being true. How little we can actually do, know, or contribute to the bigger picture, as our basic human freedoms are pulled from under us for the narrative we've been sold.

This same 'convincing' that we've been subjected to is what I think is the very same reason that we don't think what we do matters. That what we add to people's lives means anything. So, no matter what your view of the conspiracy aspect of this indoctrination we've been controlled by it is how it manages to unconsciously persuade us of the limits our own value that disturbs me more than anything. We matter immensely to the people that are in our lives, but until we realise how much we will never do what we do with appropriate vigour. What we are doing now is our purpose – we are doing it - and what we do matters. We seem to suffer under this cloud of illusion that unless we are famous, or wealthy, or stand at the highest levels of government, that we have no purpose. Our life has no meaning, and we shouldn't be bothered too much about the insignificant and 'dumb' stuff that we do. We're not changing anything, and no one cares about us or what we do. And the truth is they don't. No one cares about you or what you do - **but you ought to** – this is your life. We make a difference, and no matter how infinitesimal they have convinced us our contribution is – we matter.

I think that in our hearts we all want some very similar things – the freedom to live the way we want to and raise healthy, contributing, children. Is it only because we lack a common voice that we find ourselves so manipulated and small? Because we're divided by such trivial matters that we fail to recognise what we gain in unity and being able to put aside those differences for what we strive for in common? How did we become so brainwashed by this manipulation that we can't even smell the BS when it's waved right under our nose. That we have no intelligence to speak of and have neither any idea of what's going on - or any right to say so. And I am not including these ideas in the hope of shinning a light on some unknown conspiracy, but the inherent suggestion that constricts our apparent rights and minimalizes our intelligence. What's being forced on us is the self-infecting belief that we don't have any rights, nor any ability to do anything about anything.

We don't think we can help anyone or add anything of value. We seem convinced by the structure of our societal values that we can only measure our worth in terms of the money or attention that we get. We have effectively divorced ourselves from our internal senses, from the all-knowing intelligence within us that reminds us of our value and connection to something larger. We imagine our sense of worth can only be reflected back to us from the outside - by what other people see in us. This has become the social norm because of how our leaders, and advertisers alike, replay the subliminal 'background' idea that we are damaged, dumb, and incomplete. That we're incapable of seeing the big picture. They have an enormous interest and reason for pushing this 'lack of worth' story onto the populous they wish to control. We don't believe we are worth listening to, or being given the truth.

The job of the marketing industry is to make us feel incomplete – like we have a need that is not being met. To convince us how much better we'll feel when we have their product. That we don't know what we're missing, and we'll feel so much better in owning what they offer. Something we never even thought about buying, now becomes our new must have, and much of it by the trickery of advertising. Our greater salvation can never lie in what anyone else can offer us, and almost certainly can't happen by reducing ourselves to the opinion other people might have of us.

Nor can our value be defined by what we have done – it comes by our own assessment of how we are going with our goals, by our connection to ourselves, and the extent to which we keep those small but meaningful promises to ourselves. Our worth can only be measured by us, and that we remain in the pursuit of something important to us. Our commitment to doing what we think needs solving – what we do is what the world needs more than anything – so just smile in that fact. **By what matters to us – 'we matter'.** We matter to ourselves and find meaning and satisfaction in what we do. We certainly don't have to prove anything, or impress anyone to consider ourselves of value. We just have to know that we've played our part and done what matters to us to both bend reality to our will, and have peace in our hearts. We have to be clear what we value and make a stand for it at every opportunity.

I tend to think that we are treated like we are ignorant little children by our leaders. That we are held in contempt by the fact that we've offered them our co-operation. (Obedience?) Like we are the little people who don't matter, and we've been covertly conned out of our rights and voice. I have no intention of making any political statements here, but our governments no longer appear to be the 'representatives of our will' they were elected to be. Or to be the upholders of a law that applies to everyone equally? **It doesn't look like they are doing what we employed them to do?** Rather our modern system of governance reflects something that is looking more and more like a dictatorship than a democracy. When corporations become our law makers, we have by default entered a communist regime disguised as a democracy. The 1215 document called the Magna Carta, came to represent the idea that the people can assert their rights against an oppressive ruler and that the power of a government can be limited to protect those rights. It was the first document to put into writing that the King and his government were not above the law. This is the founding idea that western society is grounded in, but with how things are turning it really makes one wonder.

It would seem that we have become subjected to the will of unelected officials who now run the world – like the WEF, and the WHO to name a few. The systems that were set up to protect us have been overthrown in a behind the scenes coup d'état where the wealthy have taken it upon themselves to enslave us 'mere mortals' within our own system.

I had to add this chapter not to bring light to my personal views of some conspiracy but if we are to become more conscious, it must also be to the plight of our communities, nations, and all of humanity. Not just more conscious of our own minds, but of those who seek to undermine our ownership of it at the most subconscious levels. To fully appreciate our personal value, we have to be conscious of the covert narrative that profits from and seeks to increase its power by diminishing of ours. We do have value, and we do have a say. And we do offer our clients, communities, and families far more than anyone will ever be able to measure in gold. As clichéd as it might seem, it is because of our binding subconscious agreement of money to be our only measure of value, we've become blind to the 'salt of earth' treasures we provide each other. In our connection and compassion, we hold something far greater than any other measure of our wealth.

We've become divorced from our greater senses of not just the higher human qualities and moral principles, but our alchemic abilities for us to turn ordinary moments into lasting memories. We don't appreciate the effect we can have on people. We forget that these are the best times of our lives as we are living through them. Our ability to turn ordinary happenings into extraordinary times is the highest skill of all but we could never attempt to measure it. What lies within us can transcend the ordinary feelings, but people rarely ever care to look there. It reminds me of the story where the Gods wanted to leave a treasure on earth for us, but feared that it would be found too easily. So they hid it where we would never think to look.

Devil Inside? So too is Heaven.

> *"The highest and most beautiful things in life are not to be heard about, nor read about, not seen but if one will, are to be lived."*
> **Soren Kierkegaard**

Shame of it is we are probably surrounded by something far more pleasing to our senses than we know but the need for our instant and personal gratification, and how we might look to others, forbids us from looking or seeing it. We're dopamine freaks who can't go an hour without our phones, or a day without killing the pain of boredom with sex, drugs, or shopping. If our personal appreciation dared to delve beyond those normal social values we might look weird from the outside because no one could ever see 'our kingdom'. It might look like we were dancing with shadows. We fail to go to the place where we can unlock what will transform how the world around us seems. Because we have all been hoodwinked into what really has value, we don't use our eyes to see.

Maybe if we were able to just wake up and cherish those golden moments of our lives when they were happening we wouldn't need all the stuff we think we are striving for. That fulfilment is so much simpler than we're making it – so much cheaper, and more available to us than it seems, because of how we've brainwashed by those shared societal values. The values that have become ingrained, and grew on each other for generation after generation to move further away from the source of true gold that we harbour within. What if, little by little, we were able to deposit those golden moments (potentially every moment.) into a kind of spiritual bank account - a vault that starts to look far more favourable than the carrot reward we might otherwise be coaxed by.

What if we became more awake to the 'manufactured' panic when the evidence just doesn't seem to support it? How foolish would we look if we became so convinced, we were in a hotpot of doom because we were conned into believing in ideals that have no real value to us? If the things that could make our lives complete are sitting right beside us - but we've been outwitted into believing they have no value. What if we didn't need these 'essential' things they are forcing down our throats in order to feel the way we want to? What if we could live without the things they said we can't live without? We hold the keys to feeling the way we want to in every moment regardless of circumstances – what is it that has us so convinced otherwise? What if it turns out that they had convinced us we were in hell, when the reality is we can turn it into heaven when we know how. That heaven is far closer than we ever thought?

How foolish would we be to think that anyone could care more than we do about our lives and what we are doing in them? If we got ourselves all down about the state of the world because it appears to lack the compassion, we thought it should have? If it were to appear to us that 'nobody cares', it should be even more reason for us to care. Nobody should, or could, care more about what we are doing than we do. It's not their life – it's ours. But somehow that mindset, or perception, that nobody cares has become translated as 'we can't make a lick of difference to anything', so we shouldn't go getting ourselves all 'riled' up over anything'. But some things should boil our blood – some things should bother us.

To be 'care-free', or to care-less is to rob our lives of meaning, the reason we came here, and our 'God' granted ability to turn it into something it wasn't before we got here. It's by what matters to us, by the act of us having a meaning and purpose that we are able to bend what is real in the world. And we could never expect to have any sense of satisfaction without something have some meaning for us. It would be unlikely we'd even want to get out of bed if nothing mattered to us. But it is when something does matter enough to us that things that might seem to be getting in our way - a habit that might seem hard to break, or hill that was too high to climb, just crumbles into dust. When we have something that matters to us or we care about enough, anything in our way gets miniaturised. Among all of the other things purpose offers us – it shrinks our problems. If we care about something enough, our reasons will steam-roll anything in the way. We just have to care enough about the result and the work required becomes straight forward, if not effortless.

To not care about anything deeply is to ensure that we never know the joy of a triumph. That we're doomed by never wanting to do battle - be in the fight for ourselves – or for something even greater than ourselves. We grow by those reasons, and we shrink without them. To not care is the recipe for an emotionless and bored stiff life. Emotions are never the enemy – they are both our compass and the creative catalyst that forms, and can transform, the world around us.

> *"All things by immortal power. Near or far, to each other linked are, that thou canst not stir a flower without troubling of a star."*
>
> Francis Thompson

We might not be going to start the revolution but that pebble that we drop in the pond makes waves that we could never rightly fathom the effect of. We cannot know the effect of every small thing we do. How, when we smiled at that newborn in a pram, we changed their impression of how the world is. And as it is said even those who ignore us might still be inspired by us. We may not be getting showered in accolades, but we are always planting a seed that grows into something that will outlast us. By being our 'stupid' selves we might well be giving someone just the push prod impetus they needed – the 'permission' to be nonchalant, carefree, or pursue that idea they thought everyone would laugh at.

The art we create, or the project we begin, may not seem like it is going to make big waves in the ocean, but its ripples may change someone's outlook or give them all the inspiration they needed to make a start on something great. It would be arrogant to think we could know how our piece of the puzzle, the part we add, fits into that greater puzzle. To understand all of the people we indirectly affect - how we affect someone who affects someone else and becomes an unbroken chain that ripples through time indefinitely. We all emit a frequency that affects the entire connected world forever in every moment.

We shouldn't need to have 'all eyes on us' to realise ourselves as performers in every moment. To know that everyone indirectly sees all of our actions, and hears every thought in our head. We shouldn't need our 'work' to be considered so important that it would be carried on after our death before we make the decision to create something. As in "I'm not going to do anything if I don't think it is going to have some profound impact". I'm willing to bet that Colonel Sanders could have never envisioned that his brand of chicken flavouring would be established in 145 countries around the world when he was taking his 'silly' secret herbs and spices door to door back in 1952. He was apparently knocked back over a thousand times, but persevered through with vision and stamina. We can never know the impact of what we create – we just need to create what comes to our heart.

We can't all be the next Nelson Mandela, or Elvis Presley, or Lionel Messi but if we were able to see the whole butterfly effect of the ripple we send out I think we'd certainly behave differently. We'd act more consciously. Be more courteous and be naturally more cautious of what we send out. Not paranoid but free. We'd be more fearless in what we create. We'd care less about the people that don't 'get' or approve of who we are. We'd always have something better to do than concern ourselves with the opinion of the 'spectators' and critics. There will always be people who think they know who we are and what we are doing from the 3 minute window of our life that they witness.

> *"No pessimist ever discovered the secret of the stars, or sailed to an unchartered land, or opened a new doorway for the human spirit".*
> Helen Keller.

The power of a unified voice.

You may well be one person and one small voice against the heckling and judgement of the world, but we are all waiting for you. We are all waiting for you to show us what you've made. To show us what someone who is unashamedly themselves looks like. Who's not afraid to make a fool of themselves if it means representing their truth. We never look as stupid in the eyes of others as we think. Most people aren't even watching and couldn't care less what we do. It has often been reckoned that most of our psychological ailments can be derived from an over exaggeration on our part of how much other people care about what we do. German philosopher Friedrich Nietzsche has quoted **'Everything I do is wrong'** which may seem at first to be pessimistic and defeatist, but it also grants us the freedom to do whatever it is we want to.

If it's all 'wrong' then what do I have to fear? And not in the sense that it will have no consequences, but if we are starting from a position of careless freedom, then we understand that anything we add is far better than nothing. What we want to do might very well go wrong, but it is far better than doing nothing. If everything we did had to have an awesome outcome we'd hardly ever move. And it has often been noted as a trait of all successful people of their proclivity and willingness to fail. To fail, but fail forward in order to learn a better way.

> "Those who have won major victories realised that all of the resources to win are within, and that most knowledge needed to succeed is acquired after action."
>
> Brendon Burchard.

We humanoids may be vastly different in our values and beliefs, but we also have so much more in common than we realise. If it were possible to have a world-wide consensus, I think that everyone would place peace on earth and in mind at the very top of their lists. But it seldom occurs to us when the obstacle is us, or how easily this can change. Out of all the ways we feel, we never seem to question or get to the bottom of why we feel the way we do, so can't know what might be required of us to change it. We may well be standing behind meaningless conclusions, often out of outdated habits, that forbid the peace we claim to want so badly. While we may claim we'd be willing to do whatever it took to have peace, justice, equality – making the necessary lifestyle and belief changes remains completely off the table. **We can't change what we don't know is stopping us.**

Would we be willing to grant others absolute freedom in their choice of lifestyle if that meant we could also enjoy the same privilege? Would we be willing to make the necessary sacrifices it would take to bring peace to our minds? Would we be willing to pay any price to have the things that stand at the top of our values? It often seems that, when we are faced with even the smallest of conflicts in our lives, we're unable to recognise these troubles as a starting point to having peace of mind. And that surely carries as a contributor to peace on earth. We want world peace more than anything else but when some 'mongrel' cuts us off in traffic, they are going to pay – big time. We can't see the relationship between our peace and these apparently 'little things'. Or how whatever we see as being wrong in the world has anything to do with us. How the disruptions to our peace influences the whole. How an elevation in our conscious state can actually change what's going on in us - and for us. Changing us changes the world according to us.

We absolutely want the freedom to live the way we want to and claim to understand the built-in agreement that this also means allowing everyone else that same privilege. But when push comes to shove, we have a huge list of problems with what other people do and how they are. It would never occur to us that peace starts in our own hearts and how our light expands outwards to the corners of the globe. That the very best thing we can do for the world is to grow ourselves in a spiritual sense. Is peace on earth 'unrealistic'? Not if we are united enough in its value and recognise all of those 'small' starting points - all of the parts that we can control and manage that contribute towards it. Understand the starting point as us. But then "He said this about me, and his ancestors did this" – these are where this desire for peace breaks down at its roots.

Not recognising these small things as part of a bigger problem are the very ideas that make it impossible. How we, in our tiny little lives, are contributing to the violence and division? And deny how much we can be a part of the solution? What are the beliefs that we hold that contribute to the division and contribute to the indifference that we can't let go of? We can't consider a world at peace because we can't imagine we have anything to do with it – but that ignorance may be the only thing standing in the way.

When it comes down to it what are our options? I know none of us 'apparently' have any say in the human outcome (that's the privilege of our authorities) but how do we see this human conundrum panning out? What would have to happen for it to not end in war and us be left to pick up the pieces of a decimated world? This is the reason I wanted to add this chapter before tying all of the ideas together, because we have not only been duped out of our greatest source of intelligence, and convinced that we aren't smart, or good enough, but that we don't play a part in how this all goes down. This is our world and the history of humanity that we, in our daily lives, are bringing to pass in every action we take and belief we hold. "We the people" means far more than we think. The closer we get to a common cause, the more unstoppable we become in playing our part in the human future.

> "A house divided against itself cannot stand. I believe this government cannot endure permanently half slave and half free. I do not expect the Union to be dissolved – I do not expect the house to fall – but I do expect it will cease to be divided. It will become all one thing or the other."
>
> **Abraham Lincoln**

And I sure as shit know that in the hands of our megalomanic 'authorities', our future does look glum. And yes, I agree that it is not by our doing, but it is by both our lack of concern and our belief we can't do anything about it. It is not by our choice that our rights become eroded away, but by our ignorance and compliance when it is happening right under our noses. By our lack of choice when we do have one, but then get convinced by shadow tactics that these choices are not ours to make. We are the numbers and the more we are united by a common need, and are willing to let go of the insignificant obstacles to these shared ideals, the more we can take the reins of our future. It would seem the authorities have a vested interested in our squabbling and we so readily take the bait – never realising who's behind the conflict or what we are losing on a greater scale in our less than important differences.

> "It is not our differences that divide us. It is our inability to recognise, accept, and celebrate those differences."
>
> **Audre Lorde.**

We hold the power in the form of the base line values we share and agree upon. When we speak with a unified voice on a singular and overriding need, we become an unstoppable force to any form of poorly conducted authoritarianism. We are the people and, when we aren't divided and fighting each other over incidentals, we will remember that we are the ones who hold the platform on which our leaders stand on. Were they not elected to serve the peoples will? And if they aren't performing that function, it represents a decay of both our social system and their power will go with it.

If our system is not actively serving the will of the people, then what people is it really serving? If it is not born from the principles of justice, equality, and the sovereignty of the individual then the decay has already begun. It has been known since the birth of our earliest civilisations that in order for larger communities to come together and benefit from the increased diversity of skills that a larger community offers – it can only thrive by its upholding of a common law. In order for that utopian ideal to prosper it must be founded in a system of justice that applies equally to all people. The degree to which this justice is lacking or not apparent is to the same degree that ensures a societies decline. The system collapses and a new fairer system has always taken its place. If the system is not founded in justice and equality it cannot last. It is like us thinking that we could survive if we cut off major body parts. For the human body to thrive it needs all of its systems in co-operation, and the same applies to the larger system of our society.

> "The rights of every man are diminished when the rights of one man is threatened."
> **John F Kennedy**

A civilisation can only thrive under a banner of co-operation, equality, and justice. If a society lacks these fundamental ideals and fails to honour the rights and choices of its citizens, it is showing the first signs of its demise. And this is not a statement of my personal political views – but of the metrics that determine the health of a society. If a society's health is deteriorating then it won't survive, no matter how clever the perpetrators of tyranny imagine they are. I have no intention of making any form of political statement. This is a book about becoming more conscious. But that consciousness is not confined to what goes on inside us, but also what is occurring in our world at large.

We cannot turn a blind eye to the state of our society and hold firm to the idea that we are conscious, any more than we could claim to pride ourselves on being compassionate whilst we gorge ourselves in front of the starving.

We all play a role in the betterment of human consciousness, by ensuring our human rights, choices, and freedoms are upheld. And challenging whatever ways we think they are being taken from us against our will. We have to stand and be counted in the face of any obvious threat to those freedoms if we are to maintain we are conscious of the underlying principles that serve our society at large. We all play a role in the collective future of our planet - and its people. As Frances Wright stated –

> *"Equality is the soul of liberty; there is, in fact, no liberty without it."*

What we are armed with.

> *"Man is not made for the State but the State for man. And it derives its powers only from the consent of the governed."*
> **Thomas Jefferson.**

If I'm to write on the subject of consciousness, it wouldn't seem adequate for that to be just referring to a consciousness of our own minds but to raise an awareness of those who have the intention of hijacking them. Meaning those who have the will to con us out of, not just our own choices and freedoms, but obscuring the truth of the role we play in the human future. Those who would have us believe that we are not even smart enough to know when we are being forced into giving up our human freedoms for some half-baked version of the 'greater good'. We are being brainwashed into believing those at the helm have our best interests at heart by the same 'leadership' that are trying to convince us that we are all in some grave danger of everything from everywhere. In danger from everything except those that invoke the fear.

Those who deal in fear just keep winding up the seriousness of the threats that they themselves have created. Much like the imaginary war effort that the residents in George Orwell's '1984' novel were asked to make sacrifices for and forgo their basic freedoms. Have we arrived at Orwell's 'fantasy'? Our awareness is constantly being bombarded constantly a biased narrative aimed at convincing us of both our helplessness, and our inability to do anything about it. Requiring of us to disregard our intuitions and intelligence, and reminding us of the need to sacrifice our free will to the people who are 'looking after' us and 'know better'.

We are being systematically exploited by an agenda aimed squarely at devaluing our rights to speak and make our own judgements. There is an obvious agenda to divide us, and secretly cheat us out of our own will to choose. Our enemy is not just our conditioning, but those in power who hold us in contempt for the very act of believing we have any rights. We are in the trenches of a psychological war the likes of which have never been seen, and we are unfortunately not privy to the scope of the tactics this war on our minds uses. Their arsenal is packed with tools to not just take away our choices but lead us to be thankful we have such brave leaders steering us into the oblivion of our own demise.

We are gaslighted, deceived, and led by half-truths into a labyrinth of tangled lies about who's really in charge, and what the plan is. The 'group think' cues that we are being subconsciously manipulated by. It unfortunately will not occur to the majority of trusting souls who imagine most people are just as kind and thoughtful as they are – and that our leaders must be even more so – or they would have never become elected. We all have an instinctive tendency to look towards authority figures for how we might best serve the greater good. We look to who is in charge of the tribe for direction, so we can understand how to do our part.

But it seems the more unbelievable the lie we are expected to swallow, the more human consciousness becomes dumbed down into this bizarre and obscure world of deceit. Where it would seem the bigger and more outrageous the falsehood the further they are able to lead us down this rabbit hole of deception. It is a war on our consciousness and the gradual but purposeful stupification of human beings. Where we are fed an ever-deepening divide in the truth, where it is a case of 'get them to believe this' and then turn their attention elsewhere and away from realising how questionable these stories really are. That Oswald shot Kennedy 3 times with a bolt action rifle – that Pearl Harbour was a surprise attack – or that the Pentagon was hit by a 'disappearing' plane. And if you don't agree with the outlandish stories, you will be labelled by the masses a 'conspiracy theorist'. I mean really!

This nullifying of our common sense is paralleled to the leading process demonstrated in the show called 'Push' by the English mentalist Derren Brown. Whereby the participants are set into an experiment to expose just how compliant the average person can become when they are led little by little into agreeing with increasingly worse or more detrimental acts of falsehood.

Little by little the unwitting participants are led down the rabbit hole of agreeing to play along with things that they know aren't right, but they have committed themselves by the previous act. They are guilty no matter which way they fall, right up until the last act they are asked to perform, which goes way beyond what any one of them would ever consider in normal circumstances. It is an entertaining exposé where participants are initially chosen for their level of social compliance and slowly but surely, led down a labyrinth, being asked to agree to perform acts that would clearly challenge their beliefs of right and wrong. But as these morally questionable acts begin quite innocently with swapping the labels on the vegetarian Hors d'oevres, the participants are asked to perform ever increasingly questionable acts and agree to going along with behaviours that they clearly know are wrong.

Without the build-up of those first, easier to agree to lies, the participants would never have performed the acts that they did. But the water they are in, and the 'heat' of the lies they agree to gradually becomes warmer, and they find themselves ultimately being found out for the smaller indiscrepancies if they don't perform the one last terrifying act. I'll let you watch it if you are interested – but it is an eye-opening display of just how easily ordinarily good people can be gradually led into performing unspeakable acts because of their willingness to be 'good', agreeable, compliant, and doing the 'right thing'??

It is a mind-blowing performance by Brown which I think demonstrates a similar situation in the BS we are asked to believe and participate in. We are pushed harder and harder into a corner. Into believing that lies are truth, and what should appear to us as obvious deceptions, are overlooked in the name of the greater good. They are carried by the assumption that our leaders have the interests of the masses close to their bosom. 'Push' echoes just how easily we can be led by a process of systematic conditioning into buying ever more incredulous narratives of what's happening, and at the same time blinding ourselves to the real threats in our world.

Before we know it we are duped into believing the most difficult to swallow stories of betrayal and giving up our freedoms in the process. It would seem half of the people are actually convinced that the BS is true, and the other half think they are going mad because they just can't see how the other half actually believe it. It is as if we are slowly but surely being indoctrinated into agreement that black is actually white, or risk being viewed as some sort of crazed conspiracy nut. I guess we just have to accept that the perpetrators of these increasingly harmful narratives that serve only those who exist at the highest levels of our society, could never be brought to justice within a justice system that they have governance over. We just have to accept our 'rulers' are unpunishable for the largest of crimes because of the unbelievable scale on which these crimes are enacted. It is a system that rights its own rules and has been corrupted at the highest levels.

We are bound by a powerful unconscious force to lean with the beliefs of the herd and comply with the masses. By our very nature we are unconscious and prone to wanting to be a part of the largest group to maintain our sense of belonging, intelligence, order, and safety. We can't know or realise all the forces that are at play that distract us and forbid us from imagining there can be any real harm done by the few that rule over the many. In our plight to share the truth we are not armed with, or up against, any form of 'truth'- we are up against popular opinion, however ludicrous that might become.

This fact of our nature has been demonstrated time and again - that we would rather join in on a lie, and be socially compliant, rather than be the odd one out. This happens, to varying degrees obviously, and will always be dependent on how highly we value what we are being asked to compromise. But little by little we are led slowly deeper into the web of deceit where we will one day wake up and wonder how we ever got where we are. By unconsciously tolerating incredulous lies, because we didn't see the greater ploy of our deceivers, and didn't think it would really affect us that much. And we certainly didn't want to be counted as the crazy ones.

> *"A lie doesn't become truth, wrong doesn't become right, and evil doesn't become good, just because it is accepted by a majority."*
> **Booker T Washington.**

There have been many such experiments conducted in the name of demonstrating the lengths we will go to in order to maintain the status quo. Even if we are not agreeable people it is often just easier and more peaceful to go along – in many cases it is like 'what is the harm done'. Once such demonstration was conducted where in a room of eight people, 7 of whom were *controls* of the experiment who were all told to lie about the colour of a card that was being held up. The entire group were asked to say if the sample being shown was red, orange, or pink. A card that was an obvious pink, but all of the seven controls of the group declared that it was definitely red when they were asked.

The poor old victim of the experiment was faced with two options – to either go along with the group or be the only one amongst them who was wrong. And nine out of ten times the experiment was run, the member who wasn't part of the control group would just go along rather than be 'wrong' or the odd one out.

And as innocent as this will to comply might seem in this type of experiment, the truth it points towards illustrates something far more dangerous than we might imagine. That we would rather sell someone out, or admit wrong was right, rather than stand aside from the group. Not in every instance obviously, but it is much harder than we may think for us to see any truth that might go against the beliefs of the majority. Anything that asks us to stand aside from or against the larger group. This urge towards social compliance is a much greater force than we can reckon with. To stand against a majority opinion because we can no longer tolerate it as being true, takes much more courage than we might have considered. Nor do we usually give ourselves any credit for those times when we do. We are up against an assault on our senses and, unless we operate with some level of awareness of our enemies' tactics, we may well be the ones who are buying into our own craziness.

Calm – our secret spiritual weapon.

But these are all just more tactics to take that single choice away from us. To push our buttons, and stir our emotions, over things that we think we can't do anything about. But, of course, there is something we can do. And even though the battle lines have been clearly drawn in this psychological warfare it is one that we can easily win if we know what we are fighting against and what we are armed with. No one can force us to feel any way we wouldn't choose to if we are to value our own choices and consciousness. No one can make us do anything we wouldn't want to, no matter how serious the threat. And while they can employ every plan, tactic, and intention they have of dividing us, stirring our emotions, and making us believe we might very well be going mad, we only become victims if we let it all into our minds.

This ploy can only be successful if we get stirred, divided, or think we are crazy and there is nothing we can do to oppose the injustice and psychological attack.

We only lose the fight if we buy into the game, and hand over the controls in the form of our emotional over-reactions and the anger and hatred they were hoping for. It is in our fury and frustration that we become complicit in the war and the trap they have laid for us. We stand exhausted with, no result, lots of enemies and have lost the battle in just the way they anticipated. In our being broken and emotionally distraught and helpless we have lost a battle against an unseen and unknowable enemy.

"If someone is driving you nuts, stop handing them the keys."

By going nuts about anything, we've walked straight into the mouse trap they set for us. And then we walk around even angrier trying to punch at the mist. In awareness **we have something in our armoury that is next level on what they are working with.** Your calm – your ability to see the magic where there was none - goes far beyond their arsenal and their ability to push our buttons. To see beauty and go more deeply into the majesty of our environment is our smoking pistol.

They imagine they are dealing with infants, but this is the birth of a new human era in consciousness. We are waking up to witness the power of our own creation and what we can turn the world into by our own will. And at the same time we are effectively turning the world into a place of peace - that makes their level of combat seem futile. Peace in our heart, and the expansion of each moment into joy and laughter that wasn't there before, is making magic appear from the ether – from the thin air and it is a far more advanced weaponry than the cheap trickery they are playing with. **Don't get mad – get calm.** What we are armed with is consciousness – exemplified by our choice to feel in each and every moment. What Victor Frankl referred to as the last of the human freedoms – *our will to respond.*

We shouldn't ever imagine that we are behind or can't win. Get mindful and go into the heart of whatever it is that might be making you feel that way so you can understand just how situational this issue is. We have our defences and what we are being dragged into is no match for the weapons we can now fight with. The only thing that can ever make us feel a sense of lack or powerlessness is an absence of mind. And the cure is both simple and universal.

Why did I even bring this up?

I earlier made the point of illustrating how our conditioning was actually a lie someone once convinced us was true, so that our conscious choice to feel would become an easier, and more obvious, option. That in awareness we can find it so much easier to laugh in the face of apparent circumstances, conflict, and fear. In the face of the 'evil' situations that had covertly been causing so much grief in our life for so long. To point out that we were up against a very real force that we couldn't ordinarily see or understand, that was wrong about us, and had ruined so many moments in our life. But as I have mentioned I don't believe there are any weak people. We don't lack courage we just fail to either identify what is to gain, or know the nature of our internal enemy. If we knew – if we saw it clearly in our hearts, what was the right thing to do - it wouldn't be difficult or questioned. It would be done without effort. We never lack courage – we lack awareness of the reasons we do things and the real consequences when our acts are multiplied by time. If we saw our enemy for what it was, and how it was continually sabotaging our lives we would snap its neck like a twig.

And this was the point of mentioning this covert enemy that seeks to overtake our consciousness, our good sense, and choices without us even being aware of the sacrifice we are making. I think that we find it much easier to band together against a common external enemy when we can identify what it actually is and how it means to attack us. When our need becomes even more urgent because the enemy is at our door – stealing our rights and human history before our very eyes. And **when we understand that there is one, very powerful, thing that we can do** that both benefits the 'whole' and defeats our combatant at their own game.

This is not just us feeling good more of the time – or something so hedonistic as indulging in our own pleasure. There is something far more universal and grander at stake here. This is us disarming humanities real worst enemy – this is our peaceful protest. To live in mindfulness, be clear on what matters to us, and see the beauty that can only exist because of us realising it exists in us. Being calm, living our lives by design, and noticing the magic that no one else has seen **is the very means by which we stand together against what threatens the sovereignty of everybody's mind's and freedoms**. This is how we win without ever raising a sword. And I'm not suggesting this can always be a peaceful transition, and there will never be sacrifices asked of us, but in the throne of our minds we can remain calm in knowing that we are already home. And this is precisely how we can defeat those that seek to control our behaviour with fear and servitude to something that doesn't serve us.

I believe there is a plan in action to invade our inner space - to conquer what is most sacred about us. But we are not unarmed - we are onto the ploy, and we know how we win a battle such as this. They may do everything in their power to convince us to forgo our right to choose for some fairy-tale narrative of the 'greater good' but they will never force the masses off the cliff by their own choosing. This 'greater good' they speak of does not serve the people but the elite – but how can they possibly be granted the title of elitism if they do not have the interests of everyone at heart – if they do not honour the responsibilities that must come with any positional privilege.

Our State of Mind is not a Choice.

This book is about understanding that our state of mind is not ordinarily a choice we make but repeats itself on autopilot. It is a self-regenerating energy source using our bodies as a host. As Ekhart Tolle implies "the pain-body wants to survive just as much as any living thing. It feeds off our pain and certainly doesn't want to die. (Cease to exist.)

We have all the necessary knowledge at our disposal – we know everything that we might need to in order to reclaim our inner kingdom. To value this place of sovereignty above all things on earth because it is through this kingdom of ours that everything that exists is created. To understand that making every choice we can to elevate our state of mind serves an even grander ideal than we could have imagined. There is a much greater reason and a much more urgent need. This road to our glory is also how we combat the tyrants that prey on our unconsciousness. We have an external enemy that is doing battle with us behind enemy lines, but it is a battle we are equipped for and can easily win. In mindfulness, being clear on what matters to us, and creating emotions without reason, we slay a demon that has existed on earth unhindered up until now. We now see this enemy for what it is, and we have the means to beat it at its own game. Anything in the outside world that forces a feeling in us that we wouldn't have by choice is seen for the darkness it represents. The lie we went along with because we thought we had to. And whether that force comes from strangers, colleagues, friends, authorities, or our own deceptive self-talk, our tactic remains the same. We are the captains of our souls.

I mentioned the covert brainwashing by the authorities for two reasons. So that we can apply these tactics towards an even greater cause and defeat an enemy at its own game. To remind us of the true urgency we are faced with to reclaim our inner world. To remain vigilant in our bunker of consciousness, and not be dragged into reactive situations every time they try to convince us we should. When we know what is at stake – when we know the battle lines that are been drawn for our own minds - the alternative to making conscious choices and moving closer to our inner world must seem even more 'hellish'. We are not just trying to feel good – we are winning the last war of humanity. **I included this chapter so that you have an even better reason to get clean in your aura and know how much more you are fighting for than just you feeling great and seeing the invisible beauty.** To make *the choice to feel* an even easier one than only getting one up on our devilish conditioning. To make this an even simpler, and more vital choice to make. We are the mighty and there is a lot to fight for, a lot to win, a lot at stake.

By reclaiming our inner kingdom, we win the world for all people. World war three has begun, but it is no longer a battle for physical territory but the sovereignty and consciousness of our own minds. A battle to take control over everything we think, feel, and believe until we have become little more than robot servants. Once they have entered the heart of our minds, those who do not understand our programming can be easily influenced out of their own choices, rights, and beliefs. The war has begun alright – it is on the T.V. – it is in the news and narrative the mainstream media spreads as truth. A propaganda story designed to convince us to hand over our will, life, and 'meagre' dreams in the name of the greater good – so that we can proclaim them as our gods, saviours, and masters. **We will own nothing and be happy**, say those that will own everything - our opinions included.

We have an enemy in the lies that are being fed to us, particularly in how they are trying to diminish our value and rights. In broad daylight ask us to not only eat a shit sandwich, but tell them how good it tastes. If the lies that our conditioning has been peddling about us was not enough for you to redact its power, there is indeed an even greater reason for you to choose the last of the human freedoms - the freedom to respond in the way we want to. There is an even more desperate situation brooding that demands not violence or demonstrations, but the requirement for us to see another side of this earth situation, and our role in it. A brighter and more astonishing side that has long been hidden from us by our own ignorance and unconsciousness. A gift we remained blind to because we lacked the presence of mind to see it.

There is an even greater need for us to feel the way we want to more of the time, because this is how we do battle in this new covert war. You might be very surprised how these tactics are employed through social and mass media. The subliminal means that are used to push our emotional buttons and sway our beliefs and opinions. In unconsciously reacting the way they want us to, we are handing over the keys to our kingdom. If this seems over the top to you, then watch this space as the truth unfolds, and the lies become even harder for us to deny. What is in our hands is far more than most people are ready to accept. Our choice to feel changes far more than just our surroundings and takes back something far more sacred than our mood.

The external enemy.

It is probably not news to anyone that our advertisers push our buttons without us even knowing it. We choose to buy a carton of beer because of the vibe in the ad, the number of times that add flashes past our face and subconsciously becomes embedded. We buy it because of social norms. (Most of our mates are drinking it.) But the people I'm referring to now are not our advertising gurus that are pulling our emotional strings – these are our news broadcasters, social media magnates, and the 'unelected officials' that have been granted the power to oversee the decisions and governance of multiple nations. Do they always have the nations, and our interests at heart? They don't really have to – they have an altogether 'higher' agenda that we 'mere mortals' would never really be equipped to understand. They tell the mainstream news what to say - they bias the 'random' feeds on our social media through manipulating the algorithm, and back it all up with the scientists they bought to give them the 'evidence' that their solutions are the answer. (To the problems they created.)

These people have a far greater reach and ability for subconscious manipulation than most of us (the population) could ever be aware. And I certainly don't think it would be considered a conspiracy to think that their plan for world-wide compliance probably isn't going to serve everyone. We are the enslaved who imagine ourselves 'free' because we can work, buy, and seemingly think what we like. It might come as a complete surprise to a lot of people how many of these apparent choices have been subliminally influenced by those who seemingly 'own the world'. Or at least the media outlets that give the public their opinion and tell them what the issues are we should be taking a side in. they have us fighting and arguing while they are plotting the next squabble they want to watch on their livestream. There are those in the highest levels of power who are holding our countries and societies to ransom and stand a far greater threat to our freedoms than the psychological tricksters that are selling us products.

Much like a hypnotist will manipulate the background workings of our mind to get us to overcome phobias, or personal issues (assuming they are always acting in our interest.) these people play on the deep emotional nature of our decision-making mind. We are pitted against each other over issues we often didn't even consider relevant or important. We are presented with the next 'pressing issue' and make our valiant stance **like it was a choice we made**. Never realising how trivial and unimportant this issue really is to us. That this 'problem' is going to affect us in ways they ensure us are terrifyingly real, but the danger they evoke in us is trickery at its finest.

These people aim to not only create a diversion from what is really going on, but to also polarise the population and get them fighting each other. This ensures the need for greater controls and our freedoms to be sacrificed ever further. If these degenerates can't get along, then they will need to be even more 'governed' and regulated out of their choices and freedoms. If they are still traveling and having fun, then they need to be taxed even harder until there is more of them living on the street, and desperately in need of their wonderful and caring government. We scarcely realise that they were the ones who caused the fight in the first place.

More control, more power, more deception – it will take quite a bit for us to wake up, but the cracks a certainly appearing. We are not as willing to remain blind, or believe the farfetched narratives we are fed. We've been convinced to panic over a storm in a teacup, because their control agenda relies on drama, fear, and terror. A hypnotist will offer us a choice to relax quickly or slowly, and we never get that sense where the choice whether to relax or not has been taken from us. We have a mind that basically wants to be presented with choices, and often doesn't notice when the most obvious and beneficial choice for us has been obscured in a well-produced hocus pocus.

It was never my intention to include things on this topic. It became a natural progression of what I consider expressing my truth. I felt I not only wasn't being honest with myself, but allowing the largest perpetrators engaged in extinguishing our awakening to do their worst without any consequences. I thought it would give us more to fight for and an even stronger reason to fulfill our obligation towards higher consciousness. That there are those that are intentionally trying to prevent this planets awakening is a crime that will result in enormous amounts of suffering – let me leave it at that.

My aim was only ever to help people be more in control of how they feel (defined by being more conscious) – to make the choice we have in each moment seem like a more obvious and simpler one than it was. But we humans are almost certainly and unwillingly falling victim to the greatest mass scale hypnosis that has ever occurred in our history. Subliminally conned out of our own instincts and choices. A swindle that is robbing us of our freedoms and choices just as villainously as our own conditioning is. Our worth, our voices, and our human freedoms have been taken from us without us ever committing a crime. We just had it taken from us in the hope we would forget our basic human rights, in the name of this 'great reset' that is proposed. But I can assure you it is running out of time, and the holes in this narrative are becoming a gaping crevasses when exposed to the exponentially expanding light of consciousness – to the light of the great awakening.

It is not for our own good that we need to be more regulated and brought under control – that we are being systematically divided, and a life affirming truth is being supressed. It is not for any form of 'greater good', but to further concrete our need to be governed and conned out of all of choices and freedoms. And to ensure that all money funnels up towards those in power. 'Who has the gold makes the rules', as they say. Or better said – who wins the war writes their version of how it all went down and who started it.

The Choice to Feel.

Our choices have to been taken from the table and for the most part we hardly even noticed when we were giving our authorities unprecedented power to rule over us in a dictatorship that would parallel some of the worst in history. If this subject may seem way left of centre to the subject of an inward search for higher consciousness, I don't believe they're unrelated. The word 'choice' implies consciousness, and when our choices are being covertly slipped from our menu, there should always be cause for concern. We should want to know the motives and be aware of what is happening, or we might one day wake up in an eco-dome with our only source of information coming from some eye in the sky.

We seem to respond far better to having an external enemy than we do to the cryptic ways in which our conditioning has us backed into a corner. This is the mass brainwashing of humanity. Brainwashing us out of our intelligence, say and choices, and I for one would like to remain as 'in the picture' as I can be. These people have a vested interest, and very clever means with which to supress our worth and get us to believe in our own lack and limitations. Convince us that our common-sense radar is faulty and can't be trusted. And that is precisely what is happening when we are asked to swallow BS as truth. This drive to supress our personal truth which could also be expressed as the promotion of our 'lack' plays an enormous part in why there exists unprecedented level of mental illness in our present time.

When we start to wake up to the vested interest these high-level, and often unelected rulers have in keeping us sick and diseased – ensuring we remain unaware of our internal strength, divine heritage, and how little we actually need to rely on the old measures of wealth, success, and intelligence – we begin to understand how little we really need to depend on apparent circumstances for how we feel. When we understand our connection to something truly mind-blowing, nothing situational will affect us the same. When we understand our power to generate emotion and feel the way we want to, 'the jig is up' - that 'golden carrot' that has been so long used to cast a spell over what we are worth will lose its appeal.

The tide is turning, but the bottom line is we have been denied the very knowledge, energy sources, and medicines that could have made us well – could have put us in entirely different circumstances. I include this because we need to become aware that it is not just our conditioning that is pulling the wool over our eyes as to who and what we are – this is also being carried out by a high-level dictatorship that is coercing us out of our rights, and more importantly, our self-knowing. And this particular enemy is much easier to spot and smoke out than the tricks our own mind plays on us.

When we get the sense of how we are being duped out of being able to trust in our own internal intelligence. When we get the sense that humans are being lured with consumption and entertainment – divided over issues that matter less to us than we are being convinced. When we get the sense of how we have been systematically supressed and divided to further justify being over-governed – we will collectively 'rise'. And not in the sense that we will start riots against our governments – this is the beginning of a peaceful rebellion. A new means to put our leaders on notice. Understanding how much we alter our physical environments by how we feel – letting go of those old measures of wealth and status, and understanding how we don't have to be bullied, panicked, or illegally coaxed out of our sovereign human rights. This is the rising of the new world. When we feel the way we want to, in spite of how they might be trying to get us to respond and go nuts over everything, we come into our true power. **How we respond is the last of the human freedoms.** You think those with big boats and private jets are wealthy? You think we have to be forced into a rebellion every time they push our buttons?

It will mean even more to us to awake to the consciousness and the choice we have to feel the way we want to. When we have better reasons, we are removed from what we used to consider effort. When we become aware that our efforts to feel as we would choose to go far beyond just infecting our immediate environment and the quality of just our lives, it will be the easiest choice in the world to make. There is so much at stake in the choices we are gifted with in each moment to live, think, and feel as we would choose to. And when this choice becomes deeply associated as our form of contribution, tied to how we are fighting in this war on consciousness, we will understand ourselves as **the new peaceful army**. The new uprising of wealth and wellness – the new compassionate souls who will lead the brigade into a world that may have only seemed true in dreams and prophecy.

Those choices that we have to feel electrified and hopeful of the new world become easier by degree of their importance. When we know how much our families and communities also stand to gain from us being our best selves – it doesn't make it harder or put us under more pressure. To the contrary, it becomes a super easy choice to make, and actions to take.

Likewise, when we get the sense of the enemy being external to us – denying us, our families, and communities the joy that is our privilege by birth. When we get the analogy that there is an active ploy to suppress the knowledge that could right now lead us to a more peaceful, tolerant, and mentally stable world. We will be fuming enough to do more of what we can to feel the way we deserve to. The global context of what we add, and the nature of our external enemies doesn't make it harder and puts us under more pressure – it means right, 'bring it bitches – I see your master plan. I know my choice to feel and the part I have to play in the human future'.

We have been duped out of believing in the most powerful thing we are armed with – our own infinite intelligence. We have been conned out of our instinctive ability to smell BS, and convinced that our 'bought' version of science can offer us some kind of guiding light for our futures. That we can trust that at the highest levels of government, someone up there is going to make sure there is a good future for all – is performing in the name of justice, equality, and righteousness. Whoever has their hands on the big wheel certainly doesn't have the interests of the broke, sick, and elderly at heart – of that I can assure you. But they have us convinced that they will 'keep us in the know' if there is anything we need to be aware of. Wink wink. That they have our best interests at heart. Surely we are not that naïve are we? Not so naïve that we believe that scientists have no biased towards those who sponsor them and pay for the studies. The so-called experts can 'prove' almost any narrative they are employed to find evidence of.

Science is not some great body of knowledge where all the top minds are in agreement about what is important and essential to our shared prosperity. Nor is there some universally formed, and agreed on, opinion about where we are going and how we get there. Science is owned and bought in the same way our politicians and governments are. We have an external enemy – one that is manipulating the human psyche to lose faith in the only real source of intelligence we can trust, and that is our own intuitions. We have been conned out of the enormous part we all play in deciding the future of humanity. And the bottom line is we are the people – we are the numbers, the ones who hold the balance of power in a democratic civil society.

And at heart we all want some very similar and base level needs. We don't need all of the stuff we have become so brainwashed into believing is representative of 'success'. We don't need to be right or follow the manipulative guidelines of what it apparently 'truly' means to be a responsible citizen. We all want peace, freedom of lifestyle and speech, and our children to grow up to be happy. We want the right to ingrain into the coming generation values that might lead them to an improved world, and standard of living. We want to raise a generation that has more forethought, compassion, and willingness to collaborate than the example we have shown them. Just like in the tribal and more apparently 'primitive' style of communities.

We respond far better to an external type of enemy than we ever could our inner demons. And when we start to get a true picture of the joy, and justice, that has been withheld from us, by those who hold the society they rule over in contempt – who have a disdain for humanity that would make Ted Bundy seem like he wasn't that bad a fella, we will do whatever it is we think is within our power to reclaim what is ours. And I don't know about you but the evil that has been systematically inflicted on us by these 'Gods' of the greater good makes my blood boil. I see an even more pressing need to stick to the joy that is my right that goes far beyond my personal satisfaction.

We are already in a war my friends, but it is not one that we need to arm ourselves with picks and shovels – it is a war on our own consciousness. And the knowledge that will set us on a course for the next age of human development is right before us. The need for us to awaken to our own minds has never been greater – the way has never been more defined – and the reward? Well, we are only just waking to the scope of the human imagination and the potential of a world where we sense what is within us. When we care much for the good of our tribe as we do ourselves -when self-interest is no longer the norm, but what actually harms us, we'll be living on the doorstep of a new world. This is the way we once lived, but the return does not mean we have to live in grass huts again. We will inherit the full range of emotional potential of which the mind has been designed. Lord knows what life will look like when the change begins. It will exceed anything the human mind might comprehend from our current level of awareness. The comeback always outshines the setback, as they say.

By the very ideas portrayed in 'transhumanism' – the notion that we can be controlled from beneath the skin to think and act in the ways they want us to, we are literally up against more than we really ever knew we had to be. We must be equipped with everything in our power. Be willing and able to deal with it on all levels at our disposal. To feel as we choose, isn't just a 'nice' thought, it is our only defence against an evil we cannot imagine. It is our only defence against a greater force of darkness than we know.

Proving our perfection

Acceptance – the only place we can plant any tree worth growing.

Anything worth nurturing in our life – any idea – any desire – any offering – must come from a place of peace, or it will be unconsciously marred by the state of desperation from which it was created. The desperation to prove ourselves, or to make up for lost time or the wrongs we have committed. If we're in a hurry, our results will flow from that same energy. It will feel like we are always behind and trying to catch up – each result instilled with the belief that we have a long way to go and will probably never arrive. We don't need to be seen, we just need to create, and express the beauty we feel inside. If we don't feel beauty – if our creation has not come from a place of completion we will only be creating another impatiently born offspring that wreaks of our desperation.

To sense the beauty we hold within we don't need to do anything more than turn inwards and hear that inner voice. Even if we are fortunate enough to have our creation widely appreciated, we have to realise that we never do it for other people. We don't live to be adored but to appreciate the beauty of what we are. Yes, there is evil in the world – and yes some of it we can do something about. But there is also an immense unseen beauty just beneath the surface that can only be known by the cracking open, and the destruction of the old world. Some of what is the old ways we just have to allow to die, because we understand the process of change. We can't do something about everything, but we have to mind our energy – that's the part that is our business. We have to mind what we add here and realise that we don't solve all of the wrongs in the world by being on some brave crusade, but by allowing. By being at peace with the unfolding however that happens. There is a beauty revealing itself for certain, but we have to feel beautiful to see it. To win this war we have to mind ourselves and guard our energy. We can't fight it, and we can never hope to convince anyone else of what is going wrong, or change into what we think is good. How could that ever be a pathway to peace? We just have to be ok with it all like more than just our lives depended on it.

Our only true goal is to uncover the beauty beneath the thin veil of illusion – it is so much closer than we think – we are so much closer than we think. We should never imagine that we have to prove ourselves because that's the energy that has been making human beings sick for thousands of years. All we have to do is hear our inner voice – an ancient voice crying quietly for us to know how impenetrable we really are. What this thing is that we are a part of and connected to - that doesn't ask anything of us but for us to be quiet for a second, and give our undivided attention. There is pain in the cracking open of the old world, just as there is pain in our own lives. But beneath that pain is an abundant infinite light, beckoning us to be present and calm enough to hear it without distress. To be calm enough to look within and appreciate that things need to crack open to grow.

And we must learn to watch without distress. In some ways we are being asked to just watch the cracking open of the old ways, and respect how that might happen that is both beyond what we can understand or do anything about. This is something so much bigger than the individual level where we like to imagine we can control everything. We're being introduced to an altogether mind defying reality. Some of it we just have to be strong enough to let it be – to be at peace with the fact that we don't understand. To allow people to find out all on their own – and accept that some aren't interested in going – it's not up to us.

Anything that we offer the world cannot come from a place of 'catching up', or having to prove how perfect we are. We are not coming from behind, or from the guilt of what we did wrong. We are not trying to make up for our wrongs here, or we will never be done. This can't come from shame or hating what happened to us. As hard as that might seem, we have to keep in mind what is on offer here. Perfection – heaven? However this is represented for you. It is a feeling that cannot be matched from within the human experience – it is bliss, and it is ours. It is our birth right. To sense our perfection we cannot come from a place of lack, or that the mind is less than perfect. The mind/ world/ our lives, however you want to refer to it, is already perfect – we just have to meet it where it is and move with it. Like everything is ok.

We don't yet realise or sense the full beauty or perfection of this moment but that doesn't mean it is not there. Or that we can only get there by showing how great we are to others. We only need to be still enough from time to time to recall that our own hearts are something sacred. We are not getting anywhere – we are waking up. We don't have to make up for lost time, or right our wrongs, or fix the world. We cannot get to the energy of perfection from a place of feeling like we are coming from behind, and in fear of missing out. We are where we are supposed to be, doing the most important work we know how to. We are doing the best we can with what we know – we always have been, and we need to make peace with that.

Ordinarily how we feel is not a choice – it is entrusted to that part of our mind that knows 'what's going on' automatically – it is far less in our control than we imagine. But all that changes the moment we step out of time and into peace.

We matter.

We are the heroes of our life – we are the heroes to all of the people in our life. And when we understand how much we mean to those closest to us, we won't need to prove ourselves to anyone else. We seem so convinced of how pleasurable fame would be – how joyous it must be to be loved by millions of people who really have **no idea who you are** that we diminish the golden bond we have with our friends – the people who do know us. The better they know us, and the more events and disagreements we've been through with them, the more they mean to us. It's the people that know us that matter, and when we become conscious of how much of a difference we make to their lives - even when they might not be fully aware of it, nothing else will matter as much to us. When we make the moments that we have with them count. When we get how much is going on, when it is actually going on, we won't give a damn what goes on outside of the present. We won't look back to the things that are happening now and think, those were the best days of my life. Right now, is incredible.

We matter. We matter to the people in our lives. The dreams we have matter, no matter how small we may have convinced ourselves they are. The things we do and say matter to the whole of civilisation in a much larger context than we could ever acknowledge. It's because we've been conned out of our choices, and convinced we are such a small insignificant 'little' voice that too much of the time we stumble through like nothing we do matters at all. What we think and feel and believe matters, and any notion to the contrary – well I'm pretty sure you already know where to stick that. **Our right to feel the way we choose to in this moment is not a luxury** – not something we do if we get time. It holds the fate of our species in the balance. It stands counter to the war on our minds that is in play, trying by sleight of hand, to take every choice we have away from us without realising what we gave up. Our choices to think, feel and believe as we choose. Our understanding that we are sovereign, intelligent beings that have a right and say in the human outcome.

If there is one theme that is carried throughout every chapter of this book, it is that the world outside of us is responding to us. We move the particles into an order that replicates our energy. You want peace on earth? It starts in your community - it begins in your house. **The locus of change starts in your heart – and expands outwards to infect the world.** And when it does, we will look out upon a very different seeming world. It is apparently there right now – we just lack the presence of mind to 'see' it.

Viva the revolution.

With all of this in mind I ask you to consider the cultural shift we experience when it becomes common knowledge of the minds natural propensity to assign the emotions we experience to an involuntary and automated process. Can you imagine the revolution when we catch wind of those who have gone to great lengths to, not just exploit this chink in our armour, but keep this knowledge from surfacing. Who have used the way our minds have evolved to puppeteer us towards a widespread compliance and our own demise. There will be a revolution when we understand our right to feel and manage our moods independently from the automated aspect of our minds. It is not our fault that we were born into this 'sin from our origin' to hand the wheel of the most important element of our health and life over to a part of us that is beyond our awareness and therefore our control.

We can't feel the way we want to – we can't manage our moods independently if we don't even realise, we naturally hand these to the force driving in the background of our minds. And we didn't notice this as a corruption of our most sacred gift – or that the people who did understand this would use it against us. There will be a revolution – in the way people feel – in our health – in our willingness to help – in a willingness to put our differences aside for what we know is towards a shared wish of every human being. Our right to live and speak our minds. Because that is the only thing that can evolve the ideas of humanity towards a just and improved tomorrow. When people dispose of the reasoning that their opinions are higher than anyone else's – and the belief that this gives them the right to muzzle other people and restrict our language. There will be a revolution and we won't all be scared of the things they tell us we should be scared of. We won't either need the vices we've been destroying our health with. We'll be able to choose emotion rather than having it done for us at levels of mind we don't have access to. We won't need to put things in our mouth, lungs and veins because we can't control our state.

They used our minds against us, but only because we weren't putting them to good use. There will be a revolution and we will be the masters of our fate, how we feel, and understand the intimate connection between these two. It's coming around and it's here for you in the next breath you take. If you want it.

Chapter 12 – Summary

- There is something of a conspiracy going on trying to convince us that we lack the intelligence or our right to a say in how this human drama will unfold. That we are not smart enough – that we are insignificant and clueless.
- A conspiracy that our leaders at the helm of this ship have things under control. That there is a body of smart people at the top of all this, who are all in agreement of what is needed, have our best interests at heart and are taking us to a bright future.
- We are being duped out of our instincts and the greatest form of intelligence we possess – we are forgoing the only thing that can take us to any sort of a promising future if we buy into this deception.
- We need to reconnect with those primal instincts and our 'feelings' if we are to ever sense the 'truth' of what is happening and the opportunities that abound.
- There is a brighter future that is blossoming inside the human spirit that they are desperate to keep under wraps because it will mean an end to their tyrannical power structures.
- They may try and divide us, but the 'truth' will only gravitate to bring us together. What divides is a lie – and what unites is truth. When we remember that we are a single species we will be welcomed to a whole new world.
- To understand there is also an external enemy that we are up against that is trying to supress the 'good news' inherent in our consciousness evolving, and what this evolution means for humanity, it should be even more reason to engage in the tools we have at our disposal.
- Calm is the new spiritual weapon of choice. To not be swayed or bothered by the panic they've used to control us for hundreds of years.
- We are engaged in a war on consciousness, but we are armed with a more devastating weapon than we may have ever

known. Because we are taking back from the autonomous mind our choice to feel the way we want to and the power away from those who've been manning the control panel of human panic levels.

- We have nothing and no one to prove our perfection to. Our right to speak what we mean and feel the way we want to.
- We matter – our voice matters – and what we do matters more to this evolutionary process. We can never know how our part fits into the greater puzzle. We just have to do whatever it is in our heart like it matters to far more than just ourselves. We are a spoke in the wheel of the evolving human force. We should understand this when we are doing our work – know it with some sense of pride.

CHAPTER 13
Tying it All Together

"There is no reality without an observer – without you."

Tying it all together.

I feel like we've covered a lot of ground since the beginning of the book, so I wanted to tie all of these ideas together at the end, just to be sure the benefits were clear and how different aspects meshed with each other. Top of the hill and paramount above them all is understanding our choice to feel. How this is not ordinarily a choice we make, but regurgitated by the apparent circumstances of our life. The reactions we have and the outcomes we experience are a consequence of this dominant vibration sustaining the status quo of our lives. A deep entanglement of the beliefs that keep us safe and in a familiar mind created setting. But we can chose how we feel, and every choice we make has a corresponding effect over the reality we experience. **How we feel is the choice that changes everything.**

Our state of mind is not a conscious choice we make but assigned to a higher automatic aspect of our minds that is designed to repeat itself indefinitely, unless acted upon by us not liking how our lives are going. Our state of mind is mirrored in our environment and reflects back to us in the circumstances, events, and realities we assume we have a very limited control over. In whatever method we find most appealing the goal remains the same – to become **more conscious of mind** - which can be translated as, more sensitive to how we are feeling.

Next down our list is Mindfulness – such a focused attention to the senses in the present moment that all of the mind made drama shifts to the background and out of our awareness. **Mindfulness connects us to the subconscious and reality creating part of our mind** where we are able to see just how imagined and changeable our life situations are. We enter the ether of the creative, where our perceptions can be shifted to see our problems and blockages in a whole new light. See them for being changeable, and sometimes even silly. Mindfulness cleans the body of habit, or conditioned energy, and is a return to the innocent bliss of our infancy. The ego hates the mindful state because it loses its ability to push our emotional buttons. But it is the seat of where we can go to perform the most profound character transformations of our lives. It is the ultimate form of escapism, and represents the key to the evolution of the human condition itself. It is a direct **'Portal'** to higher and grander dimensions that exist within all of us. Where we can exist as one with the higher mind, and the states revered by all of the great spiritual traditions that have occurred throughout time.

We have much more control over the outcomes we experience than we exercise our will over, because we don't operate from the awareness of how automatically our states are recreated, or how much our state influences what we see in the world, the thinking we do, and where our attention goes. State of mind is the true 'Grail' of our experience – influencing everything from how we think, how we are treated, what we think we can do (and so will make effort towards), to the outcomes we experience. How e feel determines how we see the world, or is the filter through which we see the world. If we have a problem that is beyond us, we only need to change the filter through which we are viewing it. It is our way of seeing that creates the problem in the first place. State of mind controls the world as we know it at a higher level of mind, but because it is a higher level than the conscious mind it is impossible to change without insight.

To change our mind we have to have a goal that is bigger than who we are now. We have to entertain a goal that is beyond us in order for it to change us. Our goals also provide the filter through which we see the world. What things mean can only be known in relation to is it moving me closer or further away. Is this something that is helping me or a distraction. Clearly defined goals are what allow us to accelerate with speed towards what we want. We will never see anything in our environment that we are not looking for, and have clearly defined as desirable. We change the world outside of us into what it becomes by what we are looking for in it. By our goals we alter the fabric of the apparently material world that surrounds us. That is better represented as the 'field of potentiality'. The world outside of us is countless trillions of moving particles that are moved into formation and order by the energy that we project. A change in energy is to change the fabric of time/space itself.

Imagined states are the most underestimated and undervalued commodity on earth. They are even more powerful than the states of mind that are reproducing themselves involuntarily – because those automatic states can only be born from the conditioning that has caged our life from the first weeks and years of our life. Conditioning is the lie that was forced on us before we had developed sufficient judgement to refute it. We took the suggestion of who we were and what we were worth that came from our parents, carers, and environment as the truth, because we had no other option. We've been fighting those conditioned conclusions and trying to prove them wrong ever since. In our human instinct to improve our state we've been desperately trying to improve our sense of worth, and our conditioning wrong. When we are up against a mind that is operating on a higher level. This is not only difficult but can drive us to the edge of insanity. The mind is pre-disposed to normalise and diminish the achievement. The feeling we get from accomplishment is quickly reduced by the vibration of drive that puts us back to the bottom of a new hill to climb.

Created states, or the states we can create without reason – no matter what seems to be going on in our environment are just as real as the states we feel when we are surrounded by the physical evidence. The only difference being that they come from the truth and purity of our desire. They are unfettered by the material world and the illusion of mind. Whether the pictures we have in mind come from real time memories, or dreamed up desires, their effect on the reality we experience is identical. The subconscious (world creating mind) cannot tell the difference – or rather the corresponding feeling is the same. In this light we can implant a new version of our history and who we are. When we visualise our dreams we are implanting new memories into the subconscious mind. Visualisations done in the deeply relaxed state – where the conscious stands down and the subconscious becomes highly receptive to our visual messages is the most effective work we can engage in. visualisations that are rich in the sensory details of the dream we are looking forward to, is the greatest return on effort work we can possibly do. It takes concentration, but it is effortless and can save us years of hard slog – putting us directly into the environment where the thing has already happened.

While our ability to focus is the key, we must also take the time to relax in proportion to our concentrated efforts. We cannot spend 10 hours in the gym and expect that this is how we will get bigger. And in a world where the competition for our attention has become so overwhelming – the net effect is that our attention spans have become considerably shortened. With the advent of social media it would seem as if we are always on display. We are historically accustomed by thousands of years of our evolution to operate in one of two states – fight or flight – or rest and digest. In the thousands of years we existed in tribal communities the ratio of these states was something like 10% to adrenally charged and 90% to the latter. Sadly in the modern era those percentages have been reversed. And it would seem like we either feel like we are always on our guards and being looked at, or we have become so exhausted that we need to take some form of sedative. While concentration is the accelerator pedal of our manifestations, we rarely integrate enough rest times to be able to sustain it.

To have purpose in our lives is to have something we care about enough to want to do something about. And whether that is teaching pottery, coaching junior football, or feeding the hungry in the third world, helping others is the only antidote to a dissatisfied life. We want to help – from the core of our being we want to devote our energy to something greater than our own life and needs. And while many people have the mindset that a life of purpose must be defined by some noble cause, the lives that we are living now are no different. It is because we don't see our 'ordinary' lives as purposeful that we don't pursue them with the gusto that they deserve. We are making the world better in the way that only we can.

But a life of purpose also has many less considered but just as profound benefits. When we know what matters to us, it not only funnels all of our energy into a single-minded pursuit, we are given some of the energy of those we aim to serve. We get a kick out of helping. In a life lived with purpose we waste less time, and we never do anything out of a sense of guilt or obligation. Things that we might have otherwise been in two minds about become a far more defined and easy choice for us. A life lived with purpose helps us be certain where to turn the bow of our ship and whether any apparent storm. The meaning of any event can be twisted to suit our needs and be integrated as a part of what needed to happen to get us there more quickly. When we have a clear purpose our problems are seen as being the vehicles that were personally made for us as a means to reach our target. It never takes courage to do the things that scare us – we don't do them because we don't see the real benefit of the outcome. We don't do them because we don't care enough about the result.

It is never fear that stops us in our tracks but a lack of compassion. If we were doing it to save our kids, whatever was in the way would never even enter our minds. What are the reasons we want to do this thing? What will it mean to our life, and the lives of those we share it with. It is not being clear on these things that causes the problem to be seen from an impossible angle.

But we matter – we matter to our families, our communities, and to the world at large. Everything we do affects the entire connected world now and forever. We have sadly fallen for the story that we are so small and insignificant that anything we do will be such a tiny blip on the radar that it wouldn't matter if we did it or not. That thing you do is not a blip on your radar – it is your whole radar. And the entire world is waiting for you to show us what you've done. To show us what it looks like when one person can live their life with the freedom from judgement that crushes so many others. Our contribution maybe the very thing that helps someone in a life changing way, or gives them permission to show that piece of art they've been hiding under their bed because everyone might say it is stupid. We could never expect to be privy to the whole picture – and how our 'little' addition nudges someone who nudges someone else. All we can do is create – and in its simplest terms this is not just our civic duty – it is our part in the evolution of our species. It is the mindset that we don't matter that kills much of the beauty that might have otherwise been seen. And what the 'powers that be', have a vested interest in suppressing.

As much as we are up against the internal enemy of our conditioning. That tries to talk us off the ledge when we are about to test out our new wings, we are also up against an even covert enemy who are desperate for us to remain small, voiceless, sick, and controllable. They secretly clip our wings and take from us the freedoms and privileges that have always been the sovereign right of all individuals. They are skilled at the psychological blackmail that short circuits the highest levels of our mind, and have us squabbling with each other over things that don't even matter to us. They have us relinquishing our rights for the sake of some 'greater good' that is not our best interests but theirs. We are locked in 'The Third World War'. A war on consciousness itself.

For all of time it has stood that he who has the gold makes the rules and writes the history. But in us coming to understand just what it is that we have inside ourselves to alter the conditions of the world around us, the whole dynamic of our society is beginning to shift. We are no longer bound by those old measures of success, wealth, and superiority. We are entering a dimensions where we are waking to the full realisation of mind. That from within ourselves we can and do, affect the nature of the physical world. We change our surroundings by how we are. The Buddha was said to have done it – to turn the world into a paradise where he was surrounded by beauty. But this was a time of relative ignorance compared to the information age to which we have been plunged into. And those at the upper levels of our society who have always played to increase their dominance and power over us, are locked in a desperate race to seize the control of our own choices and minds while they still can.

While we are still asleep to this awakening process, we are at risk of swallowing the danger story they so desperately trying to spread. The fear campaign whereby we must put our heads upon the chopping block for the sake of the few. they sense the waking up – and they understand it won't be at all long before everyone wakes to how they have been making us sick for generations. How they have been supressing the very information that might serve to cure the mental disease that plagues this world. We play a part in this war. Peace on earth starts in you place of work – starts in your home and community. Peace starts in your heart and expands outwards, to not only transform the world that you look upon, but alter the world that we all share. We are of course the primary beneficiaries of entering the freely available and transformative state, but never underestimate the fact that you are winning a far greater war. Peace and consciousness is our weapon of choice, and we are armed with a far greater arsenal than they could ever imagine.

There is indeed an attempt being made on our lives. An attempt to control and influence everything we think, feel, and believe on such a subconscious level that we may not even sense how we have been infiltrated. But our minds are ours – this is our kingdom. And we will never surrender it – we will never squander our whole world for the dimes they want to trade us for it. This is the same as what is happening when we lose our minds over something trivial. We are sacrificing the only vehicle that can take us to a better land, over some spilt milk. This kingdom is all around us – we just lack the presence of mind to see it. The world can only ever reflect our state, so don't go blaming the world if we are unaware or incapable of changing our state of mind. Get practiced. Use this world transforming skill on everything – on everyone and in each moment it comes to mind. The world you know will be far better for it.

A robot is running, and often ruining our lives, but you know how to take the wheel now. Write your goals down – why do you want them? Imagine how it would feel in the receiving of them. And live there as often as you can. Sit quietly and know there is something otherworldly listening from the grandstands. That is taking our case to the boardroom within our minds. Why do we want this thing? What difference is it going to make to our lives and the lives of others. If we are genuinely in the service of others, we won't believe the force that gets behind us. That opens doors where there were only walls.

Live in the innocence of mindfulness – the direct portal to the higher mind. Go to that board meeting and watch on as your prayers and wishes are put forward.

It is Never a Question of Bravery.

We humans are good people – we love each other and want the best for the future. It is just the way the mind has evolved that it seems to be working against us. But at heart we are courageous people – it is only for the lack of knowing what is the right thing to do that we miss our mark. We are not as scared as we have led ourselves to believe. It is not fear that stops us but a good enough reason to take action. It is through a lack of awareness of the full spectrum of implications that we become frozen in time. That we haven't considered all of the beneficiaries of our improved state of mind, and all of those who are subtly inspired by our show of strength.

If we knew what a better course of action was, or a more certain path to being better at the things that excite us we would undoubtedly do them. Instead this 'mind thing' has us pushed to the brink of misery in most cases. A suffering that we've become so accustomed to we imagine it to be the norm. This mind thing is the very same one that the prophets and seers of old were using to embark on remarkable inner journeys. And even people who have endured torturous conditions in their lives manage to bring a level of joy to their lives that many of us more fortunate souls fail to realise.

What I'm saying is this mind thing has the potential for insurmountable levels of joy. Joy that can be taken from the very same surroundings that cause many people so much grief that they'd rather not be here. Does it matter to us enough to use the mind for the wonderous experience it is not only capable but was probably designed for. The mind has become our enemy because it is programmed to exaggerate dangers that no longer exist in our world. To keep us clinging to tribal members that are not always best for us. But keeping them in our lives means that we will never find our true tribe. The mind has us convinced that we shouldn't raise our vibration/ expectations too high for fear that we won't be able to cope with the fall of disappointment. So it keeps our attention trapped in trivialities as a means of keeping our vibrational state low.

There may well have been a time when it was dangerous for us to wander too far from the protection of our cave, but that time has long since passed. And we can cope with the fall of disappointment – we can cope with it even better if we are skilled with the type of emotional martial arts that have been fore mentioned. We can manipulate meanings! The world is ours.

Because of the way we have evolved we can be very easily seduced by satisfying our primal pleasure centres. By those simple drip-fed dopamine hits from social media, food, alcohol, and shopping. We can easily be deterred from ever looking further afield for greater forms of satisfaction. And believe me there are those in the upper echelons of our society who are exploiting our natural proclivity to eat the lowest hanging fruit. That understand that if they keep the group think model barely fed, believing in their own insecurities, insignificance, and fears that they will never look up. They will never look beyond the shoreline of what this mind thing is capable of. They will never believe in their own collective ability to control the outcome of the human future. And that is a diabolical shame. That a mind that was designed and has the potential of taking us to heaven, has dropped us off in hell and we've accepted it as our home.

It is a shame because we are not only good and courageous people, but the fact that this is an easier fix than has ever occurred to us. We've been blindsided by **our own minds conspiracy to keep us believing that we are in charge – that we are the ones making all of the decisions.** We are the ones doing all of the thinking, choosing how we react, and pointing our attention exactly where we want to. The minds job is not just to sustain our vibration and only being able to see the things that confirm what we already believe to be true. It is to hoodwink us into believing we have the wheel of where our lives are going – and nothing could be further from the truth. Waking to this ploy of the mind is the beginning of a liberation that will exponentially raise the collective vibration of the world. And that is exactly what we deserve.

We deserve to feel the full spectrum of emotion this mind thing is capable. To not be at the mercy of habit or fear, and to understand that we are the ones that are not only in control of the human fate, but that we all want such similar things that most of the bickering and unrest could be seen for what it is. A mixture of the powers that be turning us on each other, and the unheard and overlooked finally finding their voice. Because they have only just been heard they've started shouting and it has become intolerable, and they are the last to notice how void of reason the argument is that they are shouting for.

I find it incredibly unjust that people anxiously avoid being seen or heard because of habits and patterns that they aren't even aware are affecting them. That they imagine everyone is looking at and judging them, when in reality they are scarcely even noticed. *We allow all of the great things we have done to be over-shadowed by that one tiny block that the mind keeps in place for stability.* We have done so much – we have tried all of our lives and always done the best we can with what we know. And while we should be applauding ourselves for who we are, we are instead berating ourselves for this one thing that we are now trying to overcome. We don't lack the courage – we lack for what is the best course of action to overcome that thing that bothers us so much. The entirety of humanity seems to be beating itself up and that is a profound injustice. That is far from fair. It is like the 'pebble in the shoe' scenario – where a supremely conditioned athlete can be brought undone by tiny and incidental piece of inanimate rubbish. That one thing that bothers us the most is destroying us, and our perceived ability to deal with anything.

So how do we start with that thing that means most to us? How do we start from where we are, instead of being overwhelmed by what we think we will never be? How do we give up that feeling of being judged when nobody cares? Because we don't lack courage – we just won't give ourselves a break, or appreciate the things that we have done. We don't appreciate ourselves for the things we are ambitiously trying to move towards. Wouldn't a good person want to do the things that you have in mind? You're doing your best so give yourself and everyone else a break. Give yourself a fucking round of applause for everyone's sake.

EPILOGUE
Our shadow's taller than our souls

There is a line in the climax of one of my all-time favourite songs "Stairway to Heaven." It goes, '**As we wind on down the road, our shadow's taller than our souls.**' And it has always 'made me wonder' (unintentional pun) if they were insinuating that the part of us that was truly sacred has become overshadowed by something so superficial and fleeting that we had thrown away the 'gold' by virtue of our values, and hung onto the old sack that it came in. Had we misplaced the part of us that is eternal, everlasting, and invulnerable for something that, in reality, is little more than an empty shell? Have we valued the image of ourselves – the thing that is blown around like the wind with our changing moods, over the part of us that holds the wisdom of many lifetimes. Traded the all-knowing part of us to get things that probably won't even mean anything to us in a week?

I guess it is not dissimilar to giving our 'state of mind' trophy to an incidental event or being given a life and not steering it towards something meaningful for us. This image we hold of ourselves is so fragile that it can be shattered if we heard that someone was spreading some gossip about us. And that piss ant piece of gossip, for all it is worth, just shattered our connection – devalued something deep within us that holds us in the absolute highest regard. Why would we let dumb stuff ever counter our connection - or bring to question how the eternal within us actually feels about us. Why would we let what we own, the position we hold, or what people might say of us, come between us and – whatever you want to call it – the thing we are all connected to that is holy. Source energy runs through our bodies, but what do we feel? A lot of the time that we aren't enough. Or that the yearning hunger inside us that can only be filled by presence and connection could be replaced by a job, or 'things'.

How have we allowed something so fragile and transient to overshadow what we must feel when we sense what we are connected to. Whether we think that thing is 'out there', or within us, surely it is more than just a keel that keeps us on course when we think we have no idea where we are headed. Has this fleeting image of us, or the conscious mind we imagine is us, eclipsed the life-force within us because we never got quiet enough to experience some intimacy with it. We had no idea what this thing was that lives within us. Has the thin and 'fake' veneer of our self-image become more important to us than the depths of our mysterious and evidently 'heavenly' or extra-terrestrial origins? Have we completely lost the sense of what we are connected to in mind, or don't care?

Do we honestly care more about how we look to other people today, to what is inherent in consciousness that we would want to end it all? There is a dormant part of our minds that clearly represents an end to human suffering – but we're more interested in… well anything else. It must stand to reason that we were left with the instruction manual – as cryptic and secretive as it might even still remain, we were left with the know-how of how to become something more than just an ignorant and near-sighted scourge that caused its own demise. Surely we are more than that? A being that was so self-interested that it didn't even see it coming – the end. I just can't believe this to be the case because we have shown what love can do. And if there is anything that characterises why we got to where we are now it is that we care about each other – even if those are for the realisation of how much we need other people.

And it is not just because of how we have advanced we are in technology that I think there's more to us – that we are smart enough to reach the next level of our evolution. To the contrary, I think how technologically advanced we seem has actually blinded us to the fact of how emotionally primitive we still really are. Of the primal forces that still drive our decisions and behaviours. I don't think it is a technological breakthrough that takes us into this supposed future, but an empathetic paradigm shift that enables us to sense ourselves as a single living species. When we think with one mind, and imagine other people, who may well have the appearance of being separate from us, are known to be very much a part of us. When this shift occurs then we'd naturally act and think in terms of the collective rather than self-interest. Rather than trying to impress everyone we appreciate them. And we see the direct senselessness of ever intentionally harming anyone.

Of course, I am a sceptic just as much as you are, and I really don't know if it would ever occur to us what needs to change for us to be able to walk through the gates and into 'Eden'. I don't know what it takes, and I'm probably just as cynical as you are towards anyone who might claim to know, but I have to think the signs are there for us and it is worthy of our consideration. It is more worth of our interest than we are making it. And surely the awareness of the outside world being a projection of our state alludes to the keys for our entry point. In light of us understanding that emotions can be more of a choice for us than they have been, have we been given the keys to something far larger and more profound than just our dreams coming true? I certainly think it is a step in the right direction. To be aware that we are creators of our reality, connected to the single all-knowing source of intelligence and have the ability to project beauty onto our environment – the like we have never seen before – definitely spells hope for us. I'm only re-iterating what has both been passed down through the ages, and what is becoming a more obvious truth as we go deeper into this process of consciousness, and human evolution.

But are we even worth saving if we have pawned our very souls, for the price of a life that might look lavish to a small group of people, for a very short while? If we'd pay any price, or trade any fare – stand on top of people even, to make sure our coat is 'shiny', and people 'respect' us? Trade our honour even to impress people who don't even know or care about us. Not suggesting that this is what everyone of a seemingly high position has done – not for a minute, but the picture we take of ourselves in this moment is little more than a photograph that will be gone one day just as surely as we will. We'll die and will it matter that we did good or bad things? Could our self-image ever trump or come before what is alive in our hearts? Could it capture what things meant to us, or the character traits we portrayed? Could it show and preserve how we made people feel? Does how we look mean more to us than our sense of what we are connected to?

Do 'things' hold more value than moments? Does the ability bestowed upon us to see the magic in the normal, become redacted because we value other things more highly. We have put 'things' before the abilities of our minds. Things that crumble and don't hold their value, any more than a second-hand car does? We forego our ability to be sorcerers and make magic out of the ordinary because we are looking for… what exactly? These moments are our magic and are the very cobblestones that pave our way to 'heaven'. We can see something dimensionally more profoundly when we stare at and be present with a plant, an animal, or a person, and take something away from the interaction that surpasses anything comparably meaningful. But we don't ordinarily fill our spiritual account with moments - we're too busy with 'life'. I'm not saying we shouldn't appreciate our 'things', but what do you think was meant by our shadows have become taller than our souls?

And for me it is that the image of who we are has become far more important and valuable to us than what is eternal and sacred. We might not be able to see it but we certainly can feel it. In the quiet of our minds it whispers, 'You are home. You are loved. And we should never trade that or forget it because that would seem like a tragedy. Bad things do happen, and it can feel like we are very alone, life is unfair, and it takes a very strong faith for us to imagine there is a point to it. That there is something working behind the scenes to bring order to this chaos. But how often do we get all 'antsy' about the most trivial things, which to me is same as devaluing our inner selves because our team didn't win – or something equally as inconsequential. Are we handing the keys of a galactic cruising vessel to a chauffeur who doesn't even know how to get this thing off the ground?

Generation after generation, we've become less concerned about what we are leaving our children than our ancient ancestors were. We think indigenous people weren't 'smart' enough to live any better than they did? They respected their elders, because they carried the seed of knowing that would sustain the coming generations. They honoured the earth and the privilege bestowed upon them to act as the caretakers of the earth. They loved their children, their tribes and respected all life. And they may not have had iPhones, but they lived a sustainable existence for some fifty thousand years. And we think they lacked intelligence?

Why should it be on us to do anything about it? I just hope that we can recall our sacredness when it matters, and if we are ever faced with the choices, we act on behalf of our tribe as much as ourselves. There is obviously far more to our minds than we are conscious of and that this stands as the next frontier. To enter into the next dimension of our minds potential. And this fragile outer egg of what it might appear that we are now, might soon be broken. But surely this goes hand in hand with the fact that we are inheriting the controls of something far greater. An aspect of ourselves that has been sleeping and forgotten. By the evidence of our origins, there is so much more to us than we can answer – that goes so far beyond what we are able to fathom that it should make our hearts sing with excitement.

The veneer of what and who we are, has become the ruler over what is eternal and most sacred about us. This image that gets blown around like a candle in the wind and is the great lie about who and what we truly are, has taken precedence over our 'huge selves'. And we are consequently at the hands of an inner tyrant. All we care about is image and identity, but we never realise that it comes at the cost of actually knowing the part of ourselves that can change it all in an instant and be at peace. We forgo knowing that part of ourselves, and don't even notice the moments when we do. Don't realise what we are severing ourselves from. We say 'tell someone who cares' about that part of us that can 'move mountains' – that we are not interested. Yet we suffer, so unjustly, in our ignorance.

> *"The desire to know your own soul will end all other desires".*
>
> Rumi

ABOUT THE AUTHOR

Simon has been working in the Personal Development space for the past 5 years, and is the author of two previous titles, 'The Control Centre' and 'Seeing Your Future – Living You Dream'. He is a certified NLP and Life Coach, and his desire to share awareness of the Law of Emotional Projection in a language that people can use and understand has become something of an obsession. He believes that far too many people suffer needlessly in ignorance of the emotional feedback loop that we live in, and how involuntarily most of our lives and experiences happen. He lives in Blackwater Central Queensland with his Partner Andrea – he can be contacted via the website www.realityhacker.com.au – where you can view all of his blogs and other products available.

www.ingramcontent.com/pod-product-compliance
Lightning Source LLC
Chambersburg PA
CBHW050305010526
44107CB00055B/2108